D1559711

Tenants
AND
the American Dream

Tenants
AND
the American Dream

IDEOLOGY AND THE TENANT MOVEMENT

Allan David Heskin

PRAEGER SPECIAL STUDIES • PRAEGER SCIENTIFIC

333.338
H 58 t

Library of Congress Cataloging in Publication Data

Heskin, Allan David.
  Tenants and the American dream.

  Bibliography: p.
  Includes index.
  1. Rental housing—California. 2. Landlord
and tenant—California.   I. Title.
HD7288.85.U62C23 1983   333.33′8   82–16688
ISBN 0–03–062133–X

MLR

Published in 1983 by Praeger Publishers
CBS Educational and Professional Publishing
a Division of CBS Inc.
521 Fifth Avenue, New York, New York 10175 U.S.A.

3456789   052   987654321
Printed in the United States of America
on acid-free paper

Contents

v

Preface and Acknowledgments

There was a flurry of research activity begun in California after the passage of Proposition 13, the tax reform initiative. It was clear to many people that the dimensions of the change this reform could engender were quite major, and researchers set out to measure the effects. I had been interested in the tenant movement since I was a Legal Service lawyer in the late 1960s, and I could see a very dramatic change in that movement after the passage of the proposition. People began to say that there had been an explosion of "tenant consciousness" and that the tenant revolt that was to come would be at least of the strength of the homeowner revolt that had passed the initiative.

All of this was remarkable seen from my past experience. In the 1960s having a "real" tenant movement in California was a dream that, I suspect, even the tenant organizers of that time did not believe would come to pass. The "tenant lobby" in Sacramento, the state capital, in the late 1960s consisted of four people, something that would not have been admitted at the time. Successful tenant organizing was limited to a few college towns. It was suspected that Californians were too individualistic, too mobile, or just too timid to be organized.

In those days I participated in the process of reforming the landlord-tenant laws of California. We hoped we were making the way easier for later generations. Tenants gained access to courts through the adoption of the warranty of habitability doctrines and the protection against retaliatory eviction. In a study I did a few years before the present one, it appeared that those reforms had contributed to what the lawyers noted, even before the post-Proposition 13 tenant revolt, as an increasing aggressiveness in the tenant population. Tenants believed they had rights, a belief that would have been largely unfounded in the 1960s. Still, the level of postproposition activity was not anticipated.

It is important that the readers of this book understand that I came to this study with this background. My interest in the questions examined are not simply academic. I am personally amazed at the recent strength of the tenant movement and interested in understanding the reasons for this occurrence and in the potential of this current episode. There are undoubtedly many times when my own experiences and opinions are incorporated in the work. I do not believe, however, that this has hurt the study. If anything, I believe this has given the study more authenticity than a stranger to the movement could have managed. I have tried to derive as objective an answer to the questions posed in the book as possible. It is important to me, as well as to others I have known in the tenant movement, that this be done. What some might call bias is in the questions themselves. It was my intention that they be the questions of the movement and not the questions of observers outside the movement.

The research itself was done with the assistance of an extraordinary group of people. Among them were: Kenneth Baar, Douglas Canfield, W.A.V. Clark, Daniel Cohen, Madeline Demaria, Phyl Diri, Antelin Gomez, Gilda Haas, Robert Kass, Mary Kelly, Ned Levine, Mark Lipin, Marilyn Marquez, Peter Marris, Richard Purkey, Sandy Rahn, Edward Soja, Gale Trachtenberg, Tevfik Ulgen, Martin Wachs, George Williams, and Goetz Wolff. Their assistance was so significant that I have chosen to use the pronoun *we* in the text. I am not using the word in its regal sense, but to acknowledge the assistance of all these people.

Three groups require special mention. The first is the Institute For Social Science Research and the Survey Research Center. They helped prepare the grant proposal that obtained funding for the study, developed the questionnaire used in the study, and conducted the interviews in a professional manner. The Center for the Study of Metropolitan Problems of the National Institute of Mental Health deserves special appreciation for its funding of the project. Lastly, the publishers, Praeger, Inc. deserve special appreciation for publishing the work. I found in seeking a publisher that the nature of the study and the methods employed left it between many publishing programs. The topic was one normally dealt with within an essay format, not with quantitative analysis, and conversely, the methodology was one not normally employed in such a political study. I believe this separation is artificial and should not be maintained.

Introduction

Tenancy has never been a desirable position for residents of the United States. The drive to own has obsessed the people from the yeoman farmer to the modern suburbanite. Being a tenant had never been part of the "American dream," and the status of tenants in this society has never been secure or comfortable. Tenants have been, in an essential way, the unpropertied in a society in which property is central. In that tenants' immediate interests seem to lie in opposition to those of property, their issues appear to present conflicts basic to the ideological fabric of the country.

The role of landlords is only slightly less anomalous. The name itself seems a carry over from long ago, and while it brings the respect of ownership and enterprise, it is hardly a term that warms the hearts of the United States citizenry. No matter how modern the management, or how extreme the commodification of the rental units, the role of the landlord seems unable to shake that touch of feudalism that has never sat well in the United States. Furthermore, landlords who have commonly operated on the scarce commodity side of the interplay of supply and demand have been repeatedly open to the charge of being monopolizers and exploiters.

The struggle between landlords and tenants, first among the agrarian and then among the urban, has been a constant theme in United States history. It was the failure of feudalism to entrench itself as an ideology in the United States that was critical. What developed in its place was an agrarian society based on petty commodity production that was fiercely antifeudal, prided itself on the enterprise of the individual, and extolled the virtues of the yeoman farmer.

Without the stable tendencies of feudalism that aided in the development of a collectivist outlook in Europe, capitalism was able to assert its hegemony without a truly contending or rival ideology. The agrarian notion of individual enterprise was easily captured by capitalism. The petty commodity production of agrarianism nurtured an ideology based on a direct relationship between hard work and reward. The hardworking yeoman would succeed and provide for his family. A successful yeoman, therefore, must have worked hard. With the advent of capitalism, the centrality of the relationship between work and reward was maintained in the psyche of the people. However, in this transformation, *accumulation* became substituted for mere provision for one's family as the expected reward for work. The relationship between work and the exploitation of the labor of others and the speculation in commodities (including land) became mystified in what McPherson (1962) calls "possessive individualism."[1]

It is within the ambiguity of this capitalist mythology of work and reward combined with intense antifeudal feelings that the landlord and tenant carry out their conflicts. The questions become whether the landlord is more akin to a feudal lord or to an entrepreneur and whether a tenant is more akin to a failing or exploited yeoman. The feudal lord is seen as not entitled to either property or rent because he does not earn them through work. The entrepreneur has presumably earned title to the property as a reward for his work and is thus entitled to an entrepreneur's profit in the form of rent. The failing yeoman, having failed to accumulate property, has brought on his own problems by his lack of enterprise and is seen as dangerously covetous of those who have accumulated property through their own labor. The exploited yeoman is being restricted from accumulation by the outrageous practices of undeserving landlords who have accumulated their property through gift, inheritance, or, more likely, speculation and who do little after acquiring title in the form of maintenance or management to justify an entrepreneur's profit on their passive investment.

The overwhelming dominance of possessive individualism in the United States has derailed the development of any concrete notions of socialism. Only that which is not the product of enterprise might, with justice, be expropriated. Even then, this expropriation must be directed toward furtherance of individualistic ends. To the extent that the state might take and reallocate unearned wealth, it must use it to assist enterprise or, at best, apply it in the development of welfare capitalism for the benefit of those unable to work.

The result has been a history of an urban tenant movement that, in the main, could only challenge that which remained feudal in character, and, with the rise of laissez-faire economics, attack those aspects of landlordism inconsistent with productive enterprise and the free market. State intervention could only be sought to restrict the practices of the unproductive, improve the workings of capitalism, and assist those frozen out of the system. Only at the fringe have more radical solutions for urban tenants' problems been proposed.

Once again, tenants are facing a crisis situation in which inflation and sectoral recession have caused real wages to seriously decline. Tenants without the hedge against inflation provided by property ownership are feeling the pressure more than others and are, as in the past, reenergizing the tenant movement. How strong the current tenant movement will become and whether, as the crisis builds, tenants will remain trapped in their historic pattern of tenant consciousness or move further to the left is at issue.

II

To answer these questions, the nature of the consciousness the tenant movement has produced and the problems of "political practice" that have been faced by the movement will be investigated (Pickvance 1977). Social movements, such as the tenant movement, have been the subject of much study in recent years. These studies, however, have not focused on the questions we are addressing. They have not, according to Pickvance, investigated the process by which a "social base", the population affected by the issue at hand, becomes a "social force", and, generally, they have understated the importance of the role movements play in the transformation of social consciousness. In Mingione's words, they "usually confine themselves to clarifying the objective conditions which underly conflict and basic class interests which exist, without investigation of the way in which these interests are actually perceived by those to whom they belong . . . " (Mingione 1977, p. 104).

Social consciousness is thought of as an amalgam of two contradictory forms of consciousness (Gramsci 1971, p. 333). Everyday experience generates one form of consciousness. The other form does not come from experience, but is rather "inherited from the past and is uncritically absorbed." This form of consciousness is called "ideological hegemony." It is the all pervasive ideology of a society. For our purposes, the broad acceptance of the centrality of individual accumulation, that is, possessive individualism, is such a hegemonic force. In Gramsci's words: "It holds together a specific group, it influences moral conduct and the direction of will, with varying efficacy, but often powerfully enough to produce a situation in which the contradictory state of consciousness does not permit of any action, any decision or any choice, and produces a condition of moral and political passivity" (Gramsci 1971, p. 333).

The inclusion of the study of social consciousness and its transformation in a study of a United States social movement seems particularly appropriate. In no country in the world is the strength of the ideological hegemony of which Gramsci spoke greater (Gramsci 1971, p. 304). Hegemonic domination has been particularly evident in the U.S. tenant movement. While in Britain the tenant movement argues for nationalization of land (Massey and Catalano 1978), in the United States the tenant movement still is calling for security of tenure and rent regulation. The realities are also different. Socialized housing, which houses much of Europe's population, houses only a small fraction of the population in the United States.[2] In most areas of the United States, again in contrast to most of Europe, landlords are free to evict and increase rents without cause. Only in a relative handful of places where local struggles have taken place has a modicum of protection been won.

To Gramsci social movements had a major role to play in counteracting the total dominance of ideology over common sense. Collective political action served "to rouse the masses from passivity" (Gramsci 1971, p. 429), and the movement, once formed, was to introduce a "counter-hegemony" sufficient to fracture the past domination (Boggs 1976, p. 72). If the collective political consciousness the movement produced was not sufficient to do this, the movement was then destined to be "absorbed or channelled into reactionary populism."[3]

III

Three methodological approaches will be employed to investigate the questions posed: historical, case study, and survey research. Historical material is needed to understand the nature of social consciousness, a case study is needed to give our inquiry into the problems of political practice a concrete base, and survey research is necessary to understand the transformations of consciousness that are taking place within the tenant population.

The history that is reported and analyzed is the history of the formation of consciousness in the tenant movement and the dominance of ideological hegemony over much of this consciousness formation. The historical nature of ideological hegemony makes such an analysis essential to our problem. Before examining the consciousness of the interviewed tenants, we must understand the history they have "inherited and uncritically absorbed." As Gramsci wrote: "It is not enough to know the *ensemble* of relations as they exist at any given time as a given system. They must be known genetically, in the movement of their formation. For each individual is the synthesis not only of existing relations, but of the history of these relations. He is the precis of all the past" (p. 353).

The case which is examined in the book is the post-Proposition 13 tenant revolt in Southern California. Proposition 13 was a statewide initiative passed overwhelmingly by the voters of the state in the summer of 1978. It rolled back property taxes to their 1975 level and greatly limited the assessments and annual increases in the tax rate. Properties are reassessed only on sale. It has been estimated that the initiative saved property owners about a billion dollars in taxes (Keating 1978). Many tenants supported the proposition with the promise that tax savings would be passed on to the tenants. When the proposition passed, not only were the savings not passed on to the tenants, but in many instances, rents were increased. The revolt of the tenant population in Southern California was spontaneous and massive.

The revolt resulted in the passage of rent regulation in the County of Los Angeles, the City of Los Angeles, and several smaller cities in the county. Among these is the City of Santa Monica. In that city the revolt led to tenants becoming the dominant political force in local politics. Through the initiative process, tenants passed the strictest rent control law now in force in the United States, elected a full slate of tenant supported, rent-control board members, and replaced a conservative, landlord oriented city council with a liberal/progressive, tenant oriented governing body.

Santa Monica's story is particularly important to this study. The victories of tenants in the city have become a nationwide symbol of both what can happen if tenants become organized and the possibilities "on the left" in the United States in this conservative era. The importance of Santa Monica to the tenant movement was demonstrated at the first meeting of the National Committee for Rent Controls held in Baltimore in the summer of 1980. When the delegates from Santa Monica were introduced at the conference, they received a spontaneous and sustained standing ovation from all those in attendance. The general political climate in the city has drawn attention from such diverse media sources as the *Village Voice* and the *Wall Street Journal*. A Los Angeles paper indicated the local interest when it took the unusual step of running a series of articles on the "first hundred days" of the new Santa Monica administration. Locally, the opposition now refers to the city as

PEOPLE'5 ЯEPЦБLIC OF БДИТД МОИICД

Kevin B. Postema, "Welcome to the People's Republic of Santa Monica," Apartment Business Outlook magazine, September/October 1981: 8. Available, the Apartment Association Greater Los Angeles, 551 So. Oxford Ave., Los Angeles, CA 90020. Reprinted by permission.

Two random samples were selected from Southern California and interviewed beginning in late 1979 and ending in mid-1980. One sample consisted of 1,456 people drawn from Los Angeles County as a whole. About 7,000,000 people live in the county. A half of them rent their homes.[4] The population of the county is demographically diverse. Los Angeles is a major population center for Latinos, particularly recent immigrants from Mexico and has a long-established black population. The economy of the county is also diverse. In recent years the county has lost heavy manufacturing jobs and gained light manufacturing jobs, particularly in the garment industry and high technology jobs in the aerospace and electronics industries. Los Angeles economy has also gained jobs in the service sectors, but not to an extent greater than the rest of the United States.

The government of the County of Los Angeles is controlled by a board of supervisors with only five members elected from districts of enormous size. Their decisions regarding issues of rent control and the like, however, only affect the unincorporated areas. The largest city within the county is the City of Los Angeles, which incorporates much of the inner core of the county. Its population is in excess of 3,000,000, over 60 percent of whom are tenants. The city council has 15 members elected from districts of over 200,000 people. Over 70 other small cities also exist in the county.

The other sample, of 729 people, was drawn from the City of Santa Monica. Santa Monica has a population of 90,000 people, of whom between 70 percent and 80 percent are renters. The city is located on the western border of the county along the coast. Santa Monica has undergone several major transformations in the past four decades. Once dominated by the resort industry and stately homes, it was transformed into a working-class tenant town to house war workers during World War II. With the decline and relocation of these war industries and the construction of a major freeway linking the city to the metropolitan area, Santa Monica lost much of its working-class character and became an attractive in-town rental suburb increasingly populated by young professionals. More recently, established professionals, in an unusual form of gentrification, had begun to displace the young professionals.

Santa Monica's location and its attractiveness (see logo on p. xvii) made it one of the primary centers of real estate speculation in the county. This speculation, and the real estate and financial interests that fueled it, dominated the city's economy and politics. While the governments in the economically diverse County and City of Los Angeles adopted moderate forms of rent regulation, Santa Monica's city council refused to make even the smallest concession to its majority tenant population. The struggle in Santa Monica was an unmediated conflict between sectors of the economy particularly benefiting from inflation in real estate values and those particularly paying the price of this inflation.

As a result of the coincidence of these events, some of the most valuable land in the county was populated by tenants. Tenants fought to remain in the city, while the real estate and financial interests fought to displace them in the interest of maximizing the speculative potential of the period.

Reprinted by permission of Santa Monicans for Renters' Rights. Logo by Michael Tabor.

The tenant movement in the county as a whole has been very much a protest movement (Piven and Cloward 1977). The revolt of tenants after the passage of Proposition 13 was spontaneous. Thousands of phone calls were made by individual tenants to elected officials complaining about landlord actions, and tenants in hundreds of buildings without the benefit of an organizer from a tenant or community group, joined together to resist rent increases. The largest organization active in the City and County of Los Angeles is the Coalition for Economic Survival (CES) with about 3,000 members. It, along with other groups, only served to escalate the struggle to the level of mass demonstrations and negotiate the concessions from the local state.

The tenant movement in Santa Monica started as a protest movement. When protest did not bring concessions, it became a political movement with the aim of transforming the local state away from the interests of landed and finance capital and toward the interests of the tenant population. We have already discussed briefly the successses of the Santa Monica movement. We will see that these victories were accomplished by an extraordinary mobilization of the tenant population.

In Castell's terms, the Santa Monica experience seemed to indicate a tendency in the tenant movement "towards structural transformation of the urban system" and "towards a substantial modification of the power relations in the class struggle, that is to say, in the last resort, in the state power" (1977, p. 432). What is left unsaid, however, is whether such transformation also tended toward fracturing the ideological hegemony under which such a movement was initiated.

Having the results of the two parallel studies will allow us to compare the more usual situation in the county with the unusual and extreme situation in Santa Monica. We must keep in mind, however, that the scale of Santa Monica, along with its overwhelmingly tenant population, made it a far easier organizational target than the massive County or City of Los Angeles. In addition the particular spatial characteristics of Santa Monica as a desirable place to live and as a center of real estate speculation gave the struggle in that city a component not present in all parts of the county.

IV

The desire to determine the tenant consciousness of the population in the study areas necessitated that the social consciousness of tenants, that is, tenant consciousness, be defined with considerable specificity. References have been made to this form of political consciousness in the tenant literature, but no one has previously undertaken the task of defining the term (Burghardt, S. 1972, p. 198; Jennings 1972, p. 61). Authors have noted that initial spontaneous protests may occur without the development of collective consciousness, but it is generally acknowledged that to sustain a movement, a common consciousness must exist in the movement's social base (Reich 1972, p. 285).

The work of John Leggett was a great assistance in approaching the problem of how to specifically define tenant consciousness.[5] In *Race, Class and Labor* (1968), Leggett defines working-class consciousness in quantifiable terms. Based on his reading of Marxist literature, Leggett divided four primary dimensions of working-class consciousness: class verbalization, skepticism about the system, militancy, and egalitarianism. He then devised tests for each of these four dimensions and, employing the Guttman scaling technique, ranked the workers he interviewed according to their level of consciousness.

We also divided our definition into four dimensions paralleling Leggett's categories. Instead of measuring class verbalization, we looked at the recognition of tenants' collective interests; instead of skepticism, we were interested in the level of theoretical sophistication; instead of militancy, we looked at willingness to be active; and instead of measuring egalitarianism, we were interested in attitudes about the institution of landlordism.

The next step in the process of defining tenant consciousness, in measurable terms, was to devise tests for each of the four dimensions of tenant consciousness. At this point Leggett's work became less helpful. While he demonstrated the theoretical basis for his selection of dimensions of consciousness, he did not provide the same foundation for his selection of tests. They appeared to be consistent with the dimensions he selected, but they were also tightly bound to the particular time and location of his study.

Because there is no tenant literature that could, without considerable interpretation, provide these tests, we turned to tenant activists to assist in the selection of appropriate tests. The inclusion of the activists in this process was consistent with the overall goals of the study. We are not interested in the political consciousness of tenants in isolation or, in the first instance, in relationship to general political perspectives in the United States. Our interest, rather, is with the consciousness of tenants vis-a-vis the tenant movement. The categories created, in the first instance, have no meaning out of this context.

What we hope to understand in measuring the consciousness of tenants is the extent to which the social base of tenants can be transformed into a social force, a tenant movement. The practitioners of the transformation are the tenant activists. It is our belief that they possess particular knowledge and judgment about this process of building a movement not otherwise available. To the extent that they are poor practitioners, in this regard, our tests are also poor. To guard against this, a peer selection technique was used. Employing this process, 32 activists identified by other activists as the leaders in the field were interviewed.

With the activists' help, a technique was adopted for classifying tenants one step beyond Leggett's method for classifying workers. Leggett employed a single test for each dimension of the consciousness he was measuring. He then ordered the dimensions, according to their significance to the definition, and using the Guttman scaling technique, tested to see if his scale was statistically valid. Workers were then classified, on the basis of the number of consciousness-indicating responses they gave, into levels from high to low consciousness.

Here the activists were not only asked what the best tests of consciousness were, but also to identify the types of tenants they encountered in their activism according to responses to the test they devised.

With this information we created six "archetype" levels of tenant consciousness with varying patterns of responses on the tests devised. Discriminant analysis was then used to derive a function from the activist-created data set and applied to the results of the interviews of the randomly selected tenants in the two surveys. The details of how this was accomplished are explained in Chapter 3 and the Appendix.

V

In Part One of the book, we present the historical analysis, report on the case study, define tenant consciousness in particularity, and classify the sample populations according to their level of consciousness. In the second part of the book, the process of consciousness formation that Gramsci described is examined. Because this has never been done before within the tenant movement, the analysis is quite detailed. Some readers may want to focus on questions of particular concern and read other portions of the analysis lightly. Reference to the tables and, particularly, to the figures can quickly convey much of what has been found. Many of the most important findings are presented in the portion of the introduction which follows.

Part Two begins with an examination of the demographics of the tenant populations in the two samples. Our analysis of the demographics, however, goes beyond understanding the makeup of the social base of tenants. What we are searching for are indications of how the social structure of the United States affects the formation of tenant consciousness and mobilization of the movement (Pickvance 1977).

In the more diverse and less mobilized county sample, demographics appear to play an important role in the formation of tenant consciousness. In the more homogeneous and highly mobilized Santa Monica sample, this is less true. For example, in the county, age, gender, ethnicity (race), and class were all significant factors. Among these, only age appears to have played a role in the formation of consciousness in Santa Monica.

The significance of age in both populations points to the life cycle character of tenant consciousness. Tenancy is often thought of as a life cycle status group (Perin 1977), but our emphasis is not on the status quality of tenancy. We are concerned about the formation of consciousness and hegemonic domination. In these terms we can see how individuals at various stages of life are more or less involved in enterprise and more or less interested in petty accumulation. At the extremes are the young who are in competition with the landlord for the right to accumulate the product of their labor and the old who have severed their direct relationship to production and only want to protect as much as they can of what they have accumulated in their productive lives.

Closely related to the life cycle concept is the role of social mobility in forming political consciousness. It has long been thought that a strong mythology of social mobility has been a major factor in the weakness of working-class consciousness and working-class movements in the United States. The significance of gender, ethnicity, and class in the county suggests differentials in the strength of this myth in the face of sexism, racism, and class domination. While the Santa Monica sample is homogeneous relative to the county sample, the finding that these elements were not significant in Santa Monica seems to indicate a degree of leveling in perceptions of social mobility in the face of the intense economic exploitation of real estate in that city.

With these observations in mind, we examine two particular sources of increased consciousness in detail: the everyday experience of tenants, particularly landlord-tenant conflict, and the desire and expectation of homeownership. Landlord-tenant conflict is the expected source of tenant consciousness. Not surprisingly, we found this to have been the case. However, the relationship was not a simple one. As suggested by our analysis of the demographics of tenant consciousness, various strata and classes were differentially impacted. Also, once again the results in the two samples were different. There has been a substantially greater sharing of information about such conflicts in Santa Monica, and this appears to have collectivized the experience, raising the consciousness of tenants who have not had any problems themselves.

This inquiry into the day-to-day experience of tenants raised the question of the interaction of experience, attitudes, and consciousness. Whether or not rent is fair or a particular action of a landlord is objectionable can be affected by the tenants' level of consciousness. In this sense consciousness can lead to greater consciousness, while a lack of consciousness can reinforce a continued lack of consciousness. This problem is not resolvable in the final analysis, but our investigation of the question did turn up substantial material bases for the attitudes expressed and suggests that experience was generating consciousness. In Part Three of the book when information on the tenants' overall political identity is added, we return to this question.

In the tenant literature it is suggested that it is not the landlord's objectionable actions that raise the consciousness of tenants. Rather the consciousness-raising catalytic agent is said to be the tenant's response to these actions (Indritz 1971). We investigate the tenants' responses and find evidence that this may be the case. Once again, the results in Santa

Monica were somewhat different from those in the county. The collective nature of conflict in Santa Monica appears to have insulated the tenants' willingness to take action from the possible negative consequences of resistance to landlord actions.

The analysis moves beyond the particular experiences of the tenants inverviewed to examine their general willingness to engage in building level organizing. Activists have said for years that the fear of being evicted has inhibited tenant organizing. Authors such as Ollman (1972) have noted that even if all other elements of consciousness are present, such a fear can still prevent the formulation of consciousness and mobilization of the population in question. The amount of activity that accompanied the post-Proposition 13 tenant revolt suggests that anger has replaced fear. We tested to see if the the tenants had a fear of eviction and found little indication of such a fear. Then the analysis turned to the question of why this change had taken place.

If this book had been written a few years ago, we would have most likely stopped our search for the sources of increased consciousness at this point. However, many people today believe that the real source of the tenant revolt is elsewhere than in landlord-tenant conflict. They. suggest that frustration over not being able to buy or the difficulty in buying have created a climate within which increased landlord-tenant conflict is taking place. There is particular interest in the tenants who will never be able to buy, what is referred to as the new "permanent tenant underclass."

Our inquiry into the desires and expectations of tenants regarding homeownership proved most interesting. The first striking finding was the universality of the desire to buy and the continued belief by most tenants in the homebuying ages that they will someday buy. The consciousness levels of the new underclass, however, varied between the two samples. Once again, the movement in Santa Monica seemed to be the determinant factor. It appears that being shut off from homeownership can be as depressing as it can be consciousness raising.

Overall, the Santa Monica results, with regards to expectations of attaining ownership, fit the expected pattern, while the county results did not. Part of the explanation for this appears to be related to the tenant movement activities in Santa Monica. However, social structure also appeared to play a part in explaining the difference. Homeownership as a symbol of upward mobility seemed to be more important to whites and professional-managerial tenants, those with the most upward mobility on the production side of their lives. If racism or sexism is blocking the tenants's upward mobility on the productive side, the homebuying problem seemed to lose much of its impact.

In Part Three of the book, we return to our original questions about the potential of the tenant movement and its ability to break free of the hegemonic control found to exist in the past. In this section the tenant movement is placed in the larger political context. We determine the political identity of all those interviewed, from conservative to progressive, and relate the tenants' political identity to their tenant consciousness. There was a clear relationship between the two. However, once again, the situation was different in the two samples. The relationship is stronger in Santa Monica. The source of this difference appears to have been the polarization that has taken place in that city. The prolonged activity appears to have driven people to align their positions on tenant issues to their overall political perspective. The inference drawn is that the tenant movement will run up against the general ideological map if it becomes increasingly aggressive. We go beyond this analysis to see if the tenant movement itself could be a source of change in general political identity. Some evidence was found that it could be the source of such change.

The focus of the study then shifts to the question of whether tenant consciousness can be mobilized. In this analysis we employ the categories suggested by Ollman's (1972) work on working-class consciousness: efficacy, allegiance, and action. Again, the findings in the two samples were somewhat different. In the county, efficacy was a central variable. The greater the sense of efficacy in the movement, the higher the consciousness. In Santa Monica the question of efficacy was settled and political identity replaced efficacy as a central variable. Allegiance proved to be the best test of tenant consciousness. In both samples allegiance was remarkably high suggesting an untapped potential in the county as a whole. However, we do point out that there is a difference in the nature of the allegiance in the two samples.

Our analysis of individuals' willingness to work in the movement discloses an extraordinary mobilization of tenants in Santa Monica. This mobilization again suggests an untapped political resource in the tenant population as a whole. A clear connection between building level activity and movement level activity in both samples indicates that additional landlord-tenant conflict will lead to an ever stronger movement. We also examine the relationship between tenant activism and overall social and political activism and find a mutually reinforcing connection.

At this point we have answered our first question. We have found substantial political potential in the tenant movement. The question that remains unanswered is whether this movement, as it gains strength, will free itself from the ideological hegemony of this country. To examine this, we create a scenario that assumes a shift left in political identity and

increased tenant consciousness in the tenant population. We then reviewed the positions of tenants with various political identities on questions of housing policy and private property. The results of the analysis
indicate that an extraordinary shift in political identity and tenant consciousness would have to take place before hegemonic control over tenant issues and the tenant movement might be broken. This is
demonstrated by comparing the results of interviews with British council housing tenants on questions of egalitarianism in housing with the
views of high consciousness, left-leaning tenants interviewed in Santa
Monica. In the final chapter, we summarize and conclude our findings.

NOTES

1. In many ways the story of tenants in the United States is a concrete example of the
struggle of people caught up in Locke's 'contradiction' that places those who labour and do
not accumulate property both in and out of civil society (MacPherson 1962). In Locke's
scheme of natural rights to 'life, liberty and estates', all members of society are individuals
entitled to life and liberty and have an interest in preserving these rights through their
membership in civil society. However, only those who have accumulated property have an
interest in preserving the rights of property. To Locke, government's major function was
the protection of property, and, therefore, while all men were members of society to be
ruled, only those who had accumulated property could be members for the purpose of
ruling. This was justified by the assumption that, although all men are created equal, those
who successfully accumulate property are able, throuh the leisure property affords, to
develop fully rational minds in ways not possible for those without property. The fact that
some people accumulate property and others do not is seen as inevitable in a monetary and
market economy. Although tenants in the United States fought for and won a degree of
political equality, they accepted much of Locke's acquisitive philosophy. The inevitable
economic inequalities carry with them the social inequalities that cannot within these
confines be resolved.

2. Approximately a third of the U.S. population rents. Overwhelmingly, they rent
from private landlords.

3. The question of absorption or reactionary populism will be discussed in the final
chapter. For our purposes it is enough to point out here a debate within the social movement literature between populist and Marxist views in which it is questioned whether any
nonclass based movement can escape absorption and be successful in transforming society
(Lustig 1980). Within the populist literature the question is more one of democratic versus
reactionary movements (Boyte 1980). Their distinctions are between movement dominated
by themes of "civic idealism, cooperation, religiously motivated action on behalf of the
oppressed, pluralism, and tolerance" as opposed to movements dominated by themes of
"rapacious individualism, hedonism, and contempt for others" (p. 60).

4. California is the third most populated tenant state after New York and Hawaii. About
45 percent of Californians rent.

5. There are, of course, many studies of social consciousness. Leggett's book, however,
is particularly useful because of its attempt to quantify levels of consciousness. This is
unusual in the literature. The book also has the distinction of predicting the black revolts of
the 1960s. This seems a very strong indicator of the validity of the method.

The use of quantitative methods in such a study is itself somewhat controversial. Gramsci, for example, wrote a diatribe against the use of statistics in political analysis (1971, pp. 428–29). The main basis for the criticism revolves around the fleeting nature of what is called "psychological consciousness" (what we call social consciousness), and the dynamic character of political change. We, in large part, agree with the observation about consciousness and politics. However, the criticism is more directed at the interpretation and use of the statistics than the intrinsic wisdom of using quantitative methods.

We have tried to avoid the major pitfalls of quantitative analysis in three ways consistent with Gramsci's approach (Femia 1981, p. 78). The first is the placing of the analysis in a historical and material context. The second is the completion of two simultaneous studies of related movements at different stages of development to gain a picture of the process of transformation of consciousness. The third is, where possible, an interpretation of the results consistent with having only a single frame of the whole moving picture.

Tenants
AND
the American Dream

PART 1

Tenant Consciousness

1

The History of a Movement and an Ideology

Many early settlers came to the United States expressly to escape the institution of landlordism (Kraus 1971, p. 335). To a colonial official of 1732, these people were "the better sort" who sought to "avoid the dependency on landlords" (Warner, Jr. 1972, p. 16). If, upon arrival, colonists found themselves to be tenants, it was said that they could not be happy. As a missionary making a tour of tenanted areas in 1802 put it: "The American can never flourish on leased lands. They have too much enterprise to work for others or remain tenants, and where they are under the necessity of living on such lands, I find they are greatly depressed in mind and are losing their animation" (Christman 1945, p. 9).

Early on in most of the colonies, inexpensive land made land ownership within the reach of most people. However, in parts of New York and New Jersey, there were wealthy landowners who would not sell their land. They were attempting to build extensive manorial estates propertied by large numbers of tenants (Hofstadter 1973, pp. 9–13). In these areas it was not long before the United States had its first major landlord-tenant contests (Kim 1978).

The gist of the disputes, which dot the mid-eighteenth, on the surface was not much different from those of today. They were over evictions and rents. It was true then, as it is true today, that if a landlord attempted to evict a large number of his tenants, he was liable to meet collective resistance. In the colonial period this resistance took the form of groups of tenants attempting to forcibly prevent evictions. If unsuccessful on the spot, the groups would return at a later date, eject whomever had taken over the property and return it to the original tenant. Those who resisted the tenants often later found their homes dismantled and strewn about in pieces (Countryman 1976).

3

While the immediate goal of the tenants' efforts was to obtain fair rent and security of tenure, the underlying aim, unlike today, was to wrestle the land that the tenants worked from the landlords' ownership. After all, they had come for the promise of land and had put their enterprise into the land in question. They saw no basis for the landlords' claim to ownership in this contest. The tenants' aim earned them the title of "levelers" (Thompson 1966, pp. 22–25) and made them ideologically controversial even with members of the urban working class, some of whom were already complaining about rent gouging practices of urban landlords (Hawke 1966, p. 478; Bridenbaugh 1955).

As the revolution approached, the population of tenants was spreading beyond New York and New Jersey throughout the colonies. Land was rising in value and becoming less accessible, while the urban population was increasing (Lockridge 1971, pp. 479–80). By the time of the Revolution, tenants had become a significant enough percentage of the population to have their interests addressed in the demands for freedom from the British. Urban tenants joined with property owners in the Sons of Liberty, for the theme "no taxation without representation" had special meaning to tenants who were generally denied the vote in colonial America (Morais 1971).

TENANTS AND POLITICAL EQUALITY

The proclamation of equal rights and government by the consent of the governed in the Declaration of Independence led tenants to assume they would be granted the vote. Tenants in Philadelphia especially looked forward to that day. After the Revolution, they would be able to elect their own to office, and as a result, landlords would no longer be able to pass laws that made it so easy to evict a tenant (Williamson 1960, pp. 86, 286).

Thomas Jefferson, who wrote the Declaration of Independence, favored giving tenants the vote, but there were many who did not (Peterson 1975, pp. 356–57). They questioned whether tenants had the independence with which to govern, and, although the Continental Congress of 1776, after much uproar, advised all the states to expand the voting population, only a few responded favorably (Williamson 1960, pp. 92–93). In Virginia, Jefferson attempted to speak to the claims of dependency on the part of tenants by suggesting that all Virginians without sufficient property to qualify to vote be given enough land from the public domain to qualify. However, when the Virginia Constitutional Convention was convened, the idea was not even discussed (Peterson 1970, pp. 105–6).

The result of the failure to grant tenants equal suffrage rights in the revolutionary period may have had long lasting effects on the legal structure of the United States. Virtually no tenants had either input into the writing of the U.S. Constitution or any say in its ratification. It is Charles Beard's hypothesis that the document was written with the express purpose of protecting those in possession of large amounts of property from a feared future majority of small property owners and tenants (1913). In particular the fear was of a future majority of the urban "landless proletariat" (p. 157).[1]

In some states the principle of popular government itself was far from settled (Sisson 1974). In New York Governor Morris said that "there never was and never will be a civilized society without an aristocracy." Alexander Hamilton, somewhat more directly stated, "Your public is a great beast." The feeling was "that government was best which best provided incentive, opportunity, and security for those who could accumulate and administer wealth." That this would create an elite class was not feared (Fox 1934, pp. 5–6).

When it became clear that equal suffrage rights were not forthcoming, agitation for change began among the population (p. 12). Urban, working tenants began to draft political platforms that included universal male suffrage (Rayback 1959, p. 65). Feelings were running high in many circles about the dangers of the aristocracy of which Morris spoke. The French Revolution added fuel to a growing democratic fervor and excited many with its creeds and programs (Soboul 1965).

It was in this atmosphere that Thomas Jefferson and Thomas Paine connected the threat of an emerging aristocracy with questions of land-ownership (Peterson 1975, pp. 467–68; Williamson, A. 1973, p. 242). They both took the agrarian position that land was the common stock of all and called for economic as well as political reform to deal with what they saw as the root problem of increasing land monopoly. Paine wrote, "man did not make the earth and though he had a natural right to *occupy* it, he had no right to *locate his property* in perpetuity any part of it; neither did the Creator of the earth open a land-office, from whence the first title deeds should issue" (Williamson, A. 1973, p. 243).

Jefferson continued to call for public provision of land to the landless and said if this was not done, the time might come when "every man who cannot find employment, but who can find uncultivated land, shall be at liberty to cultivate it, paying a moderate rent" (Peterson 1975, p. 397). Paine proposed a more direct redistribution of wealth in the form of an inheritance tax to be levied on the land, as opposed to the improvements on land, equal in value to the "natural inheritance of all the people" that had been absorbed by the owner. The funds collected would be distributed in part to people reaching their majority of 21 years as a stake toward enterprise and in part to people when they reached 50 years of age who presumably could no longer work (Paine 1922).

While Jefferson's and Paine's ideas were not adopted, in New York, a powerful political club called the Tammany Society was converted to "democratic ideals" and began to work for expanded suffrage (Link 1942, pp. 18–28, 209).[2] The party's writers and orators spread the message throughout the state. At the peak of their efforts, a New York paper reported that hardly a county in the state could be found where the "siren song of French equality" had not beguiled the people (Fox 1965, p. 237).

These efforts brought the suffrage issue to a head in New York in 1821. Similar efforts by others did the same in the states of Massachusetts and Virginia later in the same decade. In each of these states very heated debates preceded the granting of suffrage rights to tenants.[3] The opposition was quite formidable, including John Adams, Daniel Webster, Chancellor Kent, James Madison, John Monroe, and John Marshall (Rossiter 1962, p. 118). They tried to characterize the debates as between propertied and unpropertied interests, with the need to protect property taking primacy over whatever rights unpropertied people might have. However, the masses of people, propertied and unpropertied alike, refused to accept that conception of society in the United States. Instead, they saw the issue as one between the emerging U.S. aristocracy and the desired democracy.

The debate in New York is most illustrative for our purposes (Carter and Stone 1821). While the language is sometimes dated, the arguments concerning the worthiness of tenants and landholders and their respective contributions to society, are very similar to those made during landlord-tenant policy debates today.

The opponents of tenant suffrage argued that in Lockeian terms the ownership of property was a good indicator of the worth of an individual. They argued that among the landlowners one could "always expect to find moderation, frugality, order, honesty, and a due sense of independence, liberty, and justice." These were the men to whom "we owe all the embellishments and comforts and blessings of life." They asked: "Who builds our churches? Who erects our hospitals? Who raises our school houses?" And, they answered: "Those who have property." Among those who owned no property they said that one found a "ringed and speckled," "motley and undefinable population" known as the "idle and profligate." To give the vote to such as these would do little to encourage the thrift necessary to acquire property and thus earn the vote.

They were convinced that either landlords or employers would be able to control the votes of this population. If not, the unpropertied would certainly be organized against the interest of property by radicals.

"Ambitious and wicked men" would "inflame such combustible material." They warned that land reform that would divide the property of those who now possessed it among those who did not would follow. The problem was, as they saw it, that "liberty without wisdom and without justice is no better than wild and savage licentiousness."

Those supporting tenant suffrage began their reply with a search for the historical basis of the claims of special privileges for those who held property. They found it in the feudal and aristocratic history of Europe. To them feudalism and aristocracy meant the selective abuse of power, prosperity or influence (Welter 1975, p. 78). As such, they had no place in U.S. society. A delegate asked those in attendance to think about the failure of societies in history. Going back as far as ancient Greece, societies had not fallen from any vice of the poor. "They were all destroyed by the wealth of aristocracy bearing down on the people." This, the delegate said, established no proof that ownership of land contributed to the "elevation of mind" or gave "stability to independence" or added "wisdom to virtue." It was not among the poor that one found the "miser," the "Shylock," or the "speculator." As to the building of churches, hospitals and schools, the delegate noted that it was not wealth but the hands of labor that built these structures, the same hands so feared by the opponents of tenant suffrage.

The opposition again tried to persuade the propertied delegates of the worthiness of their stand by emphasizing the potential split between the propertied and unpropertied. "The day may come—then the state will be convulsed with civil commotions—when we may have riots and bloodshed; and wise men are bound to provide against future evils and calamities by creating such depositories of power as shall at all times be competent to afford protection to all, by preserving the supremacy of law."

THE CALL FOR ECONOMIC EQUALITY

The dominant concept of equal rights expressed in this and other suffrage debates was largely one of equal political rights. However, there were those at the convention who indicated they might have followed Jefferson or Paine and take the concept further, into the economic realm. One delegate responding directly to accusations of Jacobinism[4] reported a conversation he had had with "that Friend of universal liberty, the patriotic Lafayette." Lafayette had expressed his exultation to this delegate that the French Revolution had brought about redistribution of his and other estates to the benefit of thousands. The delegate begged the opposition to listen to the words of Lafayette, for "This, sire, is the language of true patriotism; the language of one whose heart, larger than his possessions, embraced the whole family of man in the circuit of its beneficence.'' Another stated, ''Property, sir, when compared with our other essential rights, is insignificant and trifling. 'Life, liberty, and the pursuit of happiness'—and not property—are set forth in the Declaration of Independence as cardinal objects; property is not even named.''

While no one attending the New York convention called directly for a forced redistribution of property, even in Jefferson's or Paine's terms, there were those outside the convention who did (Pole 1978). Primary among these was Thomas Skidmore, a leader of the New York City labor movement. However, Skidmore did not downplay the importance of property, as the delegate had at the New York convention. He believed, as the opponents of suffrage did, that independence came with the ownership of property. However, as a champion of equal rights, he did not doubt the worth of those who did not have it. Following the same logic that led Jefferson to propose the provision of land to the landless in Virginia, Skidmore stated that land must be provided to those presently without this "crucial element." It was not a matter of debate with Skidmore, and he criticized Jefferson for not including a "right to property" in the Declaration of Independence instead of the ambiguous "pursuit of happiness" (Ware 1935, p. 157).

Skidmore's proposal went beyond those of Jefferson and Paine in that it called for the actual redistribution of land from those who, in Skidmore's eyes, had more than they could use to those who were landless. He reached this proposal from a conceptual premise that varied from that of Jefferson and Paine. Rather than emphasizing land as the common stock of mankind, Skidmore focused on the centrality of enterprise in U.S. society. He believed that "all men should live on their own labor and not on the labor of others" (Skidmore 1829, p. 5). This meant that, if by whatever logic, someone should be able to own more land than he could work, he should not be able to use it "to extract from others the result of their labor by charging rent." To Skidmore, someone who charged rent converted "their fellow beings into slaves for their use."

Although Skidmore argued that tenants as enslaved people "had the right no matter the law to dispossess" landlords of "their" property, he stopped short of calling for immediate direct action (pp. 4–5). Instead, in his book, The Rights of Man to Property, written in 1829, he set forth what he considered a reasonable scheme to redistribute land through regulation of inheritance. Instead of taxing the common element of inheritance as Paine proposed, Skidmore described a plan to limit all inheritances in land to 160 acres, the amount of land a man could work.

The remainder of anyone's estate would pass to the government to be redistributed to those without property.

Neither Skidmore's words nor his proposal ignited the "combustible material" as was feared. To the contrary, rather than leading to an uprising of the masses, it led to Skidmore's removal as a leader of the labor movement. He was branded a radical and an agrarianist who was taking the labor movement away from such issues of direct concern to working people as wages and hours (Rayback 1959, pp. 69–70). His ideas on the redistribution of property were specifically rejected. The General Executive Committee of the Workingman's Party did not see the conflict between property and enterprise. Instead, they saw such a restriction on accumulation of property as a brake on enterprise. They stated, "We expect the reward of our toil, and consider the right of individual property the strongest incentive to industry" (Miller 1967, p. 42).

Anti-Renters: Rural Expropriation

The rejection of Skidmore's logic by urban workers did not lessen its efficacy for the agrarian tenant. Some ten years after Skidmore's book was published, agrarian tenants in New York's Hudson River Valley, set out, as Skidmore put it, to dispossess from "the aggressor the instrument of his aggression" (1829, pp. 4–5). In 1839 a 20-year struggle began, involving the lives of some 300,000 tenants, for control of nearly 2,000,000 acres of land (Christman 1945). Known as the Anti-Rent Movement, the struggle had all the elements of a modern tenant movement: mass organization, a rent strike, and confrontations over evictions, political action, and litigation (Ellis 1946).

The tenants who took active part in the Anti-Rent Movement were, in the main, descendants of families that had lived on the contested land for at least 60 years. Many were descendants of Revolutionary War veterans. The landlords were descendants of the landlords who resisted tenant actions in the eighteenth century. Most of their land was accumulated under grants from the King of England before the Revolution. The tenants took the position that they had more than paid for their land in rent over the years (Cooper 1846, pp. 282–84; Ellis 1946, p. 241) and that the landlords were aristocrats who, as Skidmore would have put it, held the tenants in continuing feudal bondage (Ellis pp. 227–28). As a compromise, they offered the landlord the return of his original investment, but he declined their offer.

The tenants saw themselves as acting to fulfill the promises of the American Revolution and the Declaration of Independence. Their forefathers had fought what they referred to as the first Revolutionary War for the landlords. The "second Revolutionary War" would be fought for the tenants. As they stated, "Honor, justice, and humanity forbid that we should any longer tamely surrender that freedom which we have so freely inherited from our gallant ancestors. . . . We will take up the ball of the Revolution where our fathers stopped it and roll it to the final consummation of freedom and independence of the masses" (Christman 1945, p. 20).

ATTENTION!
ANTI-RENTERS'
AWAKE! AROUSE!

A Meeting of the friends of Equal Rights will be held on _____
in the Town of _____ at _____ O'clock.

Let the opponents of Patroonry rally in their strength. A great crisis is approaching. Now is the time to strike. The minions of Patroonry are at work. No time is to be lost. Awake! Arouse! and

Strike 'till the last armed foe expires.
Strike for your altars and your fires—
Strike for the green graves of your sires.
God and your happy homes!

☞ The Meeting will be addressed by PETER FINKLE and other Speakers.

From Christman, 1978: p. 108. Originally published, 1945. Reprinted by permission.

To carry out their war on the landlords, the tenants organized in Indian bands modeled after the band that participated in the "Boston Tea Party." In this instance, the issue was rent rather than a tax, and one was either a champion of equal rights or "down-rent" or a friend of the aristocrats and "up-rent." It is estimated that as many as 10,000 tenants throughout the Anti-Rent area were members of the Indian bands (p. 75). At the sound of a signal horn, the tenants massed in their groups fully disguised as Indians under Indian aliases, led by Dr. Boughton, also known as "Big Thunder." When a sheriff threatened a tenant's peaceful possession, the Indians resisted. Their favorite tactic was to tar and feather the offending sheriff and deliver him out of their territory.

The tenants formed an Anti-Rent Association and held political conventions to endorse candidates for office who would bring their economic problems into the political arena (Ellis 1946, pp. 268–312). The association brought litigation attacking the landlords' titles and the terms of leases, and lobbied the state legislature. The conventions assisted in electing Anti-Rent candidates from seven counties in the state, influenced the election of governor, forced the calling of a state constitutional convention to further "democratize" the state, and, in the end, caused the transfer of much of the land to tenant ownership.

Disguises of the Delaware Anti-Renters, 1845.

From Christman, 1978: p. 156. Originally published, 1945. Reprinted by permission.

ANTI-RENTER SONG

The Landlord's Lament

(Air: "Oh, Dear, What Can the Matter Be")

The Helderberg boys are playing the dickens!
The night of confusion around me now thickens,
Unless the rent business with some of us quickens,
We'll all have to live without rents!

> CHORUS: Oh, dear, dear, what can the matter be?
> Dear, dear, what can the matter be?
> What shall I do with my tenants?
> How shall I get all my rents?

I used to get rich through the poor toiling tenants,
And I spent all their earnings in pleasures satanic,
But now I confess I'm in a great panic,
Because I can get no more rent!

> CHORUS: Oh, dear, etc.

My tenants once to my office were flocking,
Some without a coat, or a shoe or a stocking,
But now I declare it is really shocking,
To know I shall get no more rent.

> CHORUS: Oh, dear, etc.

I must give up this business I vow it's no use to me,
It's been a continual source of abuse to me;
The friends of equal rights give no peace to me
Until they get clear of the rent.

> CHORUS: Oh, dear, etc.

E. P.
—From the *Albany* Freeholder.

From Christman, 1978: p. 325. Originally published, 1945. Reprinted by permission.

The landlords, for their part, attempted to match the tenants' efforts move for move (pp. 286–95). They formed law-and-order societies to help put down the "injuns," they organized their own assocation to raise money to fight the tenants' numbers, and when the Anti-Renters went to the legislature to begin lobbying, they found the landlords already hard at work.

While the Indian bands brought the tenants' problems to a head, the victory was won in the legislative arena. A number of legislative proposals were made. It was proposed that the state buy the disputed land using the power of eminent domain and convey it to the tenants, but few legislators supported the idea. One house of the legislature actually passed a bill related to the proposal made by Skidmore. Under this legislation, tenants could have bought their land at a predetermined price on the death of the landlord.

What was adopted had two parts. The first part was the elimination of distress for rents. Attempted distress sales were often major scenes of Anti-Rent Indian-sheriff conflict. The second part was the imposition of a special income tax on the rent the landlords derived from the property. The tax took much of the landlords' profits and was a major contributing factor in the landlords' eventual decisions to sell the land to the tenants at an accommodating price.

The Conflict Between Aristocracy and Enterprise

While the tenants mounted an extraordinary organizational and political effort vis-a-vis the landlords, it would be a mistake to see the Anti-Rent issue as an isolated struggle between the landlords and the tenants. It was a matter of public debate that was decided by public opinion and interests other than the parties to the dispute. Both contestants had their champions who attempted to popularize their positions. On the landlord side was James Fenimore Cooper, noted novelist, who wrote a series of three books speaking to the issue. The first two romanticized the efforts of a pioneer family who claimed the land later made available to tenants, and the third, entitled, *The Redskins,* was a direct attack on the Anti-Rent Movement. The National Reform Association, a radical land reform organization based in New York City sided with the tenants. The National Reformers, who were influenced by Skidmore's earlier efforts, traveled among the Anti-Renters to help organize the tenants and supported them in their publication (Christman 1945, p. 67).

Cooper, whose father was a friend of Stephen Van Rensellaer, the great patroon of the Anti-Rent area, and whose family was very much like the one he wrote about in the first two books, saw himself as the

voice of the "landed gentry" (Spiller 1931, pp. 3–7). He had many democratic sentiments, but all of them fell before the central importance of the
landed estate. Property was not something to be commodified or traded.
It was the source of stability and wisdom, to be held and cherished. He
stated that he favored equal civil and political rights, but he argued that
unequal rights of property were essential (p. 248). The landed gentry,
whom these unequal rights protected, were the source of a "high order
of civilization," and the protector of liberty. Only it had the stuff to resist
both the "royal despot" and the "vulgar tyrants," the latter being a
reference to the product of "excess democracy," in this case the Anti-
Renters (pp. 250–51).

For their side, the National Reformers asserted the importance of
democracy, equal rights, enterprise, and a concept of property consistent with industry. They spoke much as Skidmore might have. They
varied only in claiming that the Declaration of Independence already
contained the concept of property rights to which they referred. They
argued that an individual's right to life had to include "a right to land
enough to till for his subsistence" (Foner, P. 1955, p. 184). To them, the
landlords, who in this instance had received their property from the
King of England, were clearly aristocrats, and the tenants, who worked
the land, were clearly entitled to have it free of the expropriation of their
labor in rent (Cooper 1846, pp. 250–57).

These were very powerful arguments in a society that was being
transformed from the "agrarian and feudal" to the "industrial and democratic" (Spiller 1931, p. 306). The forces of industry, labor, and capital
were moving to the centers of power. There was no interest among either
labor or capital in defending those seeking to hold on to the old order.
Labor and capital disagreed about the acceptability of capital obtained
through inheritance or accumulated through speculation, but they
agreed that no person possessing mental or physical ability had a moral
right to consume that which he did not in some manner produce (Fox
1965, p. 396). Among those without the "moral right" were "aristocrats" who acquired their land through a grant from a king rather than
through enterprise.

The arguments of the National Reformers were consistent with the
interests and beliefs of industry. Thus, the New York state legislative
committee that investigated the Anti-Rent Movement came to conclusions supportive of the tenants and against the primary remaining vestiges of feudalism in the state. Their metaphors disclosed an apparent
confluence of agrarian and capitalist ideologies. They found that the rent
the tenants were paying was "a drag on enterprise," that the lack of full
ownership blunted the "spirit of initiative," and the restraints on aliena-

tion retained by the landlords under the leases prevented the "free exchange of property" (Ellis 1946, pp. 274–75).

The first two findings were a confirmation of the centrality of enterprise, while the third endorsed the commodification of land. While both the Anti-Renters and the forces of industry applauded the committee's findings, it is not clear that the parties would have agreed on the definitions of the terms used by the committee. In an agrarian context, enterprise was viewed as repesenting hard work. The yeoman farmer worked the land and in improving and enriching it deserved both the reward of the yield and increased value of improved land. With the development of capitalism, enterprise took on the additional meaning of cleverness— the ability to accumulate a fortune by the intelligent manipulation of capital and the labor of others (Blau 1946, pp. 174–204). Land, still a component in the productive process, also took on the characterization of a commodity that by itself might be traded for speculative profit. What is of import is how easily the different versions of antifeudalism intertwined, masking a very important transformation in social relations, "rules of the game," that the urban tenant now had to face, particularly the distinction between the individualized production of an agrarian society and the socialized bases of production in an industrial society.

URBAN RENT AS A COMMODITY

Although complaints about the practices of urban landlords predate the Revolution, it was only with the expansion of capitalism that urban struggles over rent took on movement proportions. This point of origin generally dates from the 1830s when urban housing began to be characterized as a major social problem (Ford 1936, p. 92). The increased criticism was brought on by bank-supported land speculation that drove urban land values up as much as 220 percent in the period between 1833 and 1837 (Raybeck 1959, p. 25). With the increase in land values came equivalent increases in rents and a deterioration in the condition of rental housing to the point of creating the beginnings of this country's first modern urban slums.

The speculative bubble burst in what is known as the Panic of 1837. Tenants were especially hard hit. Unemployment soared,and the threat of eviction and of finding one's family homeless was always near. Those fortunate enough to find space filled the almshouses and poorhouses to capacity; others were left in the cold (McGrane 1924, p. 131). Rents and evictions were not the only problems tenants faced. The prices of essential commodities were rising out of reach. In early February of 1837,

Cartoon that appeared during the Panic of 1837.

From Schnapper, 1975: p. 31. Reprinted by permission.

notices calling for a demonstration appeared about New York declaring: "Bread, Meat, Rent, Fuel! Their Prices Must Come Down! The voice of the people shall be heard, and will prevail!" "All friends of humanity determined to resist monopolists and extortionists" were invited to attend (*Niles Weekly Register,* Feb. 18, 1837). Between 5,000 and 6,000 people attended and heard speakers, who, "in most exciting manner, denounced the landlords, and the holders of flour, for the prices of rents and provisions" (Hofstadter and Wallace 1970, p. 128).

The lumping of rent with the commodities of flour, meat, and fuel points out the essential difference between agrarian rent and urban rent. To the farmer the rented property is primarily an item of production, while to the urban worker it is overwhelmingly one of consumption. Therefore, in the urban context the argument that rented property is the location of the tenant's enterprise and should, therefore, belong to the tenant breaks down. Urban rent, in contrast to rural, may be justified by this logic because the property can be seen as the location of the land-lord's enterprise, while the tenant is likely to engage in enterprise else-where (Harvey 1976).

This does not mean that urban rent is not the subject of criticism consistent with the ideological framework in the United States. Like any consumption item, particularly those that are necessities, urban rent is subject to the criticism that the price is excessive and, as in the case of the 1837 demostration, a product of monopoly and extortion. During the revolutionary era, it was common to regulate the prices of goods in short supply. Such regulations often included the control of rents that could be charged by inns, which in many cases had become boardinghouses for urban workers (Morris 1971, p. 85). While the central economic concept had already moved away from that of a "moral economy" to that of "laissez-faire" by the 1830s, the notion of a "just price" for necessities remained then as it does today (Foner, E. 1976b, pp. 146–48). Indeed, it was the concept that one may not exploit a monopoly of a necessity such as housing that was the basis for the United States Supreme Court decision *Block* v. *Hirsh* (41 Sup. Ct. 458 1919) upholding World War I rent controls.

URBAN RENT AS THE PRODUCT OF LAND MONOPOLY

This focus on urban housing as an item of consumption should not cause us to forget that housing is located on land and that the urban landlord could also continue to be classified as a land monopolist. Although rent was lumped in protests with other commodities, this observation was not overlooked in the 1840s. The symbol of urban land monopoly of that day was Jacob Astor. He was the only man in New York richer than Stephen Van Rensellaer (Beach 1845, p. 4). While Astor owned land throughout the country, the majority of the value of his real estate holdings was in New York City (Myers 1927, p. 113). He owned so much land in the city, much of which was purchased at foreclosure sales during the Panic of 1837, that he earned the title of "landlord of New York" (O'Connor 1941, p. 51; Zetnick, 1979–80, p. 76).

George Henry Evans of the National Reform Association, applying the same logic used to support the attack on the Anti-Rent landlords, noted that it was land monopoly that allowed Astor, "without labor, to amass to himself the proceeds of the labor of thousands of his fellow citizens" (*Workingmen's Advocate*, Feb. 1, 1845). When Astor died in 1848, James Gordon Bennett, editor of the *New York City Herald*, made a proposal, much like Paine's, to recapture for the people of New York that portion of Astor's estate due to Astor's monopoly of land in the city. He reasoned that the increase in value of the real estate, "one-half of his immense property—ten millions, at least," was because of the growth and development of the city, a product not of Astor's labor but, "the aggregate intelligence, industry and commerce of New York" (Zetnick 1979–80, p. 77).

The application of this criticism of land monopoly to Astor, although similar in form to the criticism of Van Rensellaer, also masks a major change in the role land was playing in the emerging industrial society. Astor and his family replaced Van Rensellaer and his family as the political kingmakers of New York and the country. Although still founded on land-based wealth, the shift in political power was indicative of the importance of urban, as opposed to rural, land that could be linked with the expansion of capitalist enterprise and result in extraordinary accumulation.

The urban tenants also seemed to be just as aware as the Anti-Renters that their rent had over time, more than paid for the property they occupied (*Young America*, April 12, 1845), and there were warnings in this period that the Anti-Renter's refusal to pay rent might spread to the cities (*Workingmen's Advocate*, Sept. 14, 1844). Facing an intense housing shortage, urban tenants, like the agrarian counterparts, organized, forming a "Tenants' League" in 1848 (*Herald*, Feb. 24, 1848). The league, which was also supported by the National Reform Association, had as its goal the protection of tenants' interests. To do this, it developed a complete housing program designed to regulate rents, protect tenants against unwarranted eviction, and encourage the construction of better quality, new housing. Although the league's rent control scheme applied to housing, land, and building, it was based primarily on the notion of land monopoly and a lack of landlord productivity, rather than on a concept of commodity price regulation. They likened rent, again as the Supreme Court did in *Block* v. *Hirsh* some 70 years later, to interest and sought a usury limit on rent at the rate of 7 percent per annum on the investment in the rental property. They called for a restriction on the "aristocratic" power of arbitrary eviction by demanding a prohibition on evictions of rent-paying tenants for the purpose of renting to another tenant. New construction was to be induced by a tax on unimproved lots, and quality of housing was to be improved by limiting lot coverage of new construction.

Although the league characterized the landlords as unproductive, that is, "fat and lazy," as opposed to the "honest, hardworking" tenants, they did not call for a Skidmorelike expropriation of the rented property by the tenants. While the lack of productive work on the landlord's part limited the justifiable return he might receive on his "unproductive capital," it did not change the understanding of who owned the property. The land was not obtained by grant from a king, and the housing was not the direct product of the tenants' labor. Even if a landlord had already expropriated enough of the rewards of a tenant's labor to more than pay for the property, the U.S. urban tenant apparently still did not feel justified in calling, as the Anti-Renters had, for the termination of rent and the transfer of title to the property to the tenant.

AN AGRARIAN APPROACH TO URBAN SUPPLY AND DEMAND

The league's proposals remained alive in tenant circles for a considerable number of years, but they had little chance of being adopted against the flow of laissez-faire, antigovernment regulation sentiment of the time (N.Y. Tribune, April 3, 1866). Instead, a National Reformer's proposal to break the eastern land monopoly through the distribution of land from the public domain in the West to the landless gained popular support. The proposal, which eventually culminated in the adoption of the Homestead Act of 1862, read a great deal like Jefferson's earlier plan. However, the concept was now shrouded in the language of supply and demand in addition to concepts of equal rights. The analysis tied the workingman's problem of low wages and high rent to an oversupply of labor in the eastern cities. The logic began with the idea that high rents from land monopoly cause demands for increases in wages. The high wages were thought to attract new workers to the area, which, in turn, drove the rents up again, while driving wages down, bringing about new demand for higher wages. As long as the land monopoly was not broken, this cycle could not be broken (Workingmen's Advocate, March 1845).

George Henry Evans believed that a substantial number of workers would prefer a farm in the West over factory life and tenancy in the East. When these workers left, the eastern tenements would empty, rents would go down, and wages would go up. He went so far as to predict that if Congress passed the legislation opening up western lands in 1851, rents in the eastern cities would be nominal by 1860 (Foner, P. 1955, pp. 184–85). When Congress acted in 1862, it was too late to serve the intended purpose, as most of the arable lands that were accessible in the West had already gone into private ownership with much of it falling into the hands of land speculators (Gates 1973, p. 156).

On the United States frontier in the third quarter of the nineteenth century, one-third of the farms were held by tenants. In some areas it was over one-half (Gates 1973). As in the Anti-Renter area, the newcomers found that massive amounts of land had been accumulated by a few individuals. Many of these rural landlords chose to exploit their control of the land with rent and eviction policies that resulted in major landlord-tenant conflict.[5]

There is considerable doubt about whether the Homestead Act would have worked any better if it had been passed in 1851. It is now generally believed that urban workers would not have moved West in great numbers even if more free land had been available. Few had the means, and it is not clear that many had the interest (Shannon 1966). In the 40 years following the adoption of the Homestead Act, the problems of urban tenants actually grew worse.[6]

INCREASING HARDSHIPS FOR URBAN TENANTS

In the eastern cities, such as New York, where the population had grown four times that of 1850 by 1890, new immigrants had a particularly rough experience as tenants. Many immigrants were met at the boats in New York by runners who brought them to landlords specializing in fleecing these new arrivals. The landlords would lock up the tenants' luggage on the pretense that it was necessary for safekeeping. When the tenants, seeking to establish themselves, soon defaulted on the rent, they found themselves on the street without their luggage, the contents of which usually represented the tenants' total possessions and life savings (Miller 1967, p. 89). In 1848 the New York Legislature adopted legislation prohibiting the practice, but it failed to stop it; theft replaced law (Ernst 1949, pp. 28–29).

The common New York practice was for the landowner to rent an entire building to an agent at a rate he felt was a "fair return" on his investment. These rates of return are said to have ranged between 25 and 45 percent in some areas (Foner, P. 1955, p. 23). The agent, who was entitled to any rent money he could secure above this amount, had every incentive to maximize the rent receipts and had no incentive to maintain the property. Thus, tenants were packed into untenable spaces at high rents in what became the most densely populated city in the western world (Miller 1967, p. 135). The exploitation of the tenants did not stop there. The agents also commonly owned local stores that provided the other necessities of life to the tenants. Controlling both the tenants' living space, food, and the like, the agents held their tenants in a "state of abject dependence and vassalage little short of actual slavery" (p. 137).

In response to the growing problems of tenants, Dr. John Griscom, known as this country's first housing reformer, began an organization of "good citizens" in the 1840s to work toward reform of the conditions in the slums (Veiller 1903, p. 76). In 1850 the New York precursor to the Carpenter's Union also called for reform. Housing construction was so shoddy that structures often collapsed, killing either workers building them or tenants occupying them. Because of this, the carpenters called for construction to be supervised by qualified workers. They also called for free night lodging for the indigent and for relief from rents on "untenable" dwellings—in effect, for the "warranty of habitability," a reform that was not common in the United States until the past decade (Ware 1964, p. 23).

It was not until after the Civil War in 1865 that public attention was successfully focused on the problems. Following a report of Griscom's organization about the continuing problems of overcrowded conditions and the threat of a cholera epidemic, newspapers in New York began to highlight the issues (Mohr 1973, p. 142). Calling the tenement houses of the day "pestilent hells," the *World* made the most dramatic statements, characterizing slumlordism as the most "diabolical, horrid, atrocious, fiendish, and even hellish system of moneymaking ever invented by the mind of man" (pp. 142–43).

In the spring of 1865, the question of what was to be done was brought to a head by tenants who rallied in protest against the conditions in which they lived (p. 143). Legislators, feeling compelled to attend, vowed their support for relief from the tenants' plight. When they returned to the legislature, they acted. Following an intensely partisan legislative fight, the United States had its first housing codes (p. 148). Unfortunately, because of a change in the prevailing political winds, the codes were never enforced, and the problems continued to build (pp. 150–51).

When the Depression of 1873 hit, tenant problems multiplied. Some 300,000 people lost their jobs in the United States, and a wave of eviction swept the cities. In New York alone it was said that about 90,000 people became homeless in early 1874 (Foner, P. 1947, p. 442). Many were housed in tents or makeshift shantytowns or spent evenings in police station buildings (Schnapper 1972, pp. 93–96). The unemployed of New York, meeting under banners that read "Equal Laws and Homes for the Industrious," demanded a suspension of evictions for nonpayment of rent in the winter months. In Chicago 20,000 marched on city hall demanding "bread for the needy, clothing for the naked, and houses for the homeless" (Foner, P. 1947, pp. 446–47).

The establishment took a hard line against the tenant actions. Armed with the new theory of "social Darwinism," they characterized tenants' problems as both inevitable and evidence of the tenants' own inadequacies (Hofstadter 1944, pp. 46–47). They turned the tenants' position on landlords back upon the tenants. It was the tenant, and not the landlord, who was lazy. The proof of the correctness of the position was found in the property of the landlords and the poverty in the tenants. John Hay, later secretary of state, argued, "That you have property is proof of industry and foresight on you or your father's part; that you have nothing is judgment of your laziness and vices, or on your improvidence" (Foner, P. 1955, p. 28).

Much as the opponents of tenant suffrage had seen the move for the vote as evidence of Jacobinism in 1821, the voices for the established order of the 1870s saw communism in the collective protest actions of

Attack on "Boss" Tweed that appeared in 1874 following Panic of 1873.

From Schnapper, 1975: p. 95. Reprinted by permission.

tenants of their period (Foner, P. 1947, p. 446). One academic, writing at the turn of the century, went so far as to claim that living in a tenement by itself forced "members of a family to conform insensibly to communistic modes of thought" (Ehrenreich and English 1979, p. 70).

A SECOND TRY WITH THE LAWS OF SUPPLY AND DEMAND

Working in New York during the hard times of the late 1860s was Henry George. According to George's son, it was George's experiences with the contrasting landed wealth and tenant poverty of New York that moved him to write his famous book, *Poverty and Progress* (George 1955, p. ix). This book, a worldwide best seller, contains a restatement of the anti-land monopoly and landlordism themes. It is, in many ways, an expansion of Paine's themes of common ownership of land in the context of an urbanized laissez-faire economy (Williamson, A. 1973, p. 243). George agreed with the Anti-Renters that landlordism was inherently aristocratic and noted that modern landlordism was even worse because it maintained the powers and benefits of feudalism but none of the obligations (George 1955, p. 35l). George also restated Evans' position that the Declaration of Independence provided an inalienable right to property, but he varied from Evans in rejecting an individual's claim to exercise that right in individual ownership of land (p. 545). He believed that any attempt at equal redistribution of land would fail, leaving an expanded group of land monopolists (p. 436).

George was concerned about the potential conservatizing nature of widespread land monopoly. He feared that once a large number of people shared in even a small part of the fruits of land monopoly, the unearned increase in land value that resulted from society's growth and unearned income in rent, it would be in their interest "to prevent the adoption or even advocacy" of reform and "strengthen the existing unjust system" (George 1955, p. 326).

He believed that spreading landlordism would also dampen the call for change among the propertiless because it would confuse them about the true nature of their exploitation. In the words of the Frenchman Laveleye, George stated, "the small landlords act as 'a kind of rampart and safeguard for the holders of large estates' and 'may without exaggeration be called the lightning conductor that averts from society dangers which might otherwise lead to violent catastrophies.'" (p. 327).

However, even with this analysis, George, like Paine and Evans, veered away from direct radical change in the landownership pattern of his day. As a strong supporter of free enterprise he saw the accumulation of land as the "natural direction of social development." He, in no way, wanted to alter that development (p. 327). Instead, he, like many of his predecessors, proposed a tax. The tax was to be on land to the exclusion

SONG IN THE SPIRIT OF GEORGE'S THEORIES

Mary Had a Little Lot

Mary had a little lot
The soil was very poor;
But still she kept it all the same
And struggled to get more.

She kept the lot until one day
The people settled down—
And where a wilderness had been
Grew up a thriving town.

They grew, as population comes,
And Mary raised the rent.
With common food and raiment now,
She could not be content.

"What makes the lot keep Mary so?"
The starving people cry—
"Why, Mary keeps the lot, you know,"
The wealthy would reply.

Then Mary rented out her lot—
(She would not sell, you know)—
And waited patiently about
For prices still to grow.

She built her up a mansion fine—
Had bric-a-brac galore—
And every time the prices rose,
She raised the rent some more.

And so each one of you might be
"Wealthy, refined, and wise"
If you had only hogged some land
And held it for the rise.

Mary C. Hudson, 1880s

of improvements. George's tax would confiscate all the unearned increment in land caused by the growth of society and all rent derived from land.

George promised more with his land tax than Paine had with inheritance tax. The land tax would be sufficient to replace all other taxes. In fact the removal of all other taxes was as important to him as levying his "single tax" on land. As much as he wanted to tax land, the "unproductive" capital, he wanted to free from taxation the "productive" capital of industry and the income of labor. This would "leave to the individual producer all that prompted him to exertion" (p. 436). It would let the laborer have the "full reward" of his labor and the capitalist the full return on his capital.

George, like Evans, promised that his scheme would solve the problems of high rents and low wages. He argued that land monopolizers, through their collective individual actions, could control the land market, siphoning off capital from the productive sphere for speculative gain. Where Evans argued that the Homestead Act woudl reduce demand, George argued the single tax would increase supply (p. 438). The tax on land would force maximum building to produce the income to pay the tax. The cutting off of unproductive avenues of investment would force capital back into productive endeavors. Housing and jobs would increase. Rents would go down and wages would go up. Greater equality would also result.

George's ideas were particularly popular in New York, a city that was then about 85 percent tenants (Glaab and Brown 1967, p. 610). When, in 1886, a labor party was formed in New York to run candidates for city office, George was a natural choice to head the ticket as labor's candidate for mayor (Foner, P. 1955, p. 120). In his acceptance speech, George referred to his earlier experience in New York that had led to *Poverty and Progress*. He reported that in those days he had vowed to "seek out and remedy the cause that condemned little children to lead such lives as you know them to lead in the squalid districts" (deMille 1950, p. 148).

The Democrats and the Republicans nominated Abram Hewitt and Theodore Roosevelt, respectively, to oppose George. Professing to speak for all "wage workers and tenants," a working-class supporter of George attacked Hewitt and Roosevelt in a letter published in the *New York Times* (Oct. 24, 1888). He stated that Hewitt and Roosevelt belonged to the employing and landlord classes and in office would support the paying of the lowest wages and collecting of the highest rents. On the other hand, he promised that George would do his utmost to "bring about legislation by which wage slavery and land monopoly shall be abolished and rent be paid only to the people at large, and not more than is needed to administer the different branches of government."

Political Cartoon during Mayorality Race of Henry George.

From Schnapper, 1975: p. 165. Reprinted by permission.

Roosevelt responded in the *Times* stating that classes did not exist "on this side of the water." He denied that he was a landlord and that he wished either high rents or low wages. Hewitt responded to George, his ideas, and the labor party, in more broad-brush fashion. He charged them all as embodying "the ideas of Anarchists, Nihilists, Communists, Socialists. . . ." To him the labor party was "the demon of discord, hate, anarchy and the enemy of all mankind . . ." (Foner, P. 1955, p. 121).

Socialists joined and supported the labor party, although they were not supporters of either the single tax or George. George, as a supporter of free enterprise, was not keen about their presence in the party or their assistance. When he placed a strong second to Hewitt in the election and it came time to regroup for the next political contest, George demonstrated his discomfort about the alliance with the socialists by excluding them from the party. The ideological conflict between George and the socialists is instructive of the difference between the basis of most U.S. tenant activism and traditional concepts of socialism (pp. 149–50).[7]

As has been seen, tenant activists have played off concepts of property, industry, and democracy in opposing landlordism. George continued in this tradition, carrying it to its extreme with the context of laissez-faire economics. He went beyond the Anti-Renters in opposing landownership even if gained through enterprise, and, although George excluded buildings from his analysis, he went beyond the Tenants' League by opposing all rent on land, even to the extent of nonusurious interest. He also agreed with his predecessors that landlordism was aristocratic but again went further, noting that the modern landlord maintains the power and benefits of the past but none of the obligations. To

Political Cartoon Commenting on George's Loss.

From Schnapper, 1975: p. 162. Reprinted by permission.

George, land monopoly and landlordism were corrupted feudal institutions that flawed capitalism. They alone stood in the way of the total success of free enterprise.

Such a position could not be adopted by socialists. They saw George as "ignoring the exploitation of labor by the industrial and financial capitalists." As Frederick Engels stated, "What socialists demand implies a total revolution of the whole system of social production; what Henry George demands, leaves the present mode of social production untouched" (Foner, P. 1955, p. 120).

From the socialist point of view, George and all the nineteenth-century urban tenant activists before him had made the mistake of accepting individualism as their central economic concept. They stated that a concept of the economy that accepted a one-to-one relationship between individual labor and individual reward might have made sense to early preindustrial reformers. However, they stated, it should have died with the transformation of the economy. With industrialization "each man's labor merged indistinguishably from others' in the stream of collective effort." The socialists did not focus on the distinction between earned and unearned income or productive or unproductive capital. The wealth generated by production was all to be allocated to the common good. "Need," not an individual's "labor," should rule the entire arena of rewards from production (Rodgers 1978, pp. 218-19).

George's demonstration of how, through emphasizing individual enterprise and reward, one can totally reject landlordism without taking a step toward socialism did not lessen the conflict landlords and tenants create within the U.S. ideological framework, nor did it resolve any of the problems. Tenants' problems continued to grow worse while the labor party disintegrated and the single tax scheme was largely forgotten. A massive number of evictions took place in the 1890s, and once again, tenants fought back (McLoughlin 1892, p. 49). As had been predicted some 50 years earlier, urban tenants began to employ the Anti-Renters' tactic of the mass rent strike (Burghardt, S. 1967, p. 15).

THE TWENTIETH CENTURY

The story of the twentieth century is one of continued tenant struggles, at times reaching riotous proportions (Piven and Cloward 1977, pp. 53–55). Peaks in tenant movement activity occurred at the turn of the century, during and after both world wars, the Depression, in the 1960s and at present. The struggles in each of these periods, including the present, have resulted in the actualization of many of the nineteenth-century ideas in increasingly modern form. In 1901 the 1867 New York Housing codes were substantially revised and became a model that spread across the country (Friedman 1968). After World War I and during and after World War II, rent control laws were adopted (Drellich and Emery 1939; Willis 1950). Rent control is again an issue in the present period (Atlas and Drier 1980). Beginning in the Depression, tax and other policies have been applied, in much the model of the Homestead Act, to effect urban land reform focused on protecting and expanding homeownership (Abrams 1946). In the 1960s tenants began to be successful in limiting the "aristocratic" powers of landlords with reforms including the warranty of habitability and just cause to evict (Rose 1973; LeGates and Murphy 1981). In the 1970s tenant activists argued for a "right to housing," much as the early radical agrarians had argued for a "right to property." Operating at the edges of the ideology, they asserted that housing is a "necessity of life" that should be subject to special protection under the Consitution. Like its agrarian precedessors, the right to housing group had little hearing. The idea was quickly laid to rest in 1972 by the United States Supreme Court in the case Lindsey v. Normet (12 Sup. Ct. 866).

In this century there have been calls for reform well beyond those demanded in the nineteenth century. Particularly in moments of crisis, some have suggested programs that range from direct government construction of housing for the poor to conversion of the present rental stock to public or community ownership. What marks these programs as different is their lack of faith in the laws of supply and demand and their intent to remove at least a part of the housing stock from the "free market" and the accumulation process.

As early as 1904, a tenant group in New York is said to have planned to build its own housing cooperatives so that it could take tenants out of the tenements,[8] and in 1909 the spirit of the populist, municipal ownership movement found its way into the report of the President's Home Commission (Woodyatt 1968, p. 15). According to the commission, if government could provide public facilities such as schools and libraries, they saw no reason why it could not provide housing to those in difficult economic straits. By 1914 the idea of municipally-owned housing had reached the point of being an issue for endorsement before the convention of the American Federation of Labor, an endorsement it did not receive (McDonnell 1957, pp. 9–10).

The overwhelming need for wartime housing for war workers and servicemen did result in a cautious move into direct provision of limited amounts of housing during World War I, but as soon as the war was over, this housing was sold to the private sector (Friedman 1968). While some reformers and some elements of labor calling for housing to be made a government fuction resisted, their efforts were swamped by free enterprisers (McGrady 1918, p. 298).

The massive housing problems of the Depression are well known. While tens of thousands of people were left homeless or were living in shantytowns, called Hoovervilles, many thousands of apartments were sitting empty with rents higher than anyone could afford. In California the situation was so severe that Upton Sinclair, in his campaign for governor, called for the government to take over the vacant apartments in the state, convert them to cooperatives, and permit tenants to manage them collectively (Sinclair, 1933).

"Hooverville," Seattle, Washington.

From Schnapper, 1975: p. 463. Reprinted by permission.

As the crisis deepened, hardly anyone was left who could argue that the laws of supply and demand, if left alone, would deal with the problem (Wood 1931, p. 1). The debate was more about what percentage of the population was in need of housing assistance: one-third, one-half or two-thirds. At the extreme was the Socialist Party that called for transfer of ownership to the people of "industry, land, finance, and natural resources." They believed we could not move too fast to the "point where rent, interest, and profit are abolished" (Warren 1974).

As late as 1932, however, the American Federation of Labor still, as it had in 1914, opposed even public housing. Calling it a foreign scheme,

From Schnapper, 1975: p. 358. Reprinted by permission.

they rejected the idea almost in the same fashion as their predecessors had rejected Skidmore's plan about 100 years earlier. Public housing and the government that supported such a role for itself "seemed counter to our ideals of individual initiative and rights." However, by 1936, as the crisis deepened, they changed their minds and supported what had become a "logical and rational form of public works" (McDonnell 1957, p. 68).

Although the broad support public housing gained during the Depression led Congress to adopt legislation enabling the construction of such housing, Congress never provided the funding necesary to make public housing the major source of shelter in the United States as such housing became in Europe. In fact Congress took steps beyond the funding level to ensure that this would never happen. As insurance against the laws of supply and demand, the enabling legislation contains the extraordinary provision requiring that public housing could be built only if accompanied by the destruction of an equal number of slum dwellings.

Under this and other constraints the experience with public housing in the United States is generally considered to be one of failure (Friedman 1968, p. 119). Much of this is attributed to the lack of support and poor management, but the Red-baiting the program repeatedly received also played a part. In Los Angeles a particulary vicious attack on planned construction in the early 1950s virtually eliminated the program in that city. The Committee Against Socialist Housing was organized to stop the construction of public housing. It saw such housing as a threat to "the rights of people" because it destroyed "the freedom of private ownership" and accomplished "the major step to communism" (Gottlieb and Wolt 1977, pp. 260–61).

Such attacks stifled housing reformers' efforts in the 1950s and early 1960s. Not until after the country had experienced the civil rights and antiwar movements and antipoverty program was the drive for alternative forms of housing renewed. In Berkeley a "radical" coalition, in the spirit of college towns of that period, was the first to call for "community ownership of housing and real estate" (Community Ownership Organizing Project 1976). Observing that in their city the private market was failing to provide affordable housing, they set forth a plan that began with the formation of tenant unions and was to lead to city-aided conversion of the rental housing stock to nonprofit, limited equity cooperatives. The plan did not, however, call for expropriation, but rather purchase of landlord's property at market value, a process that has never really begun. Interestingly, in light of public housing's history, the earlier form, cooperatives, were called for rather than public ownership.

While real estate markets in college towns were overheating, real estate markets in many eastern and midwestern central cities were beginning to cool. In these cities landlords themselves were making the call for elimination of the private landlord in the form of housing abandonment.[9] In New York activists began a debate about what should be done with this abandoned housing to replace the private landlord (Homefront 1977). The debate continues to this day with ever increasing urgency. On one side the position is that the government should take control of the housing and place it under tenant management (Hawley 1978). On the other side are calls for community ownership, as in Berkeley, in the form of tenant-owned and controlled cooperatives (Barton 1977).

The debate in New York has carried over into portions of the current tenant movement at large (Atlas and Drier 1980). The nationwide debate, however, is not based solely on the problem of what to do about abandoned housing. The stagflation of the past half decade has resulted in soaring real estate values and rents that have risen at a rate 5 percent above the growth in the real incomes of tenants (LeGates and Murphy 1981, p. 258). Landlords in increasing numbers across the country have been cashing in their inflated equities through condominium conversion, and new construction of multifamily housing has, for the same reason, not been directed at tenants but at potential owners who have been willing to pay a premium price to get on the inflationary spiral. The result of this shift in activity is decreasing rental vacancy rates, now below 5 percent nationwide, and additional pressure on rents, a pressure tenant leaders are not sure rent control alone can withstand.

The problem is seen as reaching crisis proportions necessitating forms of ownership of rental housing, whether public or cooperative, secure from this pressure. The apparent urgency of the present situation has generated new schemes for removing as much housing from the market system as possible. Primary among those drawing up such plans are Chester Hartman and Michael Stone (1981).

Hartman and Stone propose to greatly increase the quantity of publicly financed, developed, and managed housing in the United States. Their scheme does not call for the end to all private homeownership or to all roles for speculation or financial institutions in homeownership. It limits this "commodity" conception of housing to those who can afford and choose it and sets forth an alternative for others. In their alternative all financing is done by the government in return for giving up the right to trade or rent housing for profit. In their plan, however, security of tenure is ensured.

Importantly, for our purposes, part of the plan calls for the elimination of all private rental housing. They, like the Berkeley reformers, would buy the housing from the landlords, but what they would pay is quite different from that proposed earlier. Much like the Anti-Renters, who acted in an agrarian context, they would credit the tenants with having purchased that portion of the property paid for during their tenancy. The tenants would have a right to buy the units in which they live and pay only the down payment made by the landlords and the value accumulated before the tenants took possession. If the tenant chose to have the unit converted to public housing, the landlord would still get only that portion of the worth of the property, not that of the tenant. The landlord is said to be entitled only to a return on his actual investment in the property, the down payment, made when he purchased the property. The remainder of the money used to buy the building is provided by the tenant, not the landlord. Their willingness to allow the landlord to receive that portion paid by prior tenants is clearly a political and administrative compromise at variance with their logic.

For Hartman's and Stone's purposes, this would greatly reduce the cost of eliminating the landlord; for our purposes, it proposes a very different conception of urban tenancy than has, to this date, been developed (Tribe 1978, p. 24). In their conception an option to buy is implied in every rental agreement, just as a warranty of habitability is today—a concept that from traditional views of landlordism, would mean expropriation of the landlord's property.

Hartman and Stone take the step that few before them have taken. While the Hartman and Stone proposal does not deny a role in society for property accumulation, it does, as Skidmore would have put it, deny the right to expropriate another's labor through rent. In this way it is a consumption side version of Skidmore's plan. Instead of limiting accumulation to the land a person can work, it limits acumulation to the housing a person can live in.

Whether the tenant population, the latent membership of the tenant movement, facing its present difficulties, is willing to go this far remains to be seen. There is a great deal of evidence that the mainstream of the tenant movement is still directed, as in the past, toward finding a solution to the problem in programs aimed primarily at winning the battle of supply and demand, rather than such a serious interruption in the process of individual accumulation.

SUMMARY

The purpose of this chapter was to describe and analyze the history that, in Gramsci's concept of hegemony, had been "inherited and uncritically absorbed" by today's tenants. Although the tenants interviewed in this study were urban tenants living in an industrialized world, it proved necessary to begin the review of history with an examination of tenants' struggles in the prerevolutionary agrarian United States. Agrarian concepts, deep in the past of the United States, that were transformed and adapted for the needs of industrial society proved to be the source of the constraints we sought to understand.

Agrarian tenants in this country, from early on, had very strong notions of petty accumulation through productive working of the land—in their terms through enterprise. The enemy of these enterprisers was the landlord, who in his refusal to transfer the land to those who used it for production, was characterized as both"unproductive" and feudal. Although landlord-tenant conflicts of that day often appeared, as they do today, to be about rent levels and evictions, the underlying conflict was often about who was entitled to ownership of the land. The conflict was between the "unproductive" landlords' "rights of property" and the "productive" tenants' "right to property." Land was the "critical element" that meant security and possible prosperity. Without it in an agrarian society, the tenant was all but a "slave" to the landowner.

Although the urban tenant has faced very different material conditions than the agrarian tenant, much of the agrarian conception of life has remained and dominated urban tenants' struggles. Antifeudalism has been dragged up time and time again when landlords have been seen as acting in particularly onerous ways; individual enterprise and petty accumulation have remained the model to follow if success was to be attained; and tenancy has continued to be seen as inherently insecure. The continuance of these themes in light of the socialization of production and the continued commodifications of all elements of society is very much the stuff of which hegemony is made. It has constrained conceptualizing the problem and inhibited action by urban tenants in the fashion described by Gramsci.

Urban tenants, starting from an agrarian base, could not claim the rented property as their own, earned as a result of their own productive use of the property. The tenants' enterprise was usually elsewhere, and the rented property was likely purchased with the product of another's enterprise and successful accumulation. The urban tenant, as wage worker, also could not claim ownership of his workplace because the industrialist, in this theory, did not employ the unproductive capital of the landlord, but the productive capital of the enterpriser.

For the mass of this population, gaining control over the productive side of life in the agrarian model was too unlikely a possibility to satisfy the enterprisers' drive. In its place came petty accumulation on the consumption side of life, in particular, consistent with agrarianism, in the ownership of land. This meant homeownership, if not the ownership of rental property, as well. The symbol of security was still the ownership of land. It also remained the symbol of successful enterprise and accumulation, that is, emergence from slavery. The conflict between landlord and tenant was transformed, in part, from a competition over ownership of the rented land per se to a competition over petty accumulation itself. In this context rent could be seen as interfering with the tenant's right to engage in petty accumulation, that is, own his own home.

Added to this transformation was the concept of the market economy—the world of the industrial enterpriser rather than the agrarian enterpriser. Concepts of supply and demand replaced those of the "moral" economy of the preindustrial period. The disempowering concept of the self-regulated market replaced the judgmental concept of the

"just price." The "unlimited possibilities" of the market only reinforced the necessity of proving oneself a successful enterpriser and sub-
jected those who did not succeed to suspicion.

Only in times of crisis when severe market failures have taken place
has the domination of the supply and demand framework come into
question. In these times, interventionist programs such as the control of
the prices of "necessities," that is, rent control, have been reintroduced,
along with partial schemes of socialization or collectivization of housing. Even then, the primary response has been to cure the market failure
and encourage the process of petty accumulation through government
subsidies and reforms to encourage homeownership. The almost total
hegemonic domination of the concepts of individual enterprise and supply and demand, supported by expressions of state power that favor
these concepts' implicit criteria for evaluation of self and provided no
other path to security, have not allowed counterhegemonic ideas or
institutions to gain a foothold. The edges of this domination have been
highlighted by repeated "red-baiting" when the tenant movement
threatened to go "too far".

NOTES

1. The constitutional process in Pennsylvania, where tenants did obtain the vote, gives
some indication about what the constitutional debate might have been like if tenants had
had a full voice. During the constitutional period, articles appeared in local papers warning
against those who dreamed of creating "millions of acres of tenanted soil" and a system of
"Lords and Vassals or *principal and dependent,* common in Europe" (Foner, E. 1976a,
p. 208). To stop these dreams from becoming a reality, an unsuccessful proposal was made
to include provisions in the state constitution that would declare a role for the government
in discouraging large accumulations of property (p. 209). When the U.S. Constitution was
returned to the people of Pennsylvania for ratification, criticisms were made by more
radical elements concerning the lack of a land reform law, the lack of limitations on the
accumulation of wealth, and the failure to exclude the very wealthy from public office and
voting so as to not corrupt popular government (Link 1942, p. 31).

2. There is debate about whether they were converted or were politically opportunis-
tic.

3. Some states continued to refuse to grant tenants the right to vote, most notably
Rhode Island, in which tenants drafted their own state constitution. Though the tenant
constitution and slate of candidates defeated the landowner slate and an amended landowner constitution at the polls, the existing government refused to yield power. The
subsequent revolt, the Dorr War, terminated in defeat for the tenants, though three years
later the old state constitution was amended to grant tenants the vote. The Dorr War became
a symbol of the suffrage movement, aiding in sweeping away the property qualifications for
suffrage in the remaining states (Williamson, C. 1960, pp. 246-60).

4. This term arises from the French Revolution. It is the successor to "leveler" and has
been equated with Bolshevism in this century (Sisson 1974, pp. 187-89; Frost 1920, p. 16).

5. One such landlord was William Scully (Gates 1973, p. 7). His holdings were so extensive that, when a number of his Illinois tenants grew weary of battling him in that state and moved to Nebraska in search of the elusive land ownership, they found Scully in control of the available land and themselves once again his tenants (pp. 286–87). Exploitation by Scully and other Irish landlords brought legislation establishing security of tenure and rent regulation in Ireland in the 1870s (pp. 272–73). That legislation, in turn, contributed to Scully's liquidating his Irish holdings and moving to the United States. There were calls in the United States to follow Ireland's lead and adopt such legislation here (p. 296). However, prairie-state legislators, many of whom were large landlords, characterized the problem as one of foreign influences and nonresident ownership and instead adopted antialien statutes. Scully himself quickly avoided the impact of this legislation by becoming a citizen (pp. 292–94, 297).

6. The movement to the West was more than offset by the immigration of people from Europe and a continued strong migration of people from the farm to cities (Glaab and Brown 1967, pp. 136–39). While the population of the United States doubled between 1860 and 1890, the population of nonfarm wage earners and towns over 8,000 more than tripled (Schlesinger 1929, p. 276).

7. The struggle between socialists and nonsocialists in the tenants' movement has been a constant in this century. It was true in the New York mass rent strikes of the early 1900s and it is true today. For a discussion of the difficulty of expanding socialism through organizing tenants by socialists today, see the discussion of organizers' experiences in Jamaica Plain, Boston (McAfee 1979). George's analysis shows how socialist consciousness does not necessarily follow from even extended tenant struggles.

8. This is reported in an unpublished paper by Jenna Weissman Joselit, entitled "The New York City Rent Strikes of 1904 and 1907 8". This paper is part of an excellent work being conducted on the New York tenant movement in this century at the Center for Policy Studies, Columbia University, under the direction of Ronald Lawson.

9. In this period there were some activists in New York calling for driving "slumlords" out through rent strikes. This, however, was not a general call for conversion of all rental housing.

2

The Southern California
Tenant Revolt

Until recently California has not been thought of as a center of tenant movement activity. Although outbreaks of tenant activism have occurred in California during difficult years, such as during the Depression, nothing approaching a movement has ever been sustained. Aspiring tenant organizers considered the California tenant to be too individualistic and too mobile to be organized. Housing conditions were considered to be too good, the weather too mild, urban settlement too spread out, and densities of renters too low for mass collective action.

Events of the past few years have, however, changed all this. A tenant revolt of extraordinary proportions has almost overnight thrust the California tenant from near political oblivion into the political limelight. A California tenant movement has emerged that shows signs of becoming an increasingly important force in the state and a major contributor to an even more recent national tenant movement. It has already led to the election of one of the few progressive local governments elected in this conservative era. This government, in the City of Santa Monica, has become a center of international attention.

In this chapter following a brief presentation of the changing economic position of California tenants, the chain of actions and reactions that prepared organizers to respond to a spontaneous outpouring of tenant activism will be traced. The discussion will then turn to case studies of the successes of the tenant movement where it has been the strongest, in the City and County of Los Angeles and in the City of Santa Monica. We will find that the themes developed in the last chapter again find a home in these most recent episodes of the tenant movement story.

CHANGING SITUATION

California has always had the image of a housing-rich state, an image which was not always deserved, as testified to by Charles Abrams in his 1950 article on Los Angeles housing entitled "Rats Among the Palm Trees." The one period in which the reality for tenants came close to the image was during the 1960s. In this period vacancy rates were high and some landlords, primarily those that housed the middle class, complained vigorously about an "apartment glut." While the 1960s abound with stories of landlords offering a free month's rent or a free television set to attract tenants, it should not be forgotten that the poor of California never shared the benefits of this situation. While landlords of the middle class were finding it hard to locate tenants and keeping rents down, Watts exploded in riot.

In the early 1970's even the middle-class tenant began to experience a change. The influx of tenants to California and the rapid formation of new households outstripped the construction of new rental units, lowering the vacancy rates to about 5 percent. Rents, however, were not yet affected and rose, as usual, at a rate only about half that of the Consumer Price Index (CPI) (Housing Division, Community Development Department, Dec. 6, 1978, p. 6).

In the mid-1970s there was a sharp drop off in the construction of new multifamily housing units (Sternlieb and Burchell 1980, p. 238), and, for the first time in recent memory, vacancy rates dropped below the 5 percent figure, and rents increased at a rate faster than the CPI. In Los Angeles, for example, the CPI figure for 1975 was 5.7 percent, while rents increased at 6.4 percent rate, and in 1976 it became clear that a new order of things was being established when, once again, rents rose faster than the CPI, 8.2 percent compared to 7.8 percent.

In West Los Angeles where the City of Santa Monica is located and where rents were already higher than in the rest of the city, the increases were also greater (Santa Monica Planning Department, 1978). This was caused, in part by an extraordinary increase in building turnover and speculation. In the precrisis year of 1972, only 16 residential-income properties changed hands in Santa Monica, four of which were sold twice in one year. By 1974 when the market was only beginning to heat up, for example, 67 residential income properties were traded in the City of Santa Monica, 21 of these two or more times. By 1977 these numbers had increased to 183 and 53 respectively, an increase of tenfold in five years (Santa Monica City, 1979, p. 13).

Additional pressure was placed on tenants in the homebuying ages by extraordinarily accelerating home prices (a problem discussed in Chapter 7) and a reduction of the rental housing stock in a growing condominium conversion craze. Even middle-class tenants found it harder to escape tenancy. Tenants were increasingly subject to eviction and had a difficult time finding a new place to live even if they could afford substantial rent.

By 1977 the situation had worsened to the point that serious tenant organizing began to take place. It was not until 1978, however, after the passage of Proposition 13, that tenants began to win their victories. To understand what happened after Proposition 13, it it necessary to look back a few years to an unusual chain of events that set the stage for what was to come.

ACTION AND REACTION

In 1972 tenants in Berkeley, as part of their "radical" plan to create community ownership of housing, mobilized and passed a rent control charter amendment through the initiative process. Landlords attacked the Berkeley charter amendment in court in an attempt to crush any idea of spreading rent control reform and community ownership before such an effort began. While the landlords were successful in having the Berkeley charter amendment declared unconstitutional, their action actually had the effect of legalizing later efforts. The California Supreme Court, in the case of *Birkenfeld* v. *Berkeley* (17 C.3d 129 1976), found the Berkeley law unconstitutional on procedural grounds, but held that a city might, without further state legislation, adopt a rent control law.

At the time of the court decision, however, there was no tenant movement in California that was able to take advantage of the opportunity *Birkenfeld* presented. What tenant advocacy there was consisted of housing activists, public interest lawyers and lobbyists concerned with changes in landlord-tenant law, and a variety of senior citizen and community groups only tangentially concerned. The situation in this period is demonstrated by the unsuccessful attempt in 1975 of Senator David Roberti to pass rent control legislation in the state legislature. With little support, the bill of Senator Roberti died quickly and quietly in the Senate Judiciary Committee. Though the bill's author represented a heavily tenanted district in Southern California, its defeat received little notice in the press (*Los Angeles Times,* Apr. 10, 1975, p. I-1).

The real estate and apartment industries, however, were highly organized and politically powerful in the state capitol. Having, in effect, lost in the courts they moved to the legislature to stamp out the threat the *Birkenfeld* decision presented. Legislation, Assembly Bill (AB) 3788, was introduced to prohibit local jurisdictions from enacting rent controls. Their power was demonstrated when AB 3788 passed the assembly in June 1976, the same month the Supreme Court handed down its decision (*Los Angeles Times*, Aug. 31, 1976, p. I-3; *Sacramento Bee*, June 27, 1976, p. A-3).

From Shelterforce, *1980 4(3): p. 14. Reprinted by permission.*

The passage of AB 3788 through the legislature was a classic example of big money lobby efforts by the real estate industry. The bill was backed by the newly formed California Housing Council (CHC), an association of the largest corporate landlords and apartment developers in the state, which hired polished public relations firms and experienced lobbyists for the effort. Campaign contributions exceeding $43,000 were made to key votes, including $1,500 to Assembly Speaker Leo McCarthy and to Assembly Housing and Community Affairs chairman Peter Chacon. The total expended by the real estate industry on the campaign exceeded $100,000 (*Sacramento Bee*, June 27, 1976, A-3; also Lowe 1977).

Public interest advocates in Sacramento informed the few tenant groups that existed in the state of the danger posed by AB 3788 as it moved through the senate in late summer. As it passed its first committee vote in the senate, tenant groups belatedly took their message to the press (Lowe 1977). In Los Angeles Cary Lowe, of the Community Information Project, and Lucy Fried, of the Coalition for Economic Survival, denounced AB 3788 at a press conference in an attempt to alert tenants to the danger (*Los Angeles Times*, Aug. 17, 1976, p. I-3; Aug. 19, 1976, p. II-3). Even the *Los Angeles Times* (hereafter called *LAT*), which had maintained a consistent antirent control editorial position, called for the defeat of AB 3788, claiming that the decision on rent control should be left to the communities affected (*LAT*, Aug. 17, 1976, p. II-6).

The effort was too little too late. With the aid of the intense lobbying efforts of the real estate industry, AB 3788 passed the senate on August 30 by a vote of 21 to 14 (*LAT*, Aug. 3l, 1976, p. I-3). An opponent of AB 3788, Senator John Dunlap, from Northern California, interpreted the attitude of the legislature toward the issue of rent control when he said, "by passing this bill we are saying to local governments we haven't the guts to do anything about rent control and we aren't going to let you do anything about it either" (*LAT*, Aug. 3l, 1976, p. I-3).

Those conducting the fight now had to look to the governor for a veto. Carole Norris, of the hastily formed California Renters Coalition, and John Henning, of the California Federation of Labor, called on Governor Brown to veto the bill, charging it had been "bought" by the CHC (*LAT*, Sept. 14, 1976, p. I-20). At the last minute, with the help of pressure from the State Department of Housing and Community Development, Brown was convinced to veto the legislation (Lowe 1977).

The landlords' efforts had again failed to achieve their end and as with the *Birkenfeld* case, actually prepared the way for the later formation of the California tenant movement. Housing and tenant activists loosely brought together to stop AB 3788, realized that they could not rely on the governor's veto indefinitely to stop future attempts by the real estate industry. The campaign against AB 3788 demonstrated a clear need for a system to monitor the real estate lobby's activities in Sacramento, to establish their own lobby, and to organize a channel of information between interested tenant groups.

Two months after the veto, a small group of key housing and tenant activists from around the state met in Berkeley to discuss the organization of a coalition of housing rights groups and community organizations. To those in attendance, it was clear that such a group would have to grow beyond an assortment of public interest lawyers and activists if it were to have any impact in Sacramento. Tenants and other low-income housing consumers needed to be organized into a strong statewide grassroots movement to counter the power of the real estate lobby.

The result was the California Housing Action and Information Network (CHAIN), which was "to function as an umbrella for the organizing, education, and advocacy work of housing rights groups throughout the state" (*Shelterforce*, Spring 1977). On January 22, 1977, some 250 activists met in Los Angeles to discuss the structural organization of CHAIN and future plans of action (*Property Management Journal*, Feb. 1977).

The major focus of the new organization was to encourage local tenant organizing. They were convinced that real power in Sacramento could be built only on strong tenant organization in local legislative districts. As rent increases began to push tenants to their financial limits by early 1977, the timely formation of CHAIN in reaction to the landlords' legislative efforts provided a network to channel, direct, and assist the outbreak and organization of local tenant activity around the state.

EARLY MOVEMENT EFFORTS

The year 1977 was an important one to the tenant movement in the Los Angeles area, as it grew in power from a few locally isolated organizations into a bona fide political force. While they did not have many victories in that year, they did lay the foundation for what was to come. In April 100 tenants rallied in a West Los Angeles park to protest rising rents—the first tenant demonstration in Los Angeles in years (*Brentwood*

Hills Press, Apr. 21, 1977, p. 1). With the assistance of CHAIN, the rally was organized by Margaret Thurman, a West Los Angeles tenant who had organized a local tenant organization and counseling service after receiving repeated rent increases herself. By mid-1977 community organizers increasingly began working with tenant groups fighting rent increases and poor maintenance (*CES Newsletter*, April, May, and June 1977; *Herald Examiner*, July 8, 1977, p. 6). The issue of rent control soon surfaced when the Gray Panthers, a militant senior citizens group, rallied outside of Los Angeles City Hall, demanding that the city council pass a rent control law.

Nothing documents the growing activity of tenants at this time more clearly than the fact that rent increases and protesting tenants suddenly became "news." The *Santa Monica Evening Outlook* and neighborhood newspapers began to carry news of rallies such as the one in April 1977 as front page news. The *Los Angeles Herald-Examiner* carried an in-depth piece on the growing tenant movement in Southern California (*Herald-Examiner*, July 8, 1977, p. A-6). The *Los Angeles Times* ran lengthy news articles concerning the establishment of a landlord-tenant court and tenant rent strikes over rent increases (*LAT*, July 11, 1977, p. IV-1; July 25, 1977, p. VI-1). A hearing held by a local Assemblymember in the largely senior citizen, predominantly tenant Fairfax area attracted over 600 tenants testifying to rent hikes while demanding the enactment of rent control. The *Los Angeles Times* covered the hearing, not on the back pages of the human interest section, but in the first section with the news (*LAT*, Aug. 16, 1977, p. I–20).

As the newspapers began to catch on to the growing anger of tenants, organizers were laying plans for action. In heavily tenanted Santa Monica, a tenants organization formed in the spring and designed plans for the circulaton of a rent control initiative. In the city of Los Angeles, the Coalition for Economic Survival (CES), a grassroots political organization that organized around consumer issues including food prices and utility rates, increasingly found itself working with renters, and set tenants rights as a major portion of their program. In June CES launched a petition drive demanding that local governments enact rent control (*CES Newsletter*, June, 1977; *LAT*, Nov. 26, 1977, p. II-1).

The pressure applied by tenants led to a series of hearings before the Los Angeles City Council in late summer of 1977 on Councilmember Joel Wachs' "antirent-gouging" ordinance. On August 11 tenants and landlords filled the council chambers; the tenants demanded stronger rent control while Howard Jarvis and other real estate industry voices labeled the Wachs proposal "rent control" and predicted that it would serve as the "death knell" of the rental housing industry in Los Angeles (*LAT*, Aug. 12, 1977, p.II–1). The following week, the *Los Angeles Times* ran the first of what would be a series of editorials against rent control, while tenant protesters, led by the Coalition for Economic Survival, returned to the city council demanding an immediate rent freeze, presenting the council with a petition signed by 30,000 tenants (*LAT*, Aug. 16, 1977, p. II-6; *LAT*, Aug. 17, 1977, p. II-1; *Herald-Examiner*, Aug. 17, 1977, p. 3). In the next two months the city's Governmental Operations Committee held hearings and discussions. However, Wachs' motion failed to get any other vote on the committee but his own, sparking a demonstration by 200 angry tenants which forced the committee to hastily adjourn (*LAT*, Nov. 4, 1977, p. II-8; Dec. 2, 1977, p. I-20).

Tenant groups continued to pressure the city council for relief. In March 1978 Councilmember Wachs again pushed for consideration of his antirent-gouging ordinance and was able to get it out of committee. Before an overflowing crowd, the council as a whole debated Wachs' proposal to limit rent increases to once a year, with increases not to exceed an amount tied to the consumer price index. The proposal received only six of the required eight votes for passage and an antispeculation tax was defeated as well, on a five to five vote (*LAT*, Mar. 22, 1978, p. I-1). Tenant groups, including CES, demanded a 90-day freeze during which the council could consider further action. However, approval of a powerless mediation board, labeled "no solution" and a "ploy to divert public attention from government inaction" by CHAIN coordinator Cary Lowe, was as far as the council was willing to go (*LAT*, Mar. 21, 1978, p. I-23; Mar. 25, 1978, p. II-1).

While battles over rent control raged in the council chambers in Los Angeles, tenant activists in Santa Monica launched a campaign in September 1977, to place a rent control initiative on the June 1977 ballot (*Evening Outlook*, Sept. 28, 1977, p. 1). The campaign to place the issue on the ballot was to take on what was to become a standard formula for rent control and related campaigns. On the landlords' side a well-financed campaign was managed by an advertising public relations firm; while on the tenants' side, a low-budget campaign staffed by volunteers relied on door knocking (*LAT*, May 18, 1978, Westside-1).

Elsewhere in California, tenants were also on the move. The Santa Cruz Housing Action Committee circulated rent control and antispeculation initiatives for the November 1978 ballot. In Santa Barbara, San Diego, and Long Beach as well, organizers circulated rent control initiatives for November (*LAT*, June 6, 1978, p. II-1). The previous year, tenant activists in Berkeley returned to the electorate with a new rent control initiative conforming with the guidelines set by the *Birkenfeld* decision, only to lose heavily at the hands of a well-organizd landlord campaign, which spent over $100,000 to defeat the initiative, outspending tenants

20 to one. Despite the loss, tenant activists felt things were now swing-
ing their way (*Housing Law Project Bulletin*, April/May 1977, p. 11).

PROPOSITION 13 AND THE TENANT REVOLT

In the spring of 1978, however, rent control slid out of the political
limelight and was replaced by Proposition 13, the property-tax relief
measure associated with Howard Jarvis. Apartment owners attempted to
link the resolution of the crisis in rental housing with property-tax relief.
In a political mailing Jarvis, chief executive of the Apartment Association of Los Angeles County, urged landlords to "convince your tenants
that lower property taxes mean lower rents" (*LAT*, Mar. 30, 1978, p. II-
6). A month before the election, Howard Jarvis formalized the campaign
promise that tenants would benefit from Proposition 13 by announcing
an agreement between the Apartment Association and the California
Apartment Association to share Proposition 13 property-tax savings with
tenants should it pass (*LAT*, May 11, 1978, p. I-3). The agreement called
for the membership of the two groups, numbering some 80,000, to rebate
50 percent of December's rent to their tenants.

This announcement was greeted with skepticism not only from tenant spokespersons, but also by the CHC, whose number one priority was
the defeat of local and statewide rent control efforts (*LAT*, July 13, 1978,
p. I-1). This politically astute organization ran advertisements in newspapers throughout the state two days after the Jarvis announcement,
stating that they could not guarantee rebates to tenants (*LAT*, May 14,
1978, p. I-3). Furthermore, the CHC urged a 'no' vote on Proposition 13,
fearful that the measure might stir sentiment for rent control. After Proposition 13 passed by a two-to-one margin, the CHC sent a statewide letter
to its members urging them to pass on the tax savings to renters. In the
letter landlords were warned that uncertainty "could have a substantial
effect on continuing attempts in the legislature and at local levels of
government to impose rent controls" (*LAT*, June 19, 1978, p. II-1).

On the same ballot that California voters overwhelmingly approved
significant tax breaks to property owners, they firmly defeated rent control proposals in two California cities. In Santa Monica voters surprisingly turned down Proposition P, the rent control initiative, 56 percent
to 44 percent; in Santa Barbara, the other city, the vote was roughly the
same (*LAT*, June 8, 1978, p. II-1). Apartment industry contributions made
these campaigns among the most expensive ever in both communities.
In Santa Monica real estate interests outspent tenants by 20 to one,

spending over $250,000 (*Evening Outlook*, Aug. 2, 1978, p. 15). Similarly, in Santa Barbara, rent control forces spent $21,000 compared to the $160,000 spent by the opposition.

However, as the CHC feared, Proposition 13 gave momentum to the burgeoning statewide tenant revolt. The aftermath of the property-tax measure appeared to demonstrate to California renters that their status as tenants separated them as a group, or class from property owners. Despite the Jarvis campaign promise, not only did most landlords fail to pass on the savings, but rent increases continued unabated. A survey conducted by the City of Los Angeles in August revealed that in just a little over two months following the election, 11 percent of Los Angeles renters received rent increases while only 7 precent were promised some benefits by their landlord (*LAT*, Aug. 22, 1978, p. I-1). With the savings of landlords statewide expected to be over a billion dollars, every rent increase notice after the election became an affront to renters.

Tenant organizers were quick to recognize the boost Proposition 13 gave to the rent control movement. In a style repeated throughout the state by other activists, spokespersons for CHAIN and CES held a press conference in Los Angeles two weeks after the election to announce that rent increases were continuing since the passage of Proposition 13, citing examples from a tenant hotline operated by CES (*LAT*, June 22, 1978, p. I-33). In Sacramento CHAIN, the Campaign for Economic Democracy (CED) and the Gray Panthers announced a "Coalition to Rollback Rents," while declaring their support for legislation, AB 2986, introduced by Assemblymember Tom Bates, that would roll back rents to pre-Proposition 13 levels and require landlords to share 80 percent of their property-tax savings with tenants (*LAT*, June 29, 1978, p. I-3). CHAIN coordinator, Cary Lowe summed up the relationship between Proposition 13 and rent control when he wrote:

> This is the most important opportunity for tenant organizing in recent years. The landlords have finally overreached with their greed and we are seeing a backlash of tenant anger against increases (*CED News*, Aug./Sept. 1978, p. 2).

The press conferences paid high dividends as newspaper and television commentators began to label any rent increase as "unjustified" and as an instance of "rent gouging." Complaints from tenants poured into offices of elected officials around the state. A renter "hotline" established by Governor Brown received 12,000 phone calls a day to register their unhappiness about recent rent increases (*Housing Law Project Bulletin*, Aug./Sept. 1978, p. 3). By the end of the summer, forms of rent control were enacted in several California cities, waiting to be voted on in upcoming elections in several others, and the subject of a major legislative battle in the state legislature.

Politicians, influenced both by the new political awakening of tenants and the actions of landlords also began to lay the blame on the avarice of landlords. When Los Angeles Mayor Tom Bradley, sensing the political shift, announced support for the rent rollback and freeze in front of the city council, he criticized landlords for making "excessive profits" on a basic need, but he was careful to denounce "some landlords . . . but not all" for their displays of "greed" (LAT, July 13, 1978, p. I-1; LA Sentinel, July 20, 1978, p. A-10). Other council members were less reserved. Council President John Ferraro thought it "unconscionable that landlords would raise rents" in the wake of Proposition 13. Councilmember Zev Yaroslavsky was hardly less severe when he termed the increases "the height of moral outrage" (Evening Outlook, July 14, 1978, p.1).

The apartment industry responded in defense, blaming government regulations and inflation for the deterioration of the housing supply (Evening Outlook, Feb. 2, 1979, p. A-2; Apr. 6, 1978, p. A-11; Aug. 21, 1978, p. A-10). The Los Angeles Times concurred with the industry assessment in an editorial, arguing that it was "landlord costs, not landlord abuses (that) are the principal cause of rent inflation" (LAT, July 13, 1978, p. I-1).

Tenant activists disagreed. They blamed many of their problems on the increase in the number of landlords looking for a quick return with minimal involvement. One Santa Monica activist, Dennis Zane, explained the nature of the problem in a neighborhood newspaper column. "More and more," claimed Zane, "the 'mom and pop' apartment building is a thing of the past." Replacing them in Santa Monica, particularly, were the speculators.

> The speculator . . . seeks a quick turnover. He or she raises the cost of financing, property values, taxes, and thus rents by continuous buying and reselling of property. Tenants absorb both the profit demands of speculators and the increased costs of everything else associated with property owners (Zane, in Ocean Park Perspective, Jan. 1978, p. 1).

Only a few individuals viewed the problem from the perspective of larger economic questions. One landlord blamed the entire crisis on the banks and mortgage payments (LAT, Aug. 29, 1978, p. II-5). A tenant activist focused criticism upon the free market and called for change in national housing policy toward the construction of public housing (LAT, Mar. 23, 1980, p. I-3).

LOS ANGELES

The flurry of reported rent increases following the approval of Proposition 13 renewed the fight for rent control in Los Angeles. Once again, Wachs introduced an ordinance, this time calling for a six-month rent freeze at pre-Proposition 13 levels. The first hurdle for the bill to clear was the Governmental Operations Committee, which had rejected a previous rent limitation proposal by Wachs the summer before. The key vote on the committee was Council member Ernani Bernardi, whose district lies in the San Fernando Valley. Bernardi had previously been an outspoken foe of rent control and a leader on the council in opposition (*LAT*, Mar 22, 1978, p. I-1).

It was in the San Fernando Valley that tenants in the city of Los Angeles reacted loudest to post-Proposition 13 rent increases. A poll conducted by the local newspaper serving the valley revealed that one out of every six valley renters received a rent hike within five weeks of the election (*Valley News*, July 14, 1978, p.1). Gregory Nelson, an aide to Councilmember Wachs, whose district also lay within the valley, reported that more complaints about rent increase were received in the last week of June than any time in the previous year (*Valley News*, June 30, 1978, p.1). Incidents of tenant organizing, particularly rent strikes, appeared in the newspaper (*LAT*,June 30, 1978, p.I–32; *Valley News*, July 7,1978, p.1; July 8, 1978, p.1; Aug. 3, 1978, p. 2).

Some valley tenants, angered by rising rents and the city council's previous refusal to take steps to remedy the situation, formed the Valley Tenants Association and decided to bypass city hall and take matters into their own hands. The group, composed primarily of senior citizens, circulated a rent control initiative designed to roll back rents to January 1977 levels and to allow rent adjustments not to exceed 10 percent return on the landlord's investment (*Valley News*, June 30, 1978, p. 1; *LAT*, Dec. 28, 1978, p. VII-1).

The tenant unrest in the valley pushed Bernardi into doing a complete turnaround on the issue. Four months after he had led the opposition to the Wachs "antirent-gouging" ordinance, Bernardi changed his mind, declaring at first that it might become necessary to adopt "some form" of controls to ensure that renters received the "benefits they are entitled to" as a result of Proposition 13, and later becoming one of the major advocates for rent control.

Bernardi's shift was crucial, for not only did the rent control movement gain another voice on the council, it also gained a majority of the Governmental Operations Committee, which Bernardi chaired. The committee passed the Wachs proposal by a two-to-one vote. The proposed ordinance was placed before the entire council for consideration.

The ordinance failed to garner immediate support. Twice it failed to obtain the necessary eight votes, partially because of the reluctance to vote for rent control while Governor Brown called for a voluntary roll-back program (*LAT*, Aug. 4, 1978, p. I-1). Bernardi accused Brown of "playing into the hands of the rent gougers," while Wachs threatened his colleagues on the council with being "thrown out of office" if they did not provide rent relief for tenants (*Valley News*, July 25, 1978, p. 1; *Evening Outlook*, Aug. 2, 1978, p. 1).

Of greater significance was the hesitancy of black Councilmembers to join with Wachs and Bernardi in support of the freeze. Councilmember David Cunningham cast the lone vote against the ordinance while it was before the Governmental Operations Committee. Now that the ordinance was before the entire council, Councilmember Robert Farrell joined Cunningham in opposition. Farrell stated that the ordinance would have to be amended to allow for rent increases for costs incurred during rehabilitation—even if it was necessary to cure housing code violations—if it was to obtain his support. Emphasizing the different housing conditions that confront the black community from those faced by whites, Farrell reasoned, "our housing shortage is not because each and every unit is occupied, but rather because there are thousands of vacant and substandard housing units in South Central Los Angeles. . . . My constituents want decent housing and a decent rent" (*Sentinel*, Aug. 10, 1978, p.1).

The *Sentinel*, the Los Angeles black community newspaper, ignored the rent control battle for the most part and failed to take a stand on the issue. Instead, the newspaper gave strong coverage to police violence, equal opportunity, and school desegregation—issues of vital concern to most of the black community.

Despite reluctance on the part of some elected black leaders to support rent control, tenants have organized in the black community. CES, which often has been militant in its demands for rent control, has the black community as a large part of its base of support. The same is true for the United Tenants Action Council (UTAC), formed in 1974, which is the longest standing tenants rights organization in Southern California. CES and UTAC, like Farrell, emphasized enforcement of housing codes but did not go along with Farrell's plan to allow rents to be raised for the deferred maintenance of, what they characterized as, slumlords (*Sentinel*, June 7, 1978, p. A-3; Interview of Jerry Pennington, UTAC coordinator).

Farrell's and Cunningham's success in amending the ordinance to include increases for rehabilitation and Governor Brown's abandonment of the voluntary rollback plan in favor of AB 2986 removed the remaining obstacles to the passage of rent control in the city. The six-month rent freeze was approved by an eleven-to-one margin (*LAT*, Aug. 31, 1978, p. I-1).

As the rent freeze ran its six-month course, interested parties began to discuss the implementation of a broader housing policy. The director of the city's housing division, Kathleen Connell, warned, "if you simply took the freeze off, there would be an explosion in rents and massive chaos. There is a need for a rent stabilization program" (*LAT*, Jan. 4, 1979, p. II-1). In January activists Tom Hayden and Cary Lowe called not only for rent control, but for an end to condominium conversions, a limit on speculation, and more public housing (*LAT*, Jan. 14, 1978, p. II-1).

The ordinance considered by the city council was substantially weaker than activists had hoped for. Instead of offering permanent rent control, the law called for one year of controls. Instead of the demanded straight 7 percent limit on rent increases, additional increments of 6 percent for each of the two previous years without an increase were allowed. In addition a landlord could address the seven-member rent adjustment commission for even larger increases in cases of hardship, without reference to a tenants' ability to pay the increased rent. The law also provided for vacancy decontrol, a mechanism that allows rents to rise to what the market will bear upon vacancy of a unit, and exempted entirely single-family residences. Landlords were given the power to evict a tenant in order to move in a relative as well, further weakening the ordinance. At a crowded hearing, CES coordinator Reverend Al Dortch denounced the proposed law, demanding "effective rent control, not just this . . . (ordinance) . . . you're considering" (*Herald-Examiner*, Jan. 20, 1979, p. 1).

Despite echoes of Dortch's unhappiness from other tenant activists over the next two months, the ordinance, largely unchanged, passed with the minimum number of votes necessary. The bill went into effect May 1, 1979. After two years of efforts toward passing a rent control law, Wachs was understandably overjoyed when he praised Los Angeles for becoming the first major city in the western United States to "have the courage to come to grips with real estate speculation" (*LAT*, Mar. 16, 1979, p. I-1).

Activists were not entirely pleased. Concerning the law's exemption of single-family residences, Dortch responded, "almost 40 percent of the dwellings in the black and brown communities are single family. All of these people are being overlooked" (*Sentinel*, Mar. 22, 1979, p. A-1). Other activists focused criticism on the provision allowing eviction in order to move in a relative. In a *Los Angeles Times* article appearing four months after the law had taken effect, Legal Aid lawyer Barbara Blanco declared, "I've never seen such creative legal maneuvering. Interstate 5 must be jammed with landlords' relatives moving into town." Pete

Savino, a CES organizer, tied the problem to vacancy decontrol, arguing, "the bottom line is that the current ordinance gives the landlord a profit motive for evicting tenants" (*LAT*, Sept. 17, 1979, p. II-1).

The enactment of the rent freeze, and later rent control, in the City of Los Angeles left unincorporated areas under county jurisdiction without protection. Most critically affected by the lack of controls and rising rents was West Hollywood, where over 80 percent of the residents are renters. The supervisor representing this area, Ed Edelman, proposed a rent rollback ordinance that failed to pick up the necessary vote to gain a majority on the board (*LAT*, Oct. 18, 1978, p. II-1; Nov. 1, 1978, p. II-1).

In response to the board's inaction, West Hollywood tenants, with the aid of CES, used mass protests and confrontation style politicking in attempts to pressure the board to accept a rent control law. State Senator David Roberti and Assemblymember Herschel Rosenthal addressed a CES organized rally, attended by a thousand tenants demanding rent control (*LAT*, Feb 12, 1979, p. II-1). Rent strikes broke out in two apartment buildings where tenants incurred large rent increases. The tenants were quick to point out the owners of both buildings saved over $15,000 each in property taxes due to the Jarvis initiative while rents were increased up to 91 percent (*Pico Post*, Mar. 29, 1979, p. 1; Apr. 5, 1979, p. 1). In mid-April the CES-led tenants stormed the County Hall of Administration, waving notices of rent increases and evictions as proof of the necessity for immediate enactment of a rent control law (*LAT*, Apr. 24, 1979, p. II-1).

The board responded to the protests reluctantly. After granting tentative approval of a measure similar to the Los Angeles rent control law on May 16, the board waited five weeks to grant final approval. Even upon passing the measure, the board displayed hesitancy, failing to grant the measure a one-fourth vote that would have put rent control into effect immediatly. The fourth vote, that of Yvonne Burke, was an abstention. Burke had recently been appointed by Governor Brown to represent a conservative district and declined to cast her vote for rent control so as not to antagonize her constituency (*LAT*, May 16, 1979, p. II-1; May 30, 1979, p. II-1; June 11, 1979, p. II-1).

Los Angeles County joined the cities of Los Angeles, El Monte, Beverly Hills, and Santa Monica as a rent controlled jurisdiction in Southern California. Tenants had battled real estate interests in an attempt to gain some control over a speculative real estate market. However, rent control was but the beginning of the battle against the real estate industry. After winning rent control, tenants continued to apply pressure on local governments to further regulate private rental housing.

Of most immediate concern was the nationwide trend of conversion of apartments into condominiums. In a report by Citicorp Real Estate,

Inc., it was estimated that 100,000 units were converted in the United States in 1978 (LAT, May 1, 1979, p. I-1). The problem led member of Congress Benjamin Rosenthal (D-NY) to introduce legislation to ban conversions, which died a quick death in committee (LAT, Sept. 1, 1979, p. I-4).

The debate over condominium conversions ignited questions over the intrinsic value of property ownership. In response to a letter from a displaced tenant, one converter replied:

> We, the converters, are giving you the chance to have something you can call your own for less than you can find in any suburbia, the tax advantages and the pride that goes with owning your own home (LAT, Aug. 8, 1979, p. II-6).

Industry spokespersons claimed that they were merely supplying the goods for a growing demand—the demand to own. A Chicago developer explained the real estate industry's attitude toward the phenomenon, echoing arguments in favor of homeownership, to the Los Angeles Times, claiming, "people want to own something in their lifetime. Condos are a hedge against inflation. They provide tax benefits and stabilize communities" (LAT, May 1, 1979, p. I-1).

Critics contended that it was not demand, but pressure and the fear of continual eviction that forced tenants to buy (LAT, May 1, 1979, p. I-1). Furthermore, the units usually sold for more than all but the wealthiest tenants could afford. Those unable to raise the down payment were forced onto a shrinking rental housing market. In Los Angeles the city planning department received applications for the conversion of 11,705 units in 1977 alone. In Santa Monica 5,000 of its 100,000 inhabitants were notified that their buildings were in the process of conversion during the two-year period, 1978–79 (Evening Outlook, Jan. 25, 1979, p. B-1).

The threat of conversion and displacement drove tenants to organize to protect their homes. Tenant unions formed to fight application approvals (Valley News, June 22, 1978, p. 8; Pico Post, Mar. 8, 1979, p. 1). In West Hollywood, tenants marched in protest, demanding a four-month moratorium on condominium conversions. And in the City of Los Angeles, CED and the San Fernando Valley Association called for similar action.

The Los Angeles City Council responded in October 1979 with an anticonversion ordinance. The law required converters to help relocate displaced tenants by paying their moving costs and subsidizing the tenant's rent for one year should it be higher than the tenant previously paid. Furthermore, owners were required to contribute five hundred dollars for each converted unit toward a fund to build more rental housing (*LAT*, Oct. 4, 1979, p. II-1). An editorial in the *Los Angeles Times* spoke for the real estate industry, claiming that the city ordinance would serve only to worsen the situation by raising the cost of housing. The subsidies paid by the converter to the tenant, the *Times* argued, would be passed on to the purchaser of the condominium unit, raising the cost and pricing more prospective owners out of the market (*LAT*, Sept. 26, 1979, p. II-4).

The Los Angeles County Board of Supervisors considered a similar measure, requiring financial reparations to displaced tenants. However, tenants, organized by CES, reacted violently to what they perceived as an attempt to buy them off rather than address the real problem—their right to affordable housing (*LAT*, Nov. 11, 1979, p. II-1; Nov. 20, 1979, p. II-1). At an early meeting tenants chanted "recall the supervisors" and "keep the money; we want our homes, not the money" (*LAT*, Sept. 21, 1979, p. II-1). Three weeks later, 200 tenant activists chased the supervisors from the meeting hall and staged a sit-down demonstration, prompting prolandlord Supervisor Pete Schabarum to retort, "it is readily apparent we have some professional agitators" stirring the crowd (*LAT*, Oct, 10, 1979, p. II-1; Oct. 17, 1979, p. II-1). The militancy of the tenants failed to sway the board, as the measure was approved in late November (*LAT*, Nov. 21, 1979, p. II-1).

Tenants also challenged the authority of landlords to refuse rentals of families. Recent court cases prohibiting landlord discrimination against children under the Unruh Civil Rights Act spurred tenant organizing in that direction (*Housing Law Project Bulletin*, Feb. 1979, p. 10). A study done by the Fair Housing Project, a group affiliated with the Los Angeles-based Center for New Corporate Priorities, found that 84 percent of the rental housing supply in Los Angeles was restricted to some age groups, while 70 percent refused children of any age (*LAT*, Oct. 1, 1979, p. II-1). Activists from both CED and CES testified before the Los Angeles City Council, claiming the adoption of an "adults only" ban would serve both to protect the rights of children and to help maintain the family. The City Council adopted the adults only ban by a 10–3 vote (*LAT*, Jan. 31, 1980, p. II-1).

SANTA MONICA

The conversion of the Los Angeles City Council and the County Board of Supervisors must be contrasted with the repeated refusal of the Santa Monica local government to adopt even the mildest protection for its tenant population. If anything, the situation should have been reversed.

Tenants make up the overwhelming majority of the Santa Monica population, about 80 percent, while they comprise only 60 percent of the City of Los Angeles and 50 percent of the county. The explanation for the failure of the Santa Monica City Council to grant relief to its renter population can be found in the makeup of the council of that period. The head of the seven-member council, Mayor Donna Swink, was vice-president of the local bank that heavily financed real estate activity in the town. Two other members of the council, John Bambrick and Seymour Cohen, were landlords. To these three people, any interference with private property rights and the free market was unthinkable. The remainder of the members were homeowners with little interest in solving renters' problems.

Faced with this situation, tenants had sought to pass a rent control initiative, but failed. However, Santa Monica's middle class tenants, many of whom voted against Proposition P, the city's first rent control initiative, because of the promises made in connection with Proposition 13, also received post-Proposition 13 rent increases. Santa Monica was one of the major focuses of real estate speculation in Southern California, and rents were already in the process of increasing rapidly before Proposition 13 passed. Immediately after Proposition 13 was passed, notices of rent increases from individuals in 37 different buildings were reported by the Santa Monica Fair Housing Alliance (SMFHA) (transcript of Santa Monica Council meeting, July 25, 1978, item 12-B, p. 2).

As elsewhere in the state, this behavior by the landlords seemed to enrage the formerly placid tenants of Santa Monica. Many of these tenants were among the 300 that packed the city council chambers when SMFHA presented a rollback proposal to the council. Tenants testified concerning rent hikes, blaming speculators for causing their problems. They went further, linking the real estate industry to the Santa Monica City Council. One elderly tenant advocated rent strikes and threatened the council with recall elections (p. 22). Another tenant foresaw the possibility of a riot:

> There's a problem here, and something has to be done about it. Nobody believed that Watts was going to blow up. Everything was pretty much under control. And this isn't Watts and it's not the sixties, but I think something has to be done about it (p. 30).

Tenants repeatedly asserted their attachment to the community. They denied that tenants were second-class citizens and asserted the rights and status of full citizens. They referred to their apartments as their homes and indicated that they felt those homes were threatened. They emphasized their desire to stay in Santa Monica, where some had lived all their lives. One tenant, a second-generation Santa Monican, expressed his ties to the community:

> My parents were born here. My grandparents have lived here for a good many years. We have had people who work here and people who have lived here and people who have paid taxes here and people who have died here, and I intend to stay here (p. 23).

CED activist Nathan Gardels echoed those sentiments, asserting that tenants had helped build Santa Monica and deserved better than displacement because of rising rents. He posed the question for the audience to the Council, "if you're not representing the renters who are 80 percent of the city, who are you representing?"

When the council reconvened one month later, the tenants had their answer. Although three members supported a mild six-month rent control ordinance in a losing gesture, the remaining four members assumed hostile postures toward the protestors. Mayor Swink, speaking for the majority, stated that the problem in Santa Monica was not high rents; the problem was one of too many renters and not enough homeowners in the city (*Evening Outlook*, Sept. 13, 1978, p. 1).

The refusal of the council to represent 80 percent of its constituency led tenants to return to the initiative process (*Evening Outlook*, Oct. 19, 1978, p. 1). The new measure, Proposition A, was far stronger legislation than the rollback measure SMFHA had presented to the council. The charter amendment, upon approval, would establish a rent control board elected by the citizenry, annual rent adjustments, a ban upon the demolition or conversion into a condominium of any rental unit, and just cause eviction requirements. Further, Proposition A lacked a vacancy decontrol mechanism, making it more difficult to landlords to evade the law by evicting tenants.

The campaign against Proposition A served to intensify the establishment's efforts to negatively stereotype tenants. Councilmember and landlord Seymour Cohen made the classic distinction between the enterprising and the lazy when he said, "some people wisely invested in property and I don't condemn them for their actions. Some of you (tenants in the audience) are too lazy to go out and do the same thing" (*Evening Outlook*, Jan. 24, 1979, p. 1).

The local newspaper, the *Evening Outlook*, wasted few opportunities to attack tenant activists and rent control. The newspaper's editorial board questioned the wisdom of enacting a law to benefit tenants "whose only stake in the community is their rent," revealing the contempt felt by the local establishment for tenants (*Evening Outlook*, Mar. 29, 1979, p. 6). Further, the newspaper maintained that the law was unnecessary. From an admittedly unscientific survey of its readers, the newspaper reported that the majority of Santa Monica's tenants were content with their current rent levels, concluding that the rent control initiative was the work of outside agitators, Tom Hayden and Jane Fonda (both Hayden and Fonda live in Santa Monica) (*Evening Outlook*, Mar. 28, 1979, p. 1).

The *Outlook* had maintained a consistent position during the tenant uprising; as far back as the presentation by SMFHA of the rollback measure to the city council, the *Outlook* questioned the motives of activists stating, "their real goal is to use the tax system as a method for redistributing wealth, or more accurately, for redistributing the poverty which would result from their profligate, collectivist spending" (*Evening Outlook*, July 12, 1978, p. 12).

At the same time tenants intensified their attacks on landlords. When one landlord notified her tenants of a large rent increase to pay for extensive refurbishing plans, the tenants organized and challenged her right to arbitrarily do so. In response to a suggestion from their landlord that they move to a less expensive suburb, tenants also chose a classic theme, noting that it was the tenants who were *the* "productive" members of the community:

> Unlike you, we work for a living; our jobs and family needs dictate where we should live . . . why is it that landlords are able to uproot families, destabilize neighborhoods, shuffle children around from school to school, and dispossess senior citizens?" (*Ocean Park Perspctive*, Mar. 1979, p. 3).

The tenant campaign to pass Proposition A was far more sophisticated and organized than their first losing effort. In the second campaign, SMFHA was joined by the local Democratic club and CED under the banner of Santa Monicans for Renters' Rights (SMRR). The addition of CED brought on the attacks against Hayden and Fonda, CED's founders, but it also brought on the resources and experience necessary to run an electoral campaign. The use of advanced electoral computer techniques along with a mass mobilization of tenants, estimated to include about 5,000 individuals in one or another phase of the campaign, offset being outspent by real estate interests $217,257 to $38,443 (*Evening Outlook*, June 19, 1979, p. 3).

Despite claims by conservatives that the initiative drive was the work of the outside agitators Hayden, Fonda, and CED, and had no support among residents, the electorate approved Proposition A by nearly a 9 percent margin. Since the previous June rent control had lost by 11 percent, the victory represented a 20 percent turnaround between

From CHAINLETTER (California Housing Action & Information Network CHAIN News-letter), 1979 3(3): p. 1. Reprinted by permission. Graphic by S. Goldstein.

the two elections. The greatest increase in support came from the Wilshire corridor area, populated by the city's wealthier and more upwardly mobile tenants. The switch of these tenants can be attributed not only to a reaction against both the refusal of landlords to allow tenants a share in the Proposition 13 tax savings and the electoral campaigning, but also to the "demolition derby" conducted by landlords in the weeks before rent control was passed. Landlords who panicked over the likely passage of rent control and demolition restrictions, physically leveled some 500 units of rental housing, mostly in the Wilshire corridor. Even conservative tenants were outraged.

Two months later, tenants followed up their victory by electing all five members of the SMRR slate to the rent control board, defeating the rival landlord slate. The tenant sweep led one landlord to comment, "the inmates are running the institution" (*Evening Outlook*, June 27, 1979, p. 1). The protenant *Ocean Park Perspective* interpreted the election differently, concluding that "suddenly civil life in Santa Monica has opened up to include the excluded" (Oct. 1979, p. 3).

The real estate industry was not yet ready to concede power and responded with Proposition Q, an attempt to water down the rent control law. The measure was presented to the electorate as the "Fair Rents Initiative," a necessary retooling of the law to make rent control constitutional. One tenant activist termed the measure an attempt to turn rent control "into a vehicle for socking tenants with huge rent increases" (*Ocean Park Perspective*, Aug. 1979, p. 1).

Proposition Q aimed at three major changes in the law. First, it exempted single-family houses. Second, it tied annual rent increases to the consumer price index, a figure that would have been more than twice that allowed by the rent control board. Finally, Proposition Q provided for vacancy decontrol, the most glaring weakness in the Los Angeles law.

Along with Proposition Q, a seat on the city council would be determined by the election. The Renters' Rights slate ran activist Cheryl Rhoden against two other major candidates: Leslie Dutton, representing a conservative homeowner faction, and Pat Geffner, the choice of the more moderate business community. Both supported Proposition Q.

The antirent control forces still refused to concede tenants a place in the Santa Monica power structure, hoping instead that they would go away. Echoing Mayor Swink's sentiments of a year before, Geffner claimed that "one of the problems in the city right now is the imbalance between renters and homeowners." She offered condominium conversions as a means to achieve a more acceptable balance (*Evening Outlook*, Oct. 16, 1979, p. 1). Property owners insisted on believing that the problem was the renter, not the level of rent.

From CHAINLETTER (California Housing Action & Information Network CHAIN News-letter), 1980 4(2): p. 6. Reprinted by permission.

For the third time in seven months, tenants defeated the real estate industry at the polls. They also elected Rhoden to the council, giving tenants a three-seat voting bloc on a seven-member council. It was clear that in little over a year, tenants had become the dominant political force in Santa Monica. Tenants had fought for and won first-class citizenship.

It turned out that Proposition Q was but a test run for a landlord statewide effort. Soon a coalition of real estate developers, building trade unions, and landlords formed to promote a statewide initiative similar to

Proposition Q. The initiative set guidelines for rent control laws to conform to as well as to wipe every existing rent control law off the books. The purpose of the initiative was the same as earlier CHC efforts in the legislature—to stop the rent control movement.

Despite the fact that the initiative enacted no rent control provisions itself, the title on the petitions was "rent control." A realtor association newsletter admitted that the title might appear "misleading," but claimed that it "is likely to make getting signatures easier since the majority of state voters appear to favor some form of rent controls" (LAT, Oct. 26, 1979, p. II-1).

Tenant activists charged the landlords with deception; Joel Wachs, who had introduced rent control to the Los Angeles city council, termed the landlord effort as "perhaps the most misleading and deceptive initiative I've ever seen" (LAT, Oct. 23, 1979, p. II-1). Southern California Coordinator for the "No on 10" campaign, Parke Skelton, articulated the strategy that tenants would use against the initiative, Proposition 10:

> The issue isn't rent control, it's fraud. They are trying to capitalize on the popularity of rent control in order to destroy it. They made it sound like they are in favor of rent control. Actually, they want to engage in profiteering in the rental housing shortage (LAT, Mar. 23, 1980, p. I-3).

While the majority of the real estate industry denied the allegations, the tenant interpretation of the measure was corroborated by Howard Jarvis, who had made a personal decision to defend the initiative by attacking rent control. In a letter to rental property owners, Jarvis argued that the passage of Proposition 10 would ensure that "apartment ownership will remain the attractive investment which it has historically been in California" (LAT, Apr. 2, 1980, p. I-3). In a letter supporting Proposition 10 sent to homeowners, Jarvis attempted to whip up a Red scare, equating the rent control movement with socialism:

> The Jane Fonda–Tom Hayden emergency exists now . . . . Radicals want goverment to control all prices—even the price for which you can sell your home. Their first step is to have statewide rent controls. Next will be food—clothing—your home. . . . If you and enough concerned Californians act right now, we can stop this Fonda-Hayden plot before it reaches your family, and your home (LAT, Dec. 8, 1979, p. II-1).

Most of the media came out against Proposition 10, including the Los Angeles Times and the Herald-Examiner, as well as radio stations KNX, KNBR, and KABC Southern California. The Los Angeles Times, consistently antirent control in sentiment, criticized the measure as an attack upon the state constitution, an abuse of the democratic process. The paper's editorial board called the advertising campaign by the landlords "the worst we have heard for years" (LAT, Jan. 2, 1980, p. II-6; May 1, 1980, p. II-6). The confusion generated by the conflicting campaigns spread to the national press. The Wall Street Journal, not realizing that Proposition 10 would only set guidelines, not rent controls, declared "this won't be the first time an industry has voluntarily submitted to government regulation as a refuge from political pressures" (Wall Street Journal, May 27, 1980, p. 24).

Tenants organized, pressuring local governments with rent control ordinances to come out against Proposition 10. Four hundred tenants in Beverly Hills met for a "No on 10" rally; one week later they applauded the city council's formal opposition to the statewide measure (Beverly Hills Post, May 15, 1980, p. 1; May 22, 1980, p. 1). In West Hollywood, a rally was organized by CES to drum up support against the landlord initiative (Pico Post, Mar. 2, 1980, p. 1). Both the Los Angeles County Board of Supervisors and the Los Angeles City Council voted to extend their rent control measures until the November election. In case the measure passed, tenants would remain protected until they had a chance to vote for a law conforming to the guidelines set by Proposition 10.

However, such extensions were unnecessary, as the tenant movement achieved a landslide victory. Outspent by 80-to-1, tenants defeated Proposition 10 by a 30 percent margin (LAT, June 5, 1980, p. I-18). Tenant activists would use the victory as evidence that the electorate approved of rent control, and continue their drive for stricter rent control laws.

In Santa Monica events led to their natural conclusion in April of 1981. In yet another electoral sweep, a set of four city council men and women were elected giving tenant representatives a five-to-one margin on the council that was once devoid of tenant representation (Evening Outlook, Feb. 22, 1981, p. 1). The tenants showed how strong they had become by not only electing their council candidates, but also defeating a homeowner anticrime measure, passing one of their own, and electing two people to the school board. In the state the battles continue. Some have been won and others have been lost; however, it cannot be denied that in the five years since the California Supreme Court handed down the Birkenfeld decision, a feeble tenant movement made up of a handful of housing activists and public interest lawyers has developed into a powerful mass political movement. Tenants organized and pressured existing governments to enact rent controls and prevent condominium conversions.

Reprinted from the Ocean Park Perspective, by permission.

In the case of Santa Monica, a stubborn city establishment forced tenants to circumvent the city council and run an initiative campaign, which resulted in the approval of the toughest rent control measure in the state. Most impressively, the tenant movement successfully defended its gains against the most powerful interests in the state and finally gained control of the city's government.

CHAPTER

3

The Consciousness of
a Movement

From reading the recorded history of the tenant movement, it appears that the differences between the tenants active in the Sons of Liberty, the Anti-Renters, and the tenants of Santa Monica are far less than the years between them would indicate. Like a daytime soap opera, one could almost tune in at anytime and hear the same repetitive themes. There appears to be a constant need to assert the worthiness of the position of tenants in this society and contrast that position with that of the land-lord. The problems of security of tenure and gouging rents seem nearly always there. In the urban context the question of the condition of the rental housing of the poor began in the early days and has contined. The variety of causes seen by tenants for their problems has remained almost the same starting with the greedy landlord, being the prime villain, followed by the speculator, and, to a lesser degree, the bank. And the tactics that tenants use to fight individually and collectively were developed quite early and repeated again and again.

These themes are much like the primary elements of class consciousness: 1) recognition of a "significant status" shared by identifiable others; 2) acknowledgment of "common problems" of this group; 3) identification of the "systematic causes" of these shared problems; and 4) commitment to "group action" toward resolution of the problems (Dolbeare and Edelman 1979, p. 350).[1] In this instance, however, it is not the expression of "class" consciousness per se that has been discovered, but the expression of a tenant consciousness.

While our review of history disclosed the stable elements of this tenant consciousness, in at least the more vocal parts of the tenant movement, it has not told us to what degree such consciousness exists in the

66

tenant population as a whole. As with other forms of political consciousness, we would expect that tenant consciousness would occur in degrees
or at various levels. Some tenants would be expected to have little or no
tenant consciousness, while others would likely have developed only
partial consciousness. While the tenant movement has had its successes
with mass action, the history did not provide us with discernible levels
or definite information about what proportion of the population has
what level of consciousness.

In this chapter, with the assistance of 32 tenant activists in California, the levels of tenant consciousness that should be found in the tenant
population will be identified. Then the extent to which each level of
consciousness exists in two randomly selected populations of tenants
will be determined. One sample was drawn from the County of Los
Angeles as a whole and the other from the City of Santa Monica. With all
the successful political activity in Santa Monica, tenant consciousness
should be quite high. In the county less is known about whether the
protestations of activists at city hall and the county building are representative of the city's and county's tenant population.

VIEWS OF TENANT ACTIVISTS

The activists were selected and interviewed for this project with the
assistance of two long-time members of the California tenant movement,
one in Northern California and one in Southern California. These two
individuals listed all the activists they knew and then ranked them according to their centrality to the movement. This process was designed
to yield 20 people who were "musts" in the effort for further definition
of tenant consciousness. Nineteen of these people were interviewed and
were, in turn, asked to identify others they thought should be interviewed. Thirteen more people were repeatedly identified and were interviewed. In all, the list of activists included 113 names. The people
interviewed were working or had worked in Berkeley, El Monte, Los
Angeles, Orange County, San Francisco, San Jose, Santa Barbara, Santa
Cruz, and Santa Monica.

The majority of the activists interviewed were male (72 percent),
white (90 percent), single (77 percent), without children (77 percent),
college educated (93 percent), from professional or managerial back-
grounds (74 percent), and tenants (87 percent). They tended to be over 30
(55 percent), to have been in California fewer than 15 years (61 percent),
and to be paid for their tenant work (55 percent). More had been involved in the tenant movement through legislative or electoral work or
tenant counseling (81 percent) than through building organizing (68

percent). More than half had been active in the tenant movement for more than two years (65 percent) but less than six years (58 percent). Slightly less than half had had a personal problem with a landlord (48 percent). Most of these people had become involved in the tenant movement as a result of this problem. Of the remainder, half had become involved after working on other housing issues (mainly urban renewal), and half were political people who had been part of the antiwar movement or the like and saw the tenant issue as the best focus for their political interests at this time. Only one of those interviewed was black and two were Latino. While there are many third-world tenants engaged in struggles with their landlords in California, this lack of representation in the interviews of activists is representative of the leadership of the tenant movement in California. There is likely an underrepresentation of women in the sample.[2] This is because of the recent move of women to leadership positions in the California movement and an emphasis in the study design on interviewing people who had been in leadership positions before the passage of Proposition 13 and who continued to be active up to the point of the interview.[3]

Although the main interest in interviewing the tenant activists was in determining the levels of tenant consciousness in the tenant population, the interview began by asking general questions about the concept of tenant consciousness: had they heard the term, did they use it, and how would they define it. Most (79 percent) of the activists had heard the term and half had used it in conversations with other activists. They stated, however, that it was an activist's term and not in the vocabulary of tenants themselves. All of the activists stated that they saw the need for the development of consciousness around tenant issues if the movement were to grow and sustain itself over time and offered a definition of the term. A few questioned the term because they worried that the term tenant consciousness itself sounded "trendy" and might cheapen a very important idea or, alternatively, confuse people about the basic class struggle they saw as transcending the tenant movement. The various definitions offered by the activists will be discussed in the context of the levels of tenant consciousness.

LEVELS OF TENANT CONSCIOUSNESS

Next, the activists were asked if there were discernible levels of tenant consciousness in the tenant population equivalent to the levels of consciousness often described in the working-class literature: revolutionary, trade union, and false consciousness. Twenty-eight of the activists said they saw equivalent levels of consciousness in the tenant population.

Those activists who stated they saw these levels were then asked to describe the components of each, particularly how tenants at each level stood on the four elements of tenant consciousness we had previously identified. They were also asked whether they thought the four elements were correct and whether they could see any alternatives. All the activists concurred on the primacy of the four elements and none offered an alternative.

Six primary levels of tenant consciousness were described by the activists. (The method used in synthesizing the activist positions is described in the Appendix.) The names *most commonly* used by the activists were given to the levels. The six types are set out in hierarchical order in Figure 3.1.

Figure 3.1. *Levels of Tenant Consciousness*

"Radicalized"
"Consumer"
"Defender"
"Individualist"
"Unconscious"
"Landlord Lover"

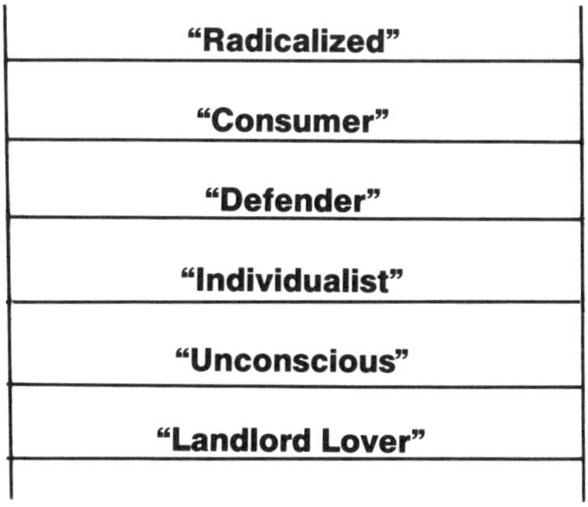

The following is a synthesis of the activists' description of each type. The language is, to the extent possible, that *used by the activists* in their descriptions:

1) At the bottom of the ladder is the "landlord lover," who identifies with the landlord position on all four elements of tenant consciousness. These tenants believe in the institution of private property to the extent that they would not restrict the landlord's "rights" in any fashion including the right to arbitrary eviction. They are willing to subvert their own material interests to those of the landlord and oppose rent control because it limits the landlord's necessary ability to maximize a return on investment. If this causes them problems, it is their fault for not owning rental property themselves. If they recognize that rents are going up, they would see it as a function of the market, inflation, and government regulation.

2) The next level of the ladder was commonly referred to as the "unconscious" tenant. Some of the views of the unconscious tenant may overlap with that of the landlord lover; however, they were seen by the activists more as "dupes" holding the landlord line than as conscious ideologues. Some of these tenants are "defeated, pliant, or fatalistic" people. Others are tenants by "choice" and have sufficient economic mobility to avoid the problems common to most tenants. It is unlikely that either consider landlords or tenants as distinct groups in society. The typical unconscious tenant would view a landlord with admiration and wouldn't mind being one—if he or she could somehow get enough money or whatever trick it takes to get rental property. While it may occur to unconscious tenants to take action if they feel wronged, they would inevitably withdraw from action for fear of eviction. The unconscious tenant knows little about tenants' rights and assumes that landlords rightly have most power. This type of tenant would know little about tenant issues, and even if she or he did vote (which is unlikely), might very well vote against rent control. They generally accept common beliefs about why rents go up if they have any theory at all. The activists predicted their reply would likely be that inflation causes rents to go up.

3) The next level was often referred to as the "individualists." These are the people who may have some awareness of tenants' problems but are not yet organizable. Most of the activists said that before Proposition 13 a great many tenants were at this level. Since the proposition, their experience has been that many of the former individualistic tenants have moved beyond this point.

The individualist believes that increasing rents are caused by more than the laws of supply and demand and inflation, but this belief does not cause them to question the market system. Knowledge that some landlords or speculators exploit scarcity and that banks have a role in stimulating rent increases does not trigger a call for reform. This is "how it is" and "one cannot fight city hall, " and, in the main, this is "how it should be." This accepting and approving attitude also dominates the individualist's view of private property. If limited housing reform is acceptable, it is not out of principle, but out of immediate self-interest. For this reason the individualist would likely oppose the power of arbitrary eviction and vote for rent control.

The individualist tenant who feels wronged by some action of the landlord might come to an initial tenant protest meeting but would not likely return for a second meeting. If anything, their contribution to an organizing effort would be to question the ability of other tenants to win in a struggle against the landlord, pointing out the possible negative outcomes of their efforts.

The least attractive type of individualist described by the activists was the "turncoat." This type of tenant would appear to go along with tenant organizing in their building while reporting on the other tenants' organizing plans to the landlord so that they could make a special deal to solve their problems. At the same time this tenant would secretly vote for rent control, while telling the landlord of his or her opposition to the idea.

4) At the next level is the "defender." This level of consciousness is the first "positive" step in the development of tenant consciousness. The defender level was said to have been the major beneficiary of the increased tenant consciousness resulting from reactions to Proposition 13. These tenants are willing to act collectively at the building level against a landlord who, for example, gave what they considered to be an "unfair" rent increase or announced intentions to convert the building to condominiums. They are not likely to participate in tenant movement activities unless they see them as directly related to their immediate problem. Further, their involvement at either the building or movement level is likely to cease once their personal problem is solved.

The defenders believe that there are landlords (perhaps including their own) and speculators who are taking advantage of a tight housing market and that this exploitation legitimizes placing some restrictions on the rights of private property. However, they still believe that the main problem in rising rents is a shortage of housing and inflation. Their moralistic approach of seeing good and bad landlords leads them to be stronger supporters of rent control than the individualists, but their general belief in the capitalist system is not much different from the individualists' general view of private property. Unless they believe they will be personally affected, they are not likely to insist on expansion of tenants' rights beyond protection from arbitrary eviction.

At the low end of this consciousness level are tenants who are afraid and will retreat to the individualistic position if things appear to be going poorly in a landlord-tenant conflict. At the high end are those who are beginning to see the need for broad reform in the landlord-tenant relationship and who are considering becoming active in the tenant movement.

5) At the next level are those tenants who have developed what was called "consumer" consciousness. The consumers have become broadly suspicious of the institution of landlordism but still accept its continued existence as an inevitable part of the overall capitalist system. The consumers' suspicions lead them to call for major regulation of rental property. Included here are laws that control discrimination, condominium conversion, and demolitions as well as rent control. In contrast to tenants with lower consciousness, their political support is not contingent

upon fear of being personally affected by injustices that proposed reforms intend to eradicate.

Compared to the defenders, the consumers have developed a populist analysis of why rents increase. They have begun to understand "how the system works" and believe that with this understanding one can make the system work better. The populist approach of the consumer tends to focus on market failures caused by "bigness." Large landlords, major speculators, and banks are considered to be at fault. At the same time this attitude leads the consumers to temper their call for reform. They believe that regulation should be directed at the major offenders and toward correcting the imbalance such offenders have created. They also fear that regulation can go too far and injure the "little guy" or the entire economic system.

The consumers are potential members of the tenant movement. Because of their reform interests, they are particularly willing to work in legislative and electoral campaigns. However, it was noted that some consumers shy away from confrontation with their own landlords. In part this is attributed to their rational legalistic approach and, in part, to a fear of eviction. It was reported that some consumers preferred to do their movement work across town where they would not encounter their own landlord.

6) At the top of the tenant consciousness ladder are several types of tenant who were generally referred to as having become "radicalized." Up to this point there has been remarkable agreement among the activists about the types of tenants at each level and the beliefs these tenants would hold. However, at this level ideological disagreements among the activists emerged. The ideological divisions generated three varying characterizations of the radicalized tenant: extreme consumer, single issue "tenantist," and the political and economic radical.

The extreme consumer, as the name indicates, is an advanced version of the consumer level tenant. The major difference is that the extreme consumers have become so critical of landlordism that they begin to call for the conversion of some private rental housing to a form of public ownership or promote the conversion of rental housing units to tenant-owned cooperatives. The tenantist and the economic and political radicals also call for such conversions; however, unlike the extreme consumer they see the conversions as a step in the long-term elimination of all privately owned rental housing. While the tenantist and radical tenants agree on this point, they probably vary from one another in their general beliefs about private property. The tenantist, like the Anit-Renter, may be opposed only to landlordism, while the political and economic radical likely favors the elimination of private property in all of its manifestations. In this vein the political and economic radical may question even cooperative ownership of rental housing and, in the Hartman-Stone mode, call for its nationalization. It is interesting to note that the activists said that even at this level, populist concern for the "little guy" may remain. Any of the radicalized tenant types may exempt the small, resident landlord from any of the proposed transformation of rental housing.

The tenantist and the economic and political radical prefer tenant organizing to electoral and legislative work. They will engage in electoral and legislative work only if they believe such work will lead to increased organizing possibilities. As a result, these radicalized tenants may oppose reforms, including some forms of rent control, that they believe would pacify rather than activate the tenant population. The most radical types may refuse to participate in the political-legal process even to the extent of refusing to register to vote. The extreme consumer, on the contrary, is very committed to change through the electoral process. This strategic difference is a major source of conflict between the types of radicalized tenants.

Extreme consumers tend to reject building organizing because they see it is futile without stronger landlord-tenant laws. The other radicalized tenants analogize the preference for electoral work as equivalent to being a football spectator who comes out on weekends (for campaigns) to cheer and stays away the rest of the week (when day-to-day organizing is done). Two activists who took this latter position argued that tenants at any level of consciousness will come out to work in an electoral campaign. Even if the tenantists or economic and political radicals agree to work in a campaign with the extreme consumer, they may still disagree on tactics of the campaign. The extreme consumer may call for a professional-technical approach and the others for a mass mobilization.

While the extreme consumer has a more sophisticated analysis of the rent problem than the consumer, it is in the same populist vein. The economic and political radicals claim to have a "systemic view." Like Engels' critcism of George, the economic and political radicals place their analysis within a criticism of capitalism. They see capitalist rent as exploitative in much the same way as the usurpation of surplus value by capitalists is exploitative. Their analysis may downplay greed as a major contributor to the rent problem because of its moralistic connotation. Instead they might emphasize the role of finance capital (banks) and the state (particularly, the tax structure that encourages real estate speculation). The tenantist on the other hand employs the traditional U.S. tenant arguments against rent examined in the first chapter. At best, landlords are unproductive members of society and, more likely, major symbols of greed. This the radical type may eschew for more sophisticated explanations.

The differences between the three types of radicalized tenants is descriptive of deep and potentially devisive ideological splits within the tenant movement. Such splits are, of course, not unique to the tenant movement. They are found in all such issue-oriented social movements. The economic and political radical tends toward "class analysis" and see the tenant movement with the more general arena of working-class struggles. The extreme consumer tends to be a pluralist who sees tenants as one among many competing "interest groups." And, the tenantist tenants tend to be U.S. radicals in the antiaristocratic tradition who see issues between landlords and tenants in terms of "democracy" and "power." Almost all of the activists interviewed used one or more of these metaphors in defining tenant consciousness, indicating that they were representative of the split among the radicalized tenants they described.[4]

The ideological division between radicalized tenants has implications beyond the strategic and problem definition differences that have already been described. They result, in a very important way, in conflicts over the composition of the social bases the activists should be trying to mobilize. This difference in conceptualizing the social base of tenants is most strongly expressed in the difference between the economic and political radical and the extreme consumer. The economic and political radical modifies the word tenant with the term working-class. This radicalized tenant is very suspicious of the activation of the middle-class tenant in times of crisis such as those faced at present. They believe that once the relatively less severe problems of the middle class are solved, they will abandon the movement, leaving the problems of the working class unresolved. They do not believe that the middle-class tenant can provide the social base for a movement that will work toward the radical social change these types of activists have as their goal. In terms of this study, such activists believe middle-class tenants have lower tenant consciousness than working-class tenants.

The extreme consumers reply to this criticism by seeing the economic and political radicals, with their class analysis, as devisive forces in the tenant movement. Some of the Northern California activists blame the radicals for the troubles the tenant movement has had in certain cities in the northern part of the state. They see the radicals and the tenantists, as well, as rejecting elements of the tenant population with the skill to bring about meaningful reform and taking unrealistic stances on the issues that are bound to lead the movement to failure.

The tenant movement in Southern California also has these divisions, but they have not been disabling. In part this is because the Campaign for Economic Democracy, that is more middle-class based, has focused its activities primarily in Santa Monica, a more middle-class city, while the Coalition for Economic Survival, that is more working-class based, has worked primarily in the City and the County of Los Angeles. To the extent that these and other such groups that exist in the San Fernando Valley must coexist in the City and County of Los Angeles, the scale of the project of organizing tenants mitigates against conflict. It has, at times, however, led to hard feelings and limited ability of the movement to present a unified Southern California front.

Another element central to defining the social base of tenants to be organized did not appear in the description of the levels of tenant consciousness but did appear in the definition of tenant consciousness. Several of the activists used the metaphor "community," rather than "class" or "interest group" in their definitions. Two of the three minority activists used this term. They seemed to be using "community" as a synonym for nationality or race. The use of this metaphor is indictive of a split in the tenant movement in California, with at least as serious ramifications as those based on class.

Until the past few years, rents in California's white neighborhoods were considered to be "reasonable." The rapid rise of rents in recent years seems to have shocked the white population and resulted in mobilization around rent control that holds out the promise of relief. Rent control is not, by itself, the solution to the problems of California's minority population. Rents in minority areas have been beyond "affordable" limits for years, and the regulation of rents will not affect the poor housing conditions that many minorities also face.

One of the activists saw the almost singular concern of the present tenant movement with rents as a expression of the racism of the movement. At the extreme, this activist said, are white tenants who, not sharing the problems of minorities, blame minority tenants and not the landlord for the poor condition of minority rental housing. Many other white tenants simply are insensitive to the minorities' problems. Another activist said this division in the tenant movement (and society) manifested itself in what was called a "racist" City of Los Angeles rent control law. The law limits general rent increases, helping the white population gain control over the problem of rapidly rising rents, but it allows the pass through of the cost of repairs to rented property even if those repairs are necessitated by housing code violations. The law does not relieve the affordability problem for minority tenants who are threatened with increasing rents if they demand even the minimum conditions of habitability required by law.

Only a few of the California organizations involved in the tenant movement are truly racially integrated. When racial mix has occurred, it has usually been because integration was the highest priortiy of that organization. A member of one such group stated that many tenant activists practice what was called "affirmative discrimination." Feeling sorry for a poor minority tenant and not wanting to add to the tenant's burdens, they do not make a maximum effort to get him or her involved in the tenant movement. Over time an organization operating from this premise becomes almost entirely white and takes on a white identity. Once such an identity is established, recruiting minority membership becomes extremely difficult.

Some of the white activists saw those who defined the social base of tenants on nationality or racial lines as divisive to the tenant movement as those defining the social base on class lines. They stated that they had difficulty trying to join in coalition with some ethnically based groups and that some were separatists to the extent that they refused to communicate on a regular basis with tenant organizations dominated by whites. Sometimes these conflicts are mixtures of ideological and ethnicity splits.

In the social base none of the activists brought up the possibility of gender as a point of division in the social base on the same level as class or ethnicity, although "sexism" expressed by male leaders of tenant organizations has more than once come to dominate internal discussions in the California tenant movement.

In examining the nature of the social base of tenants in the next chapter, all of these positions will have to be kept in mind. At present little is known in a concrete way about the varying levels of consciousness of each of these groups within the tenant population. In the final chapter after analyzing the entire results of the surveys, the importance of these divisions in the leadership will be discussed in more depth.

TENANT-CONSCIOUSNESS SCALES

While these divisions present serious questions about the future of the tenant movement, they do not interfere with the general agreement among the activists on what a tenant, at a given level of consciousness, is likely to believe and the action such a tenant is likely to take.[5] Even the disagreements about the radicalized tenants are limited in terms of the criteria of measuring their consciousness versus others levels of consciousness. Because of these substantial agreements, we were able, with some confidence, to score and scale the responses of the activists about the positions of tenants at the various levels of consciousness on the four dimensions of tenant consciousness. A five-point scale was created for each of the dimensions, and the patterns of responses for each level of consciousness was determined. The method of creating the scales is described in the Appendix.

The problem then faced was how to apply the definition of tenant consciousness and the levels of tenant consciousness to the two samples of Southern California tenants that were interviewed. The statistical device chosen to accomplish this task was discriminant analysis. Discriminant analysis is a tool for classifying individuals by predetermined criteria such as the ones we have developed for levels of tenant consciousness. For example, researchers took the voting pattern of known "radical and nonradical" MPs in the British Parliament and used discriminant analysis to see if the voting pattern of the remaining MPs were more like the radicals or nonradicals (Nie et al. 1975). Here, rather than voting patterns, the patterns of positions on the four elements of tenant consciousness for this analysis were used.

In the application of discriminant analysis, it was discovered that it was not possible to reliably discriminate between the unconsciousness tenants and landlord-lover tenants. The primary distinction the activists had given us was that of knowing the antitenant position of landlord lover versus unconscious acceptance of antitenant positions on the part of the unconscious tenant. This distinction between "ideologue" and "dupe" was too subtle to measure. The two categories were, therefore, merged into one title—Antagonist, which will be employed in the remainder of the book.

The analysis of what the activists' interviews has, in effect, produced is a formula that could be applied to the results of the surveys of the two samples to determine the tenants' level of consciousness. However, to use this formula, the responses in the survey had to be converted into scales like those constructed in the analysis of the activist interviews. The four scales that were constructed to analyze the survey results were the identification scale, the landlordism scale, the sophistication scale, and the action scale. What follows is an explanation of the process by which this was done. It is present here because it contains important findings about the attitudes and intentions of the tenant population that are helpful in understanding the nature of the consciousness of tenants.

Identification

The measure of identification as a tenant employed in both the activist and survey results was the tenants' position on rent control. In the period of the study, there were repeated campaigns, both electoral and lobbying, for rent control. It has been the central issue of the current movement.[6] With the rare exception of some too radical to support this "reform," the activists believed support for rent control was the best available indicator of recognizing the collective interests of tenants.[7]

The scale was constructed primarily with the answers to two questions. The first question asked was whether the respondent would vote for rent control, and the second asked those who stated that they would how strong a supporter they were. Because there were so many rent control elections during the period in which the instrument was administered, some of which were sponsored by landlords to weaken existing laws, the interviewer was asked to explain that the proposed law was supported by tenant groups if the respondent inquired.

Scaling the responses was complicated by some 15 percent "I don't know" answers. This problem was handled by substituting the response to what was considered a surrogate question. Later in the questionnaire, the tenants were asked whether they would vote for a candidate for a rent control board who was supported by their area tenant organization. This question had very few "I don't know" responses. The activists had stated that fewer tenants would respond affirmatively to such a question than would support rent control itself. For this reason we felt that using this surrogate response would be sufficiently conservative to ensure that the vote for rent control would not be overstated.

The points on the scale parallel being against rent control, being a mild supporter, being a moderate supporter, being a strong supporter, and being a very strong supporter. Table 3.1 sets out the support of the identification scale.

Table 3.1.   *Identification Scale**

Scale Points	Los Angeles County		Santa Monica	
5 Very Strong support	(529)	36.3%	(292)	40.2%
4 Strong Support	(357)	24.5	(152)	20.9
3 Moderate Support	(251)	17.2	(126)	17.2
2 Mild Support	(136)	9.3	(38)	5.2
1 Against	(183)	12.6	(120)	16.5

*This type of scale is known as a "Likert"-like scale, a generally accepted method of scaling (Sellitz et al. 1976, pp. 418-21).

Landlordism

To investigate the tenants' acknowledgment of tenants' common problems, a landlordism scale was constructed.[8] The name of the scale was borrowed from the historical formulation of the problem. Three sets of questions were asked toward constructing this scale. The first related to the power of eviction; the second related to tenant power; and the third related to government intervention in the housing sector, including a question about total elimination of the private sector from the rental housing field.

In both samples the tenants favored restriction of a landlord's arbitrary eviction powers. In both cases an identical 97 percent of the tenants stated that a landlord should be required to have a good reason before he or she is allowed to evict a tenant. This did not tell us, however, what these tenants would consider a good reason. Because eviction to move in a family member was an issue in the adoption of rent control in Los Angeles, we asked whether a landlord should be able to evict a tenant to move in either a distant or close relative. Over 80 percent of the respondents objected to tenants being evicted for a distant relative and more than three-quarters objected in the case of the close relative.

To see what amount of tenant power the respondents favored, we asked a series of questions about tenants having a voice in decisions affecting the property in which they lived. Tenants were asked whether they should have any say, and, if any say, less say than the landlord, equal say with the landlord, or more say than the landlord about whether renovations should be made to the property that would raise the rent, whether the property should be converted to condominiums, what the rent should be, and who should live in the building.

In both samples more than half of the respondents believed that tenants should have at least as much or more say than landlords in whether renovations should be made to the property (Los Angeles–55 percent; Santa Monica–53 percent, hereafter called LA and SM). In Santa Monica about the same number favored as much tenant voice regarding condominium conversions (52 percent), while the percentage giving these responses in the county dropped slightly (47 percent). In contrast to the question on condominium conversion, the county respondents were somewhat more aggressive on the questions about tenants having a say in what the rent should be and who should live in the building. Thirty-one percent of the respondents in the county favored tenants having as much or more voice in what the rent should be, compared to 26 percent in Santa Monica. Twenty percent of the county sample favored equal or greater tenant voice on the question of who should live in the building, while only 17 percent took these positions in the Santa Monica sample. We then created an additive scale of the responses, giving one point for stating that tenants should have some but less say than the landlord to any of the four questions; two points for equal say; and three points for stating that tenants should have greater voice. Approximately 30 percent of the respondents in both samples had a score of six out of the possible 12 points and only 5 percent of the respondents scored as many as nine points.

When we asked about government intervention in the housing sector, the county tenants called for more action in every case. More county tenants favored increased government assistance to private developers so that they could build more low- and moderate-income housing (LA–82 percent; SM–78 percent) and the construction of more public housing (LA–71 percent; SM–60 percent). Even in the more extreme position of beginning to nationalize or cooperatize the rental housing stock, county tenants took a stronger stand (LA–18 percent, favor; SM–12 percent favor). While only a few tenants went as far as favoring the elimination of all private ownership of rental housing, here again, the percentage in the county was higher (LA–4 percent; SM–3 percent).

To synthesize a scale from these questions that would approximate the scale created from the responses of the activists, the Guttman scaling technique was employed. The Guttman scaling technique provides a statistical test to see if the set of questions makes up a "scale." What this test tells us is whether there is consistency in the answers to the tenants interviewed. For example, does someone who supports nationalization or cooperatization of the housing stock also support broad tenant power, and does someone who will go as far as supporting broad tenant power also support prohibiting evictions without good reason?

Application of the technique resulted in the selection of three questions and scoring six out of 12 points on the questions regarding tenant power that had this consistency. In descending order the questions were those regarding elimination of private rental housing, support for a process of nationalization or cooperatization, scoring 6 points out of 12 on the question regarding tenant power, and opposing evictions to move in a distant relative.[9] The failure to answer any of these questions affirmatively and score 6 points on the tenant power question was taken as indicative of a prolandlordism position. Table 3.2 sets out the responses to questions employed in the landlordism scale.

While the scale passed the Guttman test, not everyone's responses were internally consistent. There were some tenants, for example, who

Table 3.2.   *Scale Questions for Landlordism Scale*

Scale Questions	Los Angeles County		Santa Monica	
Eliminate Private Rental Housing	(54)	3.7%	(21)	2.9%
Nationalize or Cooperatize	(261)	17.9	(89)	12.2
Tenant Power	(454)	31.2	(216)	29.6
Distant Relative	(1,226)	84.2	(603)	82.7

supported the government's beginning to nationalize or cooperatize rental housing and did not support the broad tenant power. In this case Guttman advises the best solution is to simply add the affirmative responses the respondents did give and place him or her at that point on the scale (Nie et al. 1975, p. 350). It is his position that this minimizes the error such inconsistency creates. This procedure was adopted.

The scale points that results can be seen in the terms used by the activists. At the top of the scale are those tenants who are clearly antilandlordism. Next comes tenants who accept the institution of landlordism but would subject landlords to heavy regulation and support programs that convert rental housing to government or tenant ownership. At point three are tenants who would only go for broad reform, such as controls on rent, condominium conversions, and demolitions. This is followed by the tenant who would support only limited self-interest reform. At the bottom of the scale are tenants who are pro-landlord. The scale is presented in Table 3.3.

Table 3.3.   *Landlordism Scale*

Scale Points	Los Angeles County		Santa Monica	
5 Antilandlordism	(27)	1.9%	(12)	1.6%
4 Heavy Regulation	(103)	7.1	(30)	4.1
3 Broad Reform	(412)	28.3	(197)	27.0
2 Self-interest				
Reform	(753)	51.7	(397)	54.4
1 Prolandlordism	(161)	11.1	(93)	12.8

Sophistication

To determine the tenants' level of sophistication regarding the causes of tenants' problems, we asked an open-ended question, which requested the one most important reason why rents sometimes go up, and a structured question, which asked the respondents about the importance, if any, of government regulation, inflation, greedy landlords, speculation, bank interest rates, and other bank policies in changing rent levels.[10]

As the activists predicted, the major responses to the open-ended question in both samples were the very general ones of inflation and supply and demand. More tenants in the county sample than in Santa Monica responded with inflation (LA–55 percent; SM–42 percent) and more tenants in the Santa Monica sample responded supply and demand (SM–17 percent; LA–10 percent). However, in both samples there were a

From SHELTERFORCE, 1976 2(1): p. 1. Reprinted by permission.

substantial number of tenants who felt landlord greed was the major cause of the problem (LA–22 percent; SM–26 percent). Few respondents stated that speculation was the primary cause (LA–3 percent; SM–8 percent), and still fewer said it was bank interest rates (1 percent in each). Of the remainder, a few blamed increasing rents on bad tenants, and still others had no idea.

The structured question resulted in translating the general responses to the open-ended question into more specific answers. However, it also reaffirmed the organizers' position that there was a lack of sophistication in the tenant population on this issue. Sixty percent of the "I don't know" responses to scale questions were from the structured questions about why rents increase.

Inflation was still the most common response of tenants in both samples. Over 80 percent of the tenants responded that it was an important reason in rent change with more than 50 percent of these tenants stating it was very important. The next most common response was landlord greed. Over 70 percent of the tenants stated that this was an important reason, with nearly 50 percent of them stating it was a very important reason. Speculation was the next most popular response. Tenants in Santa Monica gave this response 12 percent more often than in the county (SM–77 percent; LA–65 percent). Examining those who answered that speculation was a very important reason, we found an even greater difference (SM–57 percent; LA–42 percent). This may be because speculation has been more intense in Santa Monica than in most areas in the county, or it may be a product of election propaganda that has stressed the role of speculation in the communities' problems—or both. Far fewer of those interviewed stated banks were a cause. Among these, rising interest rates were seen as a more common cause (LA–47 percent;

Courtesy of Santa Monica Fair Housing Alliance. Reprinted by permission.

SM–59 percent) than other bank policies such as redlining (LA–31 percent; SM–29 percent). Fewer than a third of the respondents stated interest rates were a very important reason, and only slightly more than 10 percent stated other bank policies were a very important cause. About a third of the tenants stated government regulation was a reason, but from the general response pattern, it was difficult to tell whether these answers were meant in a conservative sense of interfering with the market and raising costs, or in a more liberal sense of criticizing exclusionary zoning in the suburbs.

Because of its greater spread of response and greater clarity, the responses to the structured question were used to construct the sophistication scale. Again the Guttman technique was employed. However, in this instance it was not possible to construct the entire scale with this method. The primary reasons were that the scale the activists had given us was not unidimensional, and that in the case of multiple responses, the relative weight given the answer was important. In particular if inflation was seen as more important than another item, it affected the activists' evaluation of the response set.

Applying the Guttman technique, we were able to scale more than 70 percent of the responses with the responses of bank interest rates and bank policies being very important, speculation being very important, and landlord greed being either somewhat or very important. Table 3.4 sets out the responses to the sophistication scale questions.

Table 3.4. *Scale Questions for Sophistication Scale*

Scale Questions	Los Angeles County		Santa Monica	
Banks				
very important	(166)	11.4%	(62)	8.5%
Speculation				
very important	(616)	42.3	(429)	58.8
Landlord Greed				
important	(1065)	73.1	(540)	74.1

At the top of the scale, in the activist terms, are tenants with a systemic view of the problem. This is followed by those who believe the market has failed and needs to be corrected. Those awarded three points were seen as moralistic, blaming exploitation of the provision of a neccessity of life in a tight market. Two and a half points were given to those who indicated fluctuations in the market (inflation) was the primary reason, but that exploitation was important too. Two points were given for those identifying market fluctuation only (inflation), 1.5 points for market fluctuations and government interference (government regulation), and a single point for government interference only. Table 3.5 sets out the sophistication scale.

Table 3.5. *Sophistication Scale*

Scale Points	Los Angeles County		Santa Monica	
5 Systemic view				
of problem	(98)	6.7%	(39)	5.3%
4 Market has failed				
and needs correction	(463)	31.8	(334)	45.8
3 Exploitation of a				
tight market	(507)	34.8	(204)	28.0
2.5 Fluctuations/				
exploitation	(319)	21.9	(130)	17.8
2 Fluctuations in				
the market	(45)	3.1	(11)	1.5
1.5 Government/				
fluctuations	(24)	1.6	(10)	1.4
1 Government interference				
in the market	—	—	(1)	.1

Action

To measure the tenants' propensity to engage in action, we asked two sets of questions. One related to what action they would consider taking if they felt wronged by a landlord, and the other related to their willingness to engage in tenant movement activity away from their building. The questions relating to action at the building level were preceded by the assumption that the tenant and others lived in a multiunit apartment building and received a rent increase that they felt was unfair. Each respondent was asked whether they would consider taking any action, ranging from the most elementary individual action to forming a tenant union.

More than 85 percent of the tenants in both samples stated they would consider talking to the landlord about the problem. Nearly as many would consider doing something more active (LA–83 percent; SM–81 percent). However, the types of additional action they would take varied in the two samples. The tenants in the county sample were more likely to say they would refuse to pay the increase (LA–37 percent; SM–31 percent), while more tenants in Santa Monica said they would consider calling the local government (SM–68 percent; LA–55 percent) or meeting with the other tenants to decide what to do (LA–67 percent; SM–71 percent).

About the same percentage of tenants who stated that they would attend a meeting with the other tenants in the building stated that they would consider joining with the other tenants to face the landlord (68 percent in both samples). When we asked how many would try to form a tenant union, the number of tenants responding affirmatively dropped off substantially (LA–28 percent; SM–30 percent).

To determine willingness to engage in tenant movement activities, we asked whether they had or were willing, if they had the time, to engage in tenant activities away from their building, such as rent control campaigns, attending public meetings, or participating in an areawide tenants' organization.[11] A surprisingly large group of those interviewed had worked in the tenant movement. In Santa Monica 13 percent had worked in a campaign, gone to a city council meeting, or the like, while 4.5 percent of those interviewed in the county had done the same. When we asked who would be willing to become involved if they had the time, and added this figure to those who had, a remarkable 44 percent of both samples had either worked in the tenant movement or expressed a willingness to do so.

The similarity between the two samples was maintained across a broad variety of types of movement activities. Figures were similar for whether or not tenants would attend a meeting of their local government (LA–40 percent; SM–41 percent), join an areawide tenant organization (LA–38 percent; SM–37 percent), work in a political or rent control campaign (LA–34 percent; SM–35 percent), contribute money (LA–32 percent; SM–34 percent), help organize tenant unions (LA–31 percent; SM–28 percent), or demonstrate at a public meeting (LA–28 percent; SM–28 percent).

Considering the unexpected large number of affirmative responses, related to movement participation, we began to wonder if the respondents had heard this question as a part of a series about how they would react to an "unfair" rent increase. The questions about attending a government meeting, giving money, or demonstrating might have been heard in a defender's frame of mind. But it would be very difficult to understand the questions about joining an area organization, campaigning, or union organizing in this light. When we examined how many of the respondents had answered affirmatively to one of these three questions, we still had a group of more than 40 percent in both samples answering affirmatively (LA–41 percent; SM–41 percent).

Once again we employed the Guttman scaling technique to select items from these responses similar to those used in the scale created from the activists' interviews. The questions selected were: willingness to organize a tenant union in response to an unfair rent increase; willingness to engage in tenant movement work; willingness to join with other tenants to oppose an unfair rent increase; and willingness to engage in individual action in response to such an increase. Table 3.6 sets out these data.

Table 3.6. *Scale Questions for Action Scale*

Scale Questions	Los Angeles County		Santa Monica	
Individual action	(1179)	81.0%	(603)	82.7%
Join with other tenants	(987)	67.8	(496)	68.0
Movement action	(610)	41.9	(300	41.2
Organize a tenant union	(404)	27.7	(216)	19.6

When the questions were scaled with one baseline point given to those not willing to take even individual action, they produced a five-point cumulative scale, as seen in Table 3.7. At the top of the scale is the potential organizer, followed by tenants who could be mobilized in the tenant movement. Next, comes the potential members of a building level tenant union, and with two points on the scale are those who would resist unfair treatment at the building level by themselves but not with others.

Table 3.7. *Action Scale*

Scale Points	Los Angeles County		Santa Monica	
5 Organizer	(298)	19.8%	(154)	21.1%
4 Movement worker	(321)	22.1	(161)	22.1
3 Tenant union member	(409)	28.1	(200)	27.4
2 Individual	(243)	16.7	(114)	15.6
1 No action	(194)	13.3	(100)	13.7

Classification

Applying the formula generated from the analysis of the activists' interviews to the results on four scales, all the tenants in both samples were classified as shown in Table 3.8. Not surprisingly, given the similarity of the responses to scale questions in the two samples, but contrary to what was expected, the Santa Monica sample did not generate higher consciousness results than the county. If there could be said to be a difference between the two samples, it would have to be that tenants in the county as a whole have slightly higher tenant consciousness than those in Santa Monica.

Table 3.8. *Levels of Tenant Consciousness*

Level of Tenant Consciousness	Los Angeles County Sample		Santa Monica Sample	
Radical	(81)	5.6%	(23)	3.2%
Consumer	(292)	20.0	(152)	20.8
Defender	(562)	38.6	(284)	38.9
Individualist	(381)	26.2	(180)	24.7
Antagonist	(140)	9.6	(90)	12.4

The mean scores of the tenants at various levels on the four scales shown in Table 3.9 reinforces the picture painted by the activists. The antagonist and individualist were generally not willing to engage in more than minimal action, while the remainder of the types expressed a willingness to engage in increasingly committed action. Only the antagonist shows little interest in rent control, and political support for rent control increases only marginally in the other categories, actually dipping slightly with the radicalized tenants in the Los Angeles sample. There is little change in the tenants attitude about landlordism until the consumer level is reached, and here only the radicalized tenants take an extreme stand. The question of why rents increase had the least variance. This is explained in part by the lack of sophistication indicated by the number of "I don't knows," and the scaling technique which collapsed the variance in the middle of the scale.

In the remainder of the book when we refer to the tenant consciousness of a group of respondents, we will be referring to their combined defender, consumer, and radicalized scores. The individualist and antagonist become nontenant-consciousness categories in the affirmative sense in which we employ the term from here on. We will also make numerous references to respondents at the "movement levels" of consciousness, meaning potentially active participants in the tenant movement. By the term movement levels we mean the combined scores of the consumers and radicalized tenants. This simplifies the analysis greatly

Table 3.9. *Mean Scores on Four Dimensions of Tenant Consciousness by Levels of Consciousness.*

Levels	Identification		Landlordism		Action		Sophistication	
	LA	SM	LA	SM	LA	SM	LA	SM
Radicalized	4.0	4.6	4.2	4.4	4.7	4.7	3.6	3.6
Consumer	4.2	4.4	3.2	3.1	4.0	4.1	3.6	3.7
Defender	4.0	4.2	2.2	2.1	3.7	3.8	3.3	3.5
Individualist	3.4	3.2	2.0	2.0	1.9	2.0	3.2	3.4
Antagonist	1.3	1.2	1.5	1.5	2.1	1.9	2.9	2.9

and is useful because very often there are only a few percent of the population being examined at the radicalized level. When there are significant numbers of respondents at the radicalized level, we will make separate note of this fact.

NOTES

1. Lukacs used the related categories in his definition of class consciousness: "Only when the *immediate interests* are integrated into a *total view* and related to the *final goal* of the process do they become *revolutionary*, pointing concretely and consciously beyond the confines of capitalist society" (Lukacs 1968, p. 71). *Emphasis added.*

2. See Lawson and Barton (1980). In this article the authors examine in depth the predominance of women in the tenant movement, but the predominance of men in leadership positions in the mid-1970's.

3. Of the total 113 activists identified, 65 were women.

4. Some of the activists who used several of the metaphors appeared to indicate a level of ideological muddle similar to that discussed by Lustig (1980) in his article "Community and Social Class." This will be discussed further in the last chapter.

5. This may be because as with class and tenants, there are many unstated modifiers. For example, a black tenant may identify the problem of tenants as white speculators or a woman may see a greedy *male* banker, but are satisfied in a survey with the unmodified terms speculators or bankers.

6. This emphasis on rent control, although appropriate in this regard, is subject to the criticism of not giving substantial weight to the problem of conditions faced, particularly by low-income and minority tenants.

7. This is the best measure of what Lukacs referred to as "immediate self interest" (Lukacs 1968, p. 71).

8. This tests to see what is the "final goal" of the tenants (Lukacs 1968, p. 71).

9. The distant relative question was selected because it met the Guttman test and would provide, it was believed, a more accurate test than the broad "good reason" question. It also was selected because it would provide more conservative results so as not to overstate the level of consciousness.

10. This is the equivalent of Lukacs "total view" (Lukacs 1968, p. 71). It is interesting in this regard to note that Lukacs makes reference to Marx lauding a group of workers for seeing "bankers" as well as "industrialists" as the source of their problems (p. 174). Lukacs sees this as an indication of higher consciousness.

11. The question included the phrase "if you had the time" to measure the total potential. Conditions and the work of organizers help determine whether people make the time.

PART 2

Toward the Tenant Movement

4

The Demographics of
Tenant Consciousness

One of the central goals of this study is the determination of the potential for mobilization of the social base of tenants. As was seen in Chapter 3, the first question which must be resolved in this inquiry is "what is the social base of tenants?" Various activists saw the tenant movement not as a movement separate and apart from other movements but rather as a subpart of class- or race-based struggles. They, in effect, modified the term tenant with class or race terminology and limited the social base accordingly. Other activists saw tenant as a primary category and all tenants, regardless of demographic characteristics, as making up the base of the movement. In investigating the demographics of tenant consciousness, we will get our first look at whose characterization of the social base of the tenants is correct.

In later chapters data will be added about the everyday experience of the tenant populations sampled, their desires and expectations regarding homeownership, and their overall political beliefs. With the analysis of this additional data, a much more complete understanding of why the social base of tenants has taken on its present configuration will be possible. In this investigation the impact of the social structure of the United States on the formations of social movements, such as the tenant movement, should be illuminated. The tenant movement, as any single-issue movement, confronts the class, race, and gender divisions present in this society.

In that this is a pioneering study of the nature of tenant consciousness, very little is now known about the demographics of this tendency. Tenancy cuts across all demographic lines. Tenancy excludes no group although certainly tenants are more likely to be young, female, minority, and low income in larger proportions than the population taken as a whole. To do this analysis of the demographics of tenant consciousness, working-class consciousness, feminist, and minority literature was often relied upon. In addition the observations and opinions of the activists were employed to interpret the findings.

ANALYSIS OF DEMOGRAPHIC CHARACTERISTICS

The similarity of the distribution of tenant consciousness in the two samples identified in Chapter 3 must be contrasted with their major demographic differences. Santa Monica's population is relatively homogeneous while the county, as a whole, is relatively heterogeneous. Santa Monica tenant population interviewed is heavily white (87 percent) and English speaking (97 percent), college educated (69 percent), and just over half either professional-managerial or petty bourgeois (51 percent). By contrast, the county population is diverse, about 40 percent Latino, black, Asian, and Native American, with a substantial minority of Spanish speakers (14 percent), a majority with no more than a high school education (56 percent), and over two-thirds working class (68 percent). Consistent with these differences, the average annual household income in Santa Monica is $2,500 higher than in the county, with 50 percent more of the Santa Monica households than in the county having over $20,000 incomes and 50 percent more of the county households having less than $10,000 incomes.

The only demographic characteristics that are similar are the average age of the respondents to the survey and the mix of men and women. Santa Monica tenants (42 years) are on average just two years older than county tenants (40 years), and the mix of men and women is identical in both samples (44 percent men and 56 percent women).

The analysis of the relationship between the demographic characteristics and tenant consciousness was done in the form of "cross-tabulations."[1] This means, for example, that it will be determined whether the level of tenant consciousness varies in a statistically significant manner among various age groups. Sometimes the analysis is taken one step further, and one variable is held "constant" while the relationship between tenant consciousness and another variable is examined. For example, looking just at female tenants, does the level of tenant consciousness vary among various age groups?

To see whether the variations in the level of tenant consciousness that are found statistically significant, the "chi-square" test will be used.[2] The chi-square test provided a statistical measure of the significance of the differences across groups in their level of tenant consciousness. The test produces a numerical result. The figure .05 will be used as the measure of the dividing line between what is significant and what is not significant. Whenever the word "significant" is used, then it means the chi-square significance is .05 or less.

Age

The literature of political and working-class consciousness suggests that consciousness is affected by an individual's position in the life cycle. Studies by Campbell, Gurvin and Miller (1954) and McKenszie and Silver (1968) arrive at this conclusion. What is usually found is that the young have the highest consciousness, that consciousness falls off

From Less Rent More Control, (Boston: Urban Planning Aid, 1973). Reprinted by permission.

through middle age, and begins to rise again among seniors. A majority of the tenant activists agreed with this position, with the other activists splitting on whether the young or the elderly would have the highest tenant consciousness.

Consistent with these findings and opinions, a significant relationship between age, the tenants' position in the life cycle, and tenant consciousness was found in both samples. The importance of age is underscored by the further finding that this is the only demographic characteristic that was found to be significant in both samples. However, contrary to the findings of the earlier researchers and most of the activists' opinions, tenant consciousness, while declining with middle age, does not increase among seniors. In fact as shown in Figures 4.1 and 4.2, consciousness continued to drop steadily with increasing age. In the county, for example, 72 percent of those under 30 years of age have tenant consciousness at the defender or higher level compared to only 53 percent of those 60 years of age or older.

Figure 4.1.   *Tenant Consciousness by Age (Los Angeles County Sample)*

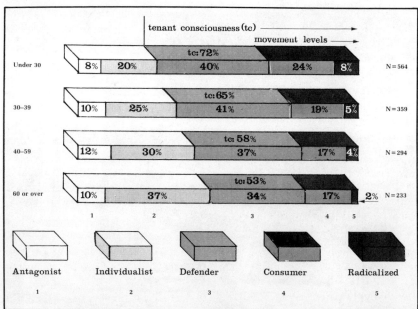

A more detailed look at the study findings in the county indicated that the results in that sample may be more consistent with the earlier studies and the activists' opinions than one would realize at a first glance. Age was not a significant factor with regards to tenant opinions about why rents increase and support of rent control. Support for rent control was remarkably consistent across all age groups, varying no more than one percentage point in the percentage of strong and very strong supporters across the various age groups. In the case of attitudes about landlordism, the scores did vary significantly with age. The scores of county tenants dropped sharply with people over 30, dipped further with the respondents between 40 and 59 years of age, but rose slightly among tenants 60 and older, leaving the seniors' scores between those of the 30 to 39 and 49 to 59 age groups. Forty-four percent of the young tenants in the county support broad reform of the landlord-tenant relationship or more, compared to 35 percent of the 30 to 39 age group, 31 percent of the 40 to 59 age group, and 33 percent of the seniors.

The lower consciousness of the seniors was not the result of any of the attitudinal responses. It came, instead, from less willingness on the part of seniors to engage in action at both the building and movement levels. For example, nearly 25 percent of the tenants in the county who are 60 and over were not willing to engage in any aggressive action in response to an "unfair" rent increase. In contrast only 15 percent of tenants between 40 and 59, 13 percent of those between 30 and 39, and 9 percent of those under 30 gave this response. As will be seen in Chapter 6, the activists indicated that seniors have a particular fear of eviction that may have caused this result.

In the same vein only 13 percent of the seniors said they would be willing to engage in tenant movement work compared to an overall average of 40 percent of the respondents. This finding is more surprising than the building level finding because senior citizens almost always comprise the majority of audiences at public hearings and government meetings where tenants' problems are at issue. The finding that they are generally less willing to engage in movement action suggests that this attendance at such meetings may be a product of their greater availability rather than consciousness and that this is the primary method of senior participation in the tenant movement, rather than being indicative of a greater, general participation.

The findings with regards to seniors raises the question of whether the seniors' lower propensity for action is an indication of lower consciousness or simply an expression of the infirmities of age suggested by the activists' observations of greater fear of eviction. It is possible that the life cycle nature of tenancy and the accumulation process is as much a factor in explaining the findings as infirmity. The frustration over difficulty in achieving the American dream is a frustration, primarily, of the young. Seniors have major problems in supporting themselves, including meeting the rent, but, as a group, they have either had their dream or long ago given up on accumulating to the point of realizing it.

Figure 4.2. *Tenant Consciousness by Age (Santa Monica Sample)*

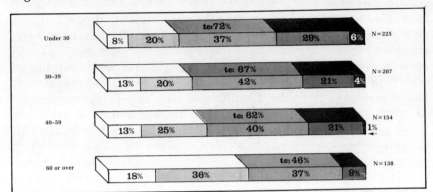

Note: *Please see Figure 4.1 for explanation of shaded bar codes. The classifications, in order, are: 1) Antagonist; 2) Individualist; 3) Defender; 4) Consumer; and 5) Radicalized.*

The finding that the attitudes of seniors on tenant questions may be more like the pattern of seniors' level of working-class consciousness than the overall results indicate did not hold in Santa Monica. About 62 percent of the Santa Monica tenants under 60 years of age were very strong supporters of rent control. In contrast only 55 percent of seniors had this level of support. There was an even sharper drop with seniors in the support for limitations of landlordism. The drop in support for rent control, while noticeable, was not statistically significant, but the drop in support for the limitation of landlordism was significant. Only 18 percent of Santa Monica seniors support broad reform of the landlord-tenant relationship or more, compared to 34 percent of the 40 to 59 age group, 40 percent of the 30 to 39 age group, and 54 percent of the Santa Monica tenants under 30 years of age. Determining why Santa Monica seniors had such low consciousness will be a matter of particular interest as other factors are added to this investigation.

Gender

Recent literature suggests that women, as a group, should have higher tenant consciousness than men. Two factors are said to cause this result. One factor stated in the literature is that traditional female responsibilities center around the physical maintenance of the home and the planned management of the household income to feed, clothe, and house family members (Lawson and Barton 1980). By focusing more on the home and often spending more of their time than their spouse or men, in general, in and around the home, the women are said to invest much of their identity in the quality and condition of their home. The other factor is that lower overall wages and overt sexual discrimination by landlords, realtors, and lending institutions inhibit the female's accessibility to the housing market (Deckard 1979). The two factors combined are thought to sensitize women to threats to their own and their family's housing well-being. Threats which include rent increases and deteriorating housing quality lead women to seek solutions to these problems.

A majority of the activists agreed with the literature and thought women had higher consciousness. In particular the activists stated that women with children have higher consciousness. Some of the activists expanded this observation to include all parents. The higher consciousness of parents was thought to be related to their experience with discrimination against children in the rental housing market (U.S. Department of Housing and Urban Development 1980).

The analysis of the results of the surveys disclosed that gender was significantly related to tenant consciousness in the county sample, but it was not a significant factor in Santa Monica. The relationship between gender and tenant consciousness in the county, however, as Figure 4.3 shows, was not exactly what the activists or the literature described. While women have slightly higher overall consciousness, measured from the defender level, the men tended to be at the extremes of consciousness, both high and low, and the women tended to be in the middle categories.

Figure 4.3. *Gender and Tenant Consciousness (Los Angeles County Sample)*

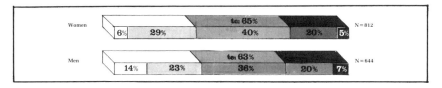

Note: *Please see Figure 4.1 for explanation of shaded bar codes. The classifications, in order, are: 1) Antagonist; 2) Individualist; 3) Defender; 4) Consumer; and 5) Radicalized.*

When the elements of the tenant consciousness scale were examined, no significant differences between the responses of men and women in the county was found on two central elements—landlordism and action. Where men and women differed was on the issue of why rents increase and on their support for rent control. The differences on the question of why rents increase were similar in pattern to the distribution of tenant consciousness. Men were both more conservative and slightly more radical. They were more likely to see inflation by itself or inflation along with some other secondary cause as the reason for why rents increase (Men–27 percent; Women–24 percent). Men were also more likely to have a systemic view of the cause of increasing rents (Men–9 percent; Women–5 percent). In contrast women were more likely to take the moralistic position, citing landlord greed or landlord greed combined with speculation as the primary causes (Women–69 percent; Men–63 percent).

On the question of rent control, the difference was more dramatic. Ten percent more women than men were strong or very strong supporters of rent control (Women–65.5 percent; Men–55 percent), and 10 percent more of the men were opposed to rent control (Men–18 percent; Women–8 percent). A step-wise discriminant analysis run with the demographic characteristics against the respondents' scores on their support of rent control indicate that gender was the primary demographic factor in determining one's level of support.[3]

The greater support for rent control among women would seem to be evidence in support of women's focus on the home as the source of their higher consciousness. However, closer analysis of the data reveals that this may not be the case. The primary source of the split in support for rent control was not even across all subgroups of men and women. Rather, the stronger support of women was concentrated among white, professional-managerial, college-educated women with between $20,000 and $30,000 annual incomes.[4] This suggests that the higher consciousness of women may not be in the focus on the home, but in the constrained opportunity structure these women face. In this case this constrained opportunity structure may be expressed in frustration over not being able to escape tenancy and attain the American dream of homeownership.

It should be noted, however, that this finding results from an analysis of the responses of all men and women interviewed in the county sample. Only a third of the county sample were married (34 percent N = 491).[5] The position that women are more focused on the home may have more importance among married men and women than in the general population. In recent years the percentage of married couples in the tenant population has been dropping. Their greater earning capacity and the inflationary pressure to buy a home have been seen as the causes for this decline (Sternlieb and Hughes 1981). In effect all the households that can escape tenancy have been choosing to escape. When the analysis is limited to those respondents who are married, evidence for the husband-wife split is found, although, again, it was only significant among the white population. Married white women had significantly higher consciousness (81 percent N = 125) than married white men (69 percent N = 133).

Children

The activists' assumption that women with children would have particularly high consciousness did not prove to be true in either sample. The consciousness of women with children was not significantly higher than that of other women. However, having children did prove to be a significant factor among men in the county sample. As shown in Figure 4.4, 68 percent of men with children had tenant consciousness. In both these groups over 80 percent of the respondents had tenant consciousness compared to 60 percent of the men without children. Much of the difference results from an unusually high percentage of fathers at the radicalized level.

Figure 4.4. *Tenant Consciousness of Men with Children and Men Without Children (Los Angeles County Sample)*

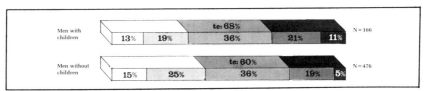

Note: *Please see Figure 4.1 for explanation of shaded bar codes. The classifications, in order, are: 1) Antagonist; 2) Individualist; 3) Defender; 4) Consumer; and 5) Radicalized.*

It is important to note that this high score was the result of exceptionally high tenant consciousness among black and English-speaking Latino fathers, a population virtually absent from the Santa Monica sample. Sixty-four percent (N = 17) of the black fathers and 46 percent (N = 28) of the English-speaking Latinos scored at the movement levels of consciousness. In both these groups over 80 percent of the respondents had tenant consciousness at the defender level or higher. No black fathers (nor black mothers) were in the antagonist category. Why these groups had such high consciousness will be a matter for further investigation. It could also relate to the difficulty of this group in following other couples out of tenancy and into homeownership.

Ethnicity

The minorities' respresentation in the county sample is more than twice that in the Santa Monica sample. Twenty-three percent of the county sample is Latino, 14 percent is black, 3 percent is Asian, and 1 percent is Native American or another minority group. In Santa Monica only 8 percent of the sample is Latino and 4 percent black. The proportion of

Asians and others is similar to that in the county. The small number of Asians and Native Americans in the samples will prohibit analysis of these groups.

If we start from the assumption that more problems correlates with higher consciousness, minorities should have higher consciousness than whites.[6] As will be seen in the next chapter, minority tenants have a harder time than whites by all measures. A study of male autoworkers in Detroit would seem to support the assumption of such a correlation. John Leggett, in the book *Race, Class and Labor* (1968), which is to a great extent the prototype for this study, found black autoworkers to have significantly higher class consciousness than white autoworkers.[7] His explanation for his higher consciousness was based, in part, on blacks' relative economic insecurity, an insecurity minority tenants share.

Beyond Leggett's survey blacks have demonstrated their militancy on tenant issues by participating in one of the major tenant revolts of this century, which took place in Harlem in the 1960s (Lipsky 1970) and later in that decade when blacks took to the streets in revolt, housing, and specifically rental housing, was cited as a major source of their discontent (National Advisory Commission on Civil Disorders, 1968, pp. 492–93). Less is known about Latinos or other minority groups with regards to tenant issues, but the logic of the studies of blacks would seem to apply.

The majority of the activists, who as must be remembered are white, did not agree with either the assumption of such a correlation or the literature. The activists stated that from their experience, whites are more organizable and have higher consciousness. In particular, the activists stated it is difficult to organize Latinos. The activists stated that language problems and the immigrant status of many Latinos created problems. The language problem makes it diffiuclt to organize Latinos and contributes to many of the Spanish-speaking tenants being uninformed of their rights and being unfamiliar or uncomfortable with the machinery of the U.S. judicial system. Because of these problems, the most successful Latino tenant organization in the Los Angeles area has organized two subgroups of its membership; one of English-speaking tenants and one of Spanish-speaking tenants.

Undocumented immigrant status is seen as a major inhibition to resisting a landlord or to becoming a visible member of a political movement, such as the tenant movement. According to the activists, some slum landlords are in complete agreement with this theory and specialize in renting to the undocumented population. In encounters between these landlords and undocumented tenants, the landlords often threaten to call the Immigration Service in an attempt to crush even minor forms of tenant resistance (Heskin 1978, p. 65). These problems lead us to expect a difference in the responses of Spanish- and English-speaking Latinos as well as between citizens and documented tenants and undocumented tenants.

This division between the literature and the activists is indicative of the division within the activists' ranks over the nature of the social base of tenants. As with the question of the nature of the social base, the resolution of the division is central to understanding the potential of the tenant movement. It is not surprising that white activists find whites more organizable, and from this experience, believe whites have higher consciousness. However, the understandable relationship could place a great limitation on the future of the tenant movement if much of the potential for organizing tenants lies in the minority populations. The potential may remain untapped if the nature of the leadership is not changed, that is, if the leadership does not arise from the social base.

Ethnicity related significantly to tenant consciousness in the county sample, but it was not significant in Santa Monica. However, the distribution of consciousness among whites, blacks, and Latinos in the county presented far from the clear picture necessary to resolve the literature-activist split. As seen in Figure 4.5, Latinos had the highest percentage of tenants at the radicalized and defender level, but the lowest at the movement levels and lowest overall consciousness. Blacks, inconsistent with Liggett's findings, had the lowest percentage at the radicalized level but the highest percentage at the movement levels. It also must be noted that they were slightly lower in overall consciousness to whites. Whites, who do not predominate at any level of consciousness other

Figure 4.5. *Tenant Consciousness by Ethnicity in County Samples (Los Angeles County Sample)*

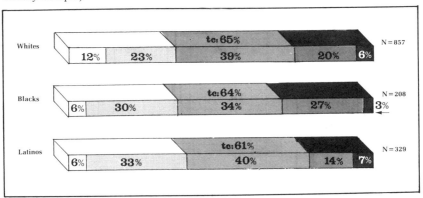

Note: *Please see Figure 4.1 for explanation of shaded bar codes. The classifications, in order, are: 1) Antagonist; 2) Individualist; 3) Defender; 4) Consumer; and 5) Radicalized.*

than antagonist have the highest overall consciousness by a single percentage point over blacks.

This ambiguous picture was altered considerably, as shown in Figure 4.6, when the contrast between the sexes in the white population suggested by the analysis of gender, and the division of language preference in the Latino population suggested by the activists' observations, are included in the analysis. English-speaking Latinos, white women, and blacks emerge as having significantly higher consciousness than white men and Spanish-speaking Latinos.[8]

Figure 4.6. *Tenant Consciousness by Ethnicity With the Interaction of Gender and Language (Los Angeles County Sample)*

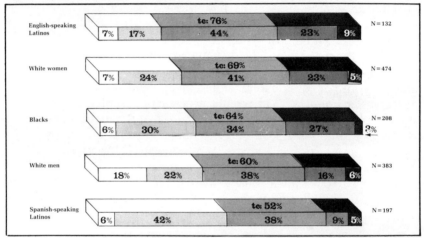

Note: *Please see Figure 4.1 for explanation of shaded bar codes. The classifications, in order, are: 1) Antagonist; 2) Individualist; 3) Defender; 4) Consumer; and 5) Radicalized.*

The difference in the level of consciousness between the three highest groups, English-speaking Latinos, white women, and blacks was not statistically significant.[9] The differences between these groups were also not significant on any of the four scales that made up tenant consciousness items, although it should be noted that the English-speaking Latinos scored highest on all four scales. There were significant differences, however, on some of the action scale questions. In response to two of the questions, whether the respondent would be willing to take individual action or join with one's neighbors in response to an "unfair" rent increase, blacks gave significantly fewer positive responses.[10]

The lower scores on these questions result in the higher percentage of blacks in the individualist category. The proportion of individualists was large enough to result in white women having higher overall consciousness even though a higher proportion of blacks were at the movement levels. A declining willingness to engage in action has been seen as accompanying advancing years; however, this is not the explanation here. If blacks and white women are compared across the age groups, a higher proportion of blacks is found in the individualist category in all age groups. Why this is so cannot be determined at this point: however, the findings will be reexamined in Chapter 6.

The grouping of minorities and white women as high consciousness in relationship to white men would seem to confirm the deprivation-consciousness correlation hypothesis and the finding of the literature. In this framework, however, the very low consciousness of the Spanish speakers is an anomaly. When it comes to class, education, and income as shown in Tables 4.1 through 4.3, white men are in the superior position and Spanish speakers in the inferior position. White men are least likely to be working class, the most likely to have gone to college and graduate school, and have $20,000 or more annual family income. Spanish speakers, in contrast, are most likely to be working class, overwhelmingly have no more than an elementary education, with most having below $10,000 a year income. It should be pointed out, however, that the correlation is not perfect. There are, for example, differences among the social positions of the three high-consciousness groups, not simply reflected in their respective levels of consciousness, that leave room for further explanation as additional data are added in later chapters.

It is important to note that the overall lower level of consciousness of white men is not simply the result of the lower support for rent control noted earlier.[11] In particular white men were also significantly less willing to restrict landlordism. For example, significantly fewer white men are willing to give an equal or greater voice than the landlord to tenants in the decision to convert an apartment to a condominium or undergo renovation.[12]

While the superior social position may be very important in understanding these attitudes and the lower consciousness of white men, the explanation of the anomalous lower consciousness of Spanish speakers can not be so easily explained and deserves particular attention.

Spanish-speaking Latinos

The low scores of the Spanish-speaking Latinos required particularly close attention because this group was, in effect, interviewed with a different survey instrument. While the Spanish instrument was translated into English without significant problems, the possibility of mistranslation cannot be overlooked. Problems with obtaining complete

Table 4.1. *Class of Ethnicity/Gender Groups (Los Angeles County Sample)*

Class	English-speaking Latinos		White Women		Blacks		White Men		Spanish-speaking Latinos	
Working	(97)	77.6%	(299)	65.4%	(150)	76.9%	(194)	52.4%	(156)	91.7%
Professional-managerial	(16)	12.8	(119)	26.0	(26)	13.3	(81)	21.9	(5)	3.0
Petty bourgeois	(12)	9.6	(39)	8.5	(19)	9.7	(95)	25.7	(9)	5.3

Table 4.2. *Education of Ethnicity/Gender Groups (Los Angeles County Sample)*

Class	English-speaking Latinos		White Women		Blacks		White Men		Spanish-speaking Latinos	
Elementary	(15)	11.4%	(28)	5.9%	(20)	9.7%	(20)	5.2%	(149)	75.6%
High School	(78)	59.1	(188)	39.7	(106)	51.2	(119)	31.2	(34)	17.3
College	(37)	28.0	(208)	43.9	(72)	34.8	(168)	44.0	(12)	6.1
Post Grad	(2)	1.5	(50)	10.5	(9)	4.3	(75)	19.6	(2)	1.0

Table 4.3. *Income of Ethnicity/Gender Groups (Los Angeles County Sample)*

Class	English-speaking Latinos		White Women		Blacks		White Men		Spanish-speaking Latinos	
Under $10,000	(62)	51.7%	(189)	43.0%	(118)	61.5%	(88)	24.4%	(134)	77.5%
$10,000-$19,999	(41)	34.2	(170)	38.6	(52)	27.1	(130)	36.1	(32)	18.5
$20,000-$29,999	(12)	10.0	(53)	12.0	(15)	7.8	(95)	26.4	(6)	3.5
Over $30,000	(5)	4.2	(28)	6.4	(2)	3.6	(47)	13.1	(1)	0.6

responses and data when interviewing the Spanish-speaking population have been noted in the survey literature (Zusman and Olson 1977). This problem deserves special attention before conclusions can be drawn from the results.

The Spanish-speaking tenants, taken as a group, comprised a true underclass in the county sample. They are very different demographically from the English-speaking Latinos. Ninety-two percent of the Spanish-speaking Latinos were working class; 78 percent have family incomes below $10,000; and 76 percent have not attended high school. In addition 50 percent of the Spanish-speaking respondents have been in Los Angeles for fewer than five years, and 82 percent have been in the city for fewer than ten years. In contrast only 20 percent of the English-speaking Latinos have been in Los Angeles for fewer than five years, and only one-third for fewer than ten years. This suggested that many of the Spanish-speaking Latinos may have been recent immigrants to the United States. The older average age of the Spanish-speaking group provided some contrary evidence (Penalosa 1971). Thirty-four percent of the Spanish-speaking Latinos are 40 or older, compared to 23 percent of the English-speaking Latinos. Fifty-five percent of the English speakers are under 30, compared to 39 percent of the Spanish speakers.

To investigate the problems of data quality and completeness of responses of Spanish-speaking respondents, the answers to questions that generate the tenant consciousness scale were examined. The answers of the Spanish-speaking Latinos were not significantly different from those of English-speaking Latinos on the questions regarding their support for rent control or their ideas about why rents increase. This was found despite the fact that Spanish speakers answered ''I don't know'' more frequently than other respondents in the sample to several of the questions which make up the why-rents-increase scale. Two-thirds of the ''I don't know'' responses by Spanish speakers were to these questions, compared to 60 percent for the remainder of the population.

The lower consciousness classification of the Spanish-speaking respondents appeared to result from the significantly lower scores they received on the action and landlordism scales. The Spanish-speaking Latinos did not have significantly more incomplete answers' than other population groups on the action scale; rather, they had fewer positive responses than others to questions about whether they would be willing to work in tenant movement activities and try to form a tenant union in response to an unfair rent increase. Positive responses to the question about forming tenant unions were found 22 percent of the time among Spanish-speaking tenants and 35 percent of the time among English-speaking Latinos. Positive replies to the questions related to movement activity were given by 35 percent of the Spanish-speaking Latinos compared to 47 percent of the English-speaking Latinos.

The activists predicted this would be the case. However, it cannot be determined whether this lower propensity for action results from a feeling that there was a language barrier between the Spanish speakers and tenant action, or from the caution required by those of undocumented immigrant status. Future surveys about collective political activity might ask Spanish speakers additional questions to clarify the issues. In particular a researcher might ask whether Spanish speakers would be willing to join with other Spanish speakers in activities, to test the language barrier hypothesis.

While there were not significantly more incomplete responses to the action scale questions, there were to the landlordism scale questions. Spanish speakers had significantly more "I don't know" responses to two of the four property scale questions, whether a landlord may evict a tenant to move in a distant relative and whether the rental housing stock should be nationalized or cooperatized.

In the case of the question regarding nationalizing or cooperatizing, 40 percent of the Spanish speakers responded "I don't know" compared to 20 percent of the English-speaking Latinos. However, if the Spanish speakers' "I don't know" answers were coded as negative responses, there was only a slight difference between the response pattern of the Spanish-speaking and English-speaking Latinos. In the case of the question about eviction for a landlord's relative, missing answers did not account for the discrepancy between the two groups. Five percent of the Spanish-speaking Latinos, compared to 2 percent of the English-speaking Latinos, answered "I don't know" to this question, while there was a 20 percent variation in their affirmative responses.

Thirty percent of the Spanish speakers would allow a landlord to evict a tenant to move in a distant relative, compared to 10 percent of the English speakers. While it appeared that in both populations, a majority of tenants would place the rights of a tenant above those of property and family, a larger minority of the Spanish speakers believed the tenant's rights should be secondary.

Several possible reasons can be given for this difference. Some of these reasons would seem to indicate that the question was an unfortunate one to place in the tenant consciousness scale, while others would seem to confirm the wisdom of the inclusion of the question. What would argue against inclusion of the question is the position that family plays a particularly important role in Latino and immigrant culture, and, therefore, inclusion of the question biases the results (del Castillo 1975; Garcia 1976). The argument on the other side would build from the special place accumulation of landed property plays in this same cultural milieu. Seen from this perspective, the responses of the Spanish speakers could be characterized much more as proproperty than profamily.

The split between the English- and Spanish-speaking Latinos on the eviction questions seemed to indicate that the preference for family over tenants was not simply "Latino." It may, however, still have been "immigrant" (Rex and Moore 1967). The immigrant influence may, however, have been more proproperty than profamily. Twenty-seven percent more of the Spanish speakers (82 percent) than English speakers (55 percent) stated they would like to own rental property. The power behind this argument was weakened by a further finding that the preference for family over tenant did not vary significantly in the Spanish-speaking population with the desire or lack of desire to own rental property. At the same time it should be noted that the group feeling most strongly about family preference and owning rental property was men under 40 years of age. Forty percent of this group would have allowed the eviction of a tenant for a family member, and 90 percent wanted to own rental property.

Perhaps it is best to characterize the Spanish speakers' responses to the eviction question as a mix of family and property preferences. A consequence of their answers to the eviction question and the action questions was that a very large proportion of this population was found in the individualist category. At this point nothing more can be done than to be aware of the possible problems the definition of tenant consciousness may have caused in interpreting the results of this study. Special note of the situation of the Spanish speakers will be made as the analysis is developed.

Ethnicity and Gender in Santa Monica

The Santa Monica population was overwhelmingly white (84 percent).[13] Focusing on the white population, it was found that, in contrast to the county sample, the overall level of consciousness of white men and women was identical (63 percent). The only difference was in the level of respondents at the movement levels. Here, the relationship was the reverse of that in the county, with white men having a larger proportion at the movement levels (white men 28 percent; white women 22 percent). With a relatively small proportion of minorities in the sample, the result of the analysis was that ethnicity by itself or ethnicity combined with gender did not prove significantly related to tenant consciousness.

Importantly, this means that in Santa Monica white men tended to have higher consciousness than their county counterparts, while in

Santa Monica white women tended to have lower consciousness. The difference results from the presence in Santa Monica of a group of high-consciousness, low-income white men on the one hand, and low-consciousness, middle-income, and senior white women on the other.[14] This later observation must be kept in mind for later investigation of why Santa Monica seniors had such low consciousness.

Class

An examination of the relationship between tenant consciousness and class first presented the problem of the definition of class. The term class can be used in many ways to describe both economic and social groups. We use the term here much as Marx conceived it, as a set of social relationships between historically situated individuals in particular relations of production (Giddens 1973). However, Marx himself never explicitly provided a definition of "the classes," leaving much room for confusion and debate about how to define and employ the concept. Some argue that there are two basic classes, capital and working (Gorz 1967; Poulantzas 1975), with petty bourgeois a third class of less importance. All other political-economic groupings of people are referred to as a strata of these basic classes.

More recently, others, taking into account the type of labor performed as well as apparent divisions in political behavior, have argued for the existence of another class. This latter group claims that the development of monopoly capitalism has given rise to a distinct professional-managerial class (Ehrenreich and Ehrenreich 1979).

A three-class model, comprised of working, professional-managerial, and petty bourgeois/capitalist classes was chosen for this analysis. Three, rather than two classes, were selected to accommodate the debate among the activists about a split in the tenant movement ranks between working-class and middle-class (what we refer to as professional-managerial) tenants. As was discussed in Chapter 3, some activists felt that tenants in the professional-managerial class, acting in their own self-interest, tend to lead the tenant movement toward ameliorative reforms and away from the more militant and comprehensive solutions to tenant problems that are needed and favored by the working class.

As defined, both the working- and professional-managerial classes are comprised of people who are employed by others—by individuals, corporations, or the government. The argument that the professional-managerial group is a separate class is based on the relative degree of autonomy that members of this class appear to have over their work and the unique relationship that they have to people in other classes. They are seen as a buffer between the working and capitalist classes and to have constructed their own class-based ideology from their middling position in the class heirarchy. As used here, the working class included both blue- and white-collar workers ranging from operators to secretaries. The professional-managerial class includes those employed by others in specialized professional and technical work, such as lawyers and dental hygienists, as well as people whose major work function is to manage or administer their work setting.[15]

Use of the term petty bourgeois indicates self-employed people who do not employ others in their work. The term capitalist is used to mean people who own a business and employ others. The analysis revealed that only a few people (1 percent) fell into the capitalist category, and their responses were similar to those classified as petty bourgeois. For these reasons, capitalists and petty bourgeois were combined into a single class for the analysis, and the label of the more numerous petty bourgeois employed from this point on.

Theoretically, the working class should be in the vanguard of all radical consciousness and practice, including the area of tenant consciousness. Marx and a host of others have placed their confidence in the idea that when this class fully realized the extent of its exploitation, it would be able to overthrow the entire capitalist system—including the institution of landlordism. While at least one study has suggested that working-class tenants are more radical than others on tenant issues (Handel and Rainwater 1964), according to many scholars who have studied the political consciousness and practices of the working class, the promise of a working-class revolution is far from fulfilled. According to these scholars, the working class is tied too strongly to the relations of domination in the United States and are, therefore, more concerned with maintaining the status quo than with social change (Aronowitz 1973).

There is also a division in the literature concerning the professional-managerial class. Some see this class as composed of people who are preoccupied with job mobility with an accompanying emphasis on income and status (Giddens 1973). Members of this group are said to place a premium on individualism, autonomy, and achievement—which are not values that one would ordinarily regard as elements of class consciousness. Others have cast this class in a more political light, seeing them as potential radicals who desire to take control of the system that they manage from those who reap the benefits of their work (Touraine 1971). A study of the New Jersey tenant movement found this class to be prominent among activists (Baar 1977). Whether this will be found in our sample population is, of course, an issue.

The petty bourgeois and certainly the capitalists have generally been found to be major supporters of private property. The petty bourgeois and the relatively minor capitalists that appear in our sample are characterized in the literature as being continually socialized and dominated by large-scale capital in their losing battle to keep things "small" (Syzmanski 1979). This situation is seen to place petty bourgeois and small capitalists in a struggle against losing their class position and slipping into the working class. The literature suggests that any threat to the status quo, including the tenant movement, is seen as a destabilizing force that can make their struggle more difficult. If this position is correct, we would expect his group to be heavily represented in the antagonist category.

As set out in Figure 4.7, class proved to be a significant variable in determining tenant consciousness in the county sample. As with many other variables significant in the county, it did not prove significant in Santa Monica. The study results in the county, however, although significant, do not conclusively resolve the disagreement between activists about whether working-class tenants or professional-managerial tenants have higher consciousness. While the professional-managerial class exhibited somewhat higher consciousness than the working class, the difference was not statistically significant, only the petty bourgeois responded as predicted. The petty-bourgeois tenants exhibited significantly lower tenant consciousness than either the professional-managerial or working class tenants, with more than twice the percentage of the other classes in the antagonist category.

Figure 4.7.   *Tenant Consciousness and Class (Los Angeles County Sample)*

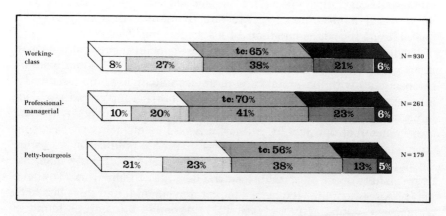

Note: *Please see Figure 4.1 for explanation of shaded bar codes. The classifications, in order, are: 1) Antagonist; 2) Individualist; 3) Defender; 4) Consumer; and 5) Radicalized.*

The similarity in the patterns of consciousness of the working-class and professional-managerial tenants would seem to indicate that the three-class model is in error. This appears confirmed by the finding that the scores of the working-class and professional-managerial tenants do not vary significantly from each other on the scales representing the four elements of tenant consciousness. This is not to say that there were not some differences. These, however, were more behavioral than attitudinal. For example, 10 percent more of the working-class tenants said that they would help organize tenant unions.

The behavior difference indicated in the greater willingness to help organize tenant unions had other manifestations. For example, in response to a question which asks what action one would take in reaction to an unfair rent increase, professional-managerial tenants were more likely to complain to the government, while working-class tenants were more likely to take direct action, such as withholding rent. These behavioral differences may be what stimulate the argument within the tenant movement about whether working-class or professional-managerial tenants have higher consciousness. Since many of the activists interviewed were organizers, they would be more highly sensitive to differences in observable behavior than tenants' beliefs and attitudes on issues.

The difference between professional-managerial and working-class tenants taken as aligned classes and the petty bourgeois is found on the support-for-rent-control and landlordism scales. This difference seems indicative of the theoretical split between the classes. Fifty-one percent of the petty-bourgeois tenants exhibited strong and very strong support for rent control, compared to 64 percent of the professional-managerial tenants and 62 percent of the working-class tenants. Examining those opposed to rent control, we find 24 percent of the petty-bourgeois tenants opposed rent control, in comparison to 12 percent of the professional-managerial and 11 percent of the working-class.

Differences between the classes on the landlordism scale is apparent if the percentage of tenants who would not restrict landlords in any of the ways proposed on the survey is examined. Twenty-one percent of the petty-bourgeois tenants did not support any of the limitations on landlords, compared to only 10 percent of the professional-managerial and 9 percent of the working-class tenants.

Before finally concluding from these findings that there is general similarity between the working- and professional-managerial classes on tenant issues and a clear difference between these two classes and the petty-bourgeois tenants, it must be remembered, that the scores for each class are a composite of responses from different strata within each class that may average out in a way that obscures the splits within each class. For example, as has been seen, there is a far greater variation between men and women of the professional-managerial class than between working-class men and women, but here the composite scores of these two classes are very similar. This does not mean that class is unimportant, but that class may have to be seen as interacting with other important variables if its meaningful expression in political attitudes is to be identified.

As shown in Figure 4.8, the addition of gender to the class analysis does not materially change the relative similarity of the professional-managerial and working-class tenants at the important movement levels. It does, however, result in the emergence of professional-managerial women as the highest overall consciousness group and leads to the discovery of a substantial proportion of professional-managerial men at the antagonist level. Why the professional-managerial women should have the highest consciousness and professional-managerial men have a high percentage of antagonists warrants further investigation. It does, at this point, seem to renew the suggestion that a sense of upward mobility is an important explanatory variable.[16]

Figure 4.8. *Tenant Consciousness of Class/Gender Strata (Los Angeles County Sample)*

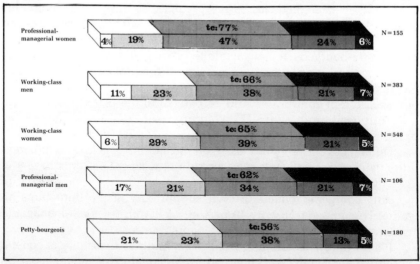

Note: *Please see Figure 4.1 for explanation of shaded bar codes. The classifications, in order, are: 1) Antagonist; 2) Individualist; 3) Defender; 4) Consumer; and 5) Radicalized.*

A heavy emphasis upon "prestige and upward mobility" has long been thought to be a characteristic of the middle class, what is referred to here as the professional-managerial class (Reissman 1959, p. 175). An important symbol of this upward mobility, achieving the American dream, is becoming a homeowner. If the theory is correct, a relationship between both the high consciousness of professional-managerial women and the concentration of antagonists among the professional-managerial men should be noted in Chapter 7 when the relationship between the American dream and tenant consciousness is examined.

Before continuing, it should be noted that over 80 percent (81.5 percent N = 119) of the professional-managerial women were white. As seen in Figure 4.9, among white women, it was the professional-managerial women who had especially high consciousness.[17] The hypothesis that frustrated upward mobility may be the cause of this high consciousness is reinforced by additional findings with regard to the high consciousness of white women. Age was a significant factor in the consciousness of white women. Consciousness was especially high among younger tenants who are still looking forward to homeownership (under 30–77 percent N = 162; 30 to 39–75 percent N = 98) and among those in the middle-income group just out of reach of ownership ($20,000 to $30,000–81 percent N = 53).[18]

Figure 4.9. *Tenant Consciousness of White Women by Class (Los Angeles County Sample)*

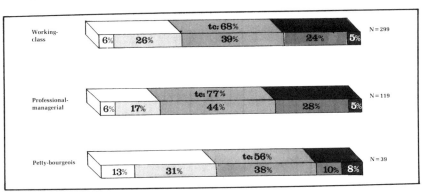

Note: *Please see Figure 4.1 for explanation of shaded bar codes. The classifications, in order, are: 1) Antagonist; 2) Individualist; 3) Defender; 4) Consumer; and 5) Radicalized.*

When the relationship between class/gender consciousness within each ethnicity/gender grouping was examined, class was found to be significant only in the case of white men.[19] Among white men, the working class had the largest proportion of respondents with tenant consciousness. However, it is worth noting that among white men, as in the whole population, there were slightly more tenants at the movement level who were members of the professional-managerial class than who are working-class tenants. Figure 4.10 presents the data for white men.

Figure 4.10.   *Tenant Consciousness of White Men by Class (Los Angeles County Sample)*

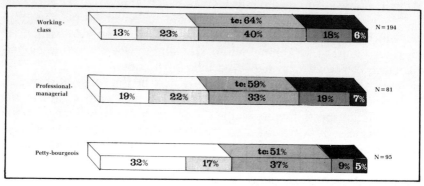

Note: *Please see Figure 4.1 for explanation of shaded bar codes. The classifications, in order, are: 1) Antagonist; 2) Individualist; 3) Defender; 4) Consumer; and 5) Radicalized.*

The singular significance of class among white men raises some central questions about the relationship between consciousness and class, gender, and ethnicity in the United States. Does the relatively favorable position of white men in this society cause class to be a more coherent factor in the political lives of white men than others? Does the relatively unfavorable position of women and minorities cause class to take a different or secondary place in the political lives of women and minorities? Does the importance of class among white men, and sex and race among others allow for coalitions or unified movements around issues such as tenancy?

While the mobilizable social base of tenants, thus far, seems broader than that seen by those activists who stressed the class or race super-structure within which the tenant movement must fit, the divisions stressed by these activists may still be present in the social base and inhibit a unified realization of the apparent potential. For example, can the high-consciousness portions of the professional-managerial female population be brought together with substantial high-consciousness portions of the minority population and selected high-consciousness portions of the white male population?

The difficulty of the problem cannot be seen in all of its dimensions at this point. The apparent similarity in the level of consciousness in these groups or the working- and professional-managerial classes may not have the same basis in experience. It could be, for example, that the high consciousness of the minority tenant comes more from the negative experience of day-to-day tenancy and the high consciousness of the professional-managerial women more from frustrated upward mobility. This together with the behavior differences already noted in the analysis of class, could create significant problems in mobilizing the apparently broad social base. As more variables are added to this analysis, the picture will become clearer.

In Santa Monica class, like gender and ethnicity, was not significantly related to tenant consciousness. Interestingly, it was not the petty-bourgeois respondents who have the lowest consciousness in Santa Monica. The consciousness level of the petty-bourgeois respondents (66 percent N = 121) and the highest-consciousness, professional-managerial respondents (67 percent N = 227) was nearly identical. It was the working-class tenants who were the lowest consciousness (61 percent N = 335). The primary source of low working-class consciousness in Santa Monica was the low-consciousness seniors, in this case, senior, white, working-class women (36 percent N = 46). They make up 30 percent of all working-class women in Santa Monica. The primary source of high consciousness of the petty bourgeois was the petty-bourgeois white women (81 percent N = 38). In contrast to the high consciousness of county professional-managerial women were a group of young middle- and upper-income, professional-managerial, white women (42 percent N = 13) in Santa Monica with unusually low consciousness. The explanation for these findings is found in Chapters 5 and 7 where tenant experience and expectation regarding homeownership are discussed.

The higher consciousness of the petty-bourgeois tenants, in addition to the professional-managerial tenants, raises an issue of the nature of the Santa Monica movement. On the one hand, the finding that class is not significant in that city can be seen as an expression of how a successful movement can unify a social base and transcend class differences. On the other hand, it may be an expression of the middle-class domination of a movement feared by some of the activists. The high consciousness of the petty bourgeois, in particular, brings to mind Engels' polemic against the petty-bourgeois character of much housing reform in the *Housing Question* (1975).

Income

The one remaining significant factor is income. In the county sample, although income significantly relates to tenant consciousness, the strong interrelationship of income with age, gender, ethnicity, and class leaves little for income by itself to explain. In addition as was seen in the analysis of class, increasing income has a different impact on conscious-ness in the various classes and other demographic groups. As seen in Figure 4.11, the result was that there was only a slight net difference in tenant consciousness across income groups. The secondary impact of income in the county sample was demonstrated by the finding that income differences did not generate significantly different levels of ten-ant consciousness in any of the ethnicity/gender categories.

Figure 4.11.   *Tenant Consciousness by Income (Los Angles County Sample)*

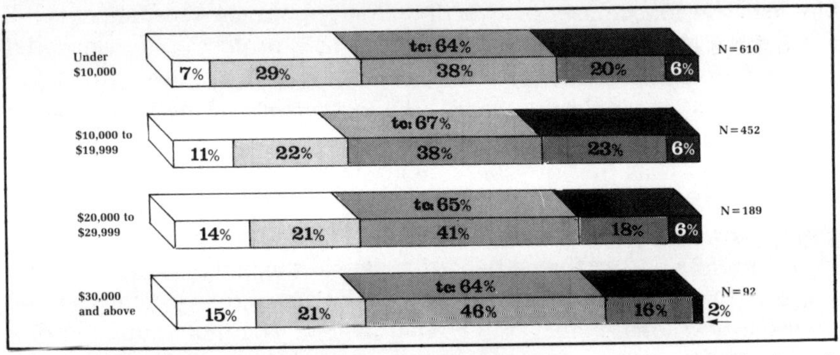

Note: *Please see Figure 4.1 for explanation of shaded bar codes.,The classifications, in order, are: 1) Antagonist; 2) Individualist; 3) Defender; 4) Consumer; and 5) Radicalized.*

In Santa Monica the story was quite different. Income was the only demographic characteristic, other than age, of importance that was sig-nificantly related to tenant consciousness.[20] What we found as set forth in Figure 4.12, is that, in contrast to the county, consciousness was higher at the low end of the income range and lower at the high end than in the county sample. The percentage of antagonists was partic-ularly enlarged in the higher income groups.

When the relationship between tenant consciousness and income was controlled by the other demographic characteristics in Santa Monica, white men appeared to be the primary source of the relationship between income and consciousness. Low-income white men in Santa Monica had quite high consciousness (74 percent N = 62), while high-income white men in that city had very low consciousness (48 percent N = 46). In the county the variance among white men was like the gen-eral figure, not so great. Low-income white men in the county sample did not have as high a consciousness (67 percent N = 88) as in Santa Monica, and county high-income white men did not have as low a consciousness (57 percent N = 47). In no other primary group or class strata were the relationships significant.

Figure 4.12.   *Tenant Consciousness by Income (Santa Monica Sample)*

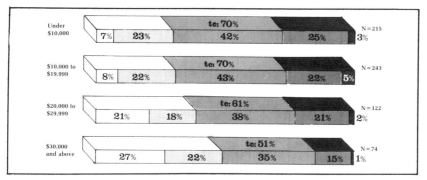

Note: *Please see Figure 4.1 for explanation of shaded bar codes. The classifications, in order, are: 1) Antagonist; 2) Individualist; 3) Defender; 4) Consumer; and 5) Radicalized.*

It should be noted that seniors had higher incomes in Santa Monica than in the county. Seventy percent (N = 205) of the seniors in the county have less than $10,000 annual income, compared to 56 percent (N = 115) of the Santa Monica seniors. At the other end of the income range, 16 percent of the Santa Monica seniors had incomes of $20,000 or more, compared to only 9 percent of the county. As noted earlier, this higher income appears to be contributing to the lower consciousness of seniors in Santa Monica. This was particularly true with senior working-class women (N = 36). None of the seniors with an annual income of $20,000 or above had tenant consciousness, and none with $10,000 or more annual income was found at the movement levels.

SUMMARY

This chapter began with the observation that the two samples are demographically very different. In investigating the relationship between the demographics of the samples and tenant consciousness, it has also been found that the relationship between the demographics and tenant consciousness in the two samples varies. The county sample can be characterized as much more demographically sensitive, with age, gender, ethnicity, class, and whether a man is a father appearing as important variables. Santa Monica, in contrast, seems much less demographically sensitive, with only age and income as important factors. The difference in consciousness cannot be explained away by the differences in the demographics. As was seen, the two white populations also proved to vary in the level of consciousness across common demographic characteristics.

As the analysis was performed, we have tried, where possible, to suggest logical explanations for what we have found. The tenants' age, their place in the life cycle and the social structure, and their apparent social mobility seemed to be important factors. In the following chapters an analysis of the experience the respondents have had as tenants, their desires and expectations about buying homes, and the political characteristics will be examined. Much of what has been found in both samples is explained by these additions.

The demographic sensitivity and coherence of the county population seems, in large part, related to the county tenant's day-to-day experience as a tenant. In the county these experiences are related to the demographics and are not mediated by the presence of as powerful a tenant movement as in Santa Monica. Santa Monica's lack of sensitivity to the demographics, in contrast, seems to be explained in large part by the success of the tenant movement and the existence in that city of an overheated housing market, which makes expectations of homeownership for all but upper-income tenants more problematic than in the county. In addition the politicalization of Santa Monica has made tenants real issues of concern. This makes political variables of primary importance in understanding the level of consciousness of tenants who live in Santa Monica. For many county tenants political concerns are far from crystalized, particularly in comparison to the lessons learned from their day-to-day experiences.

In conclusion the findings will be summarized by presenting the dominant demographic characteristics of each level of tenant consciousness. None of the levels of consciousness has a distinctly unique demographic composition, but most have an overrepresentation of one or more of the population groups examined.

Antagonist

As one might expect, men are overrepresented at the antagonist level in the county sample (1.5:1). An even higher proportion of representation is found among men who are white (1.9:1), members of the professional-managerial class (1.7:1), or with post-graduate educations (2.8:1). In contrast women from the professional-managerial class (1:2.2) and women with postgraduate educations (1:1.8) are substantially underrepresented at this level of consciousness.

Consistent with the conservative image of the antagonist stereotype, respondents at this level were more often petty bourgeois (2.1:1), between the ages of 40 and 59 (1.3:1), and with family incomes over $20,000 annually (1.5:1).

In the Santa Monica sample this group has a similar income level, but there is an additional overrepresentation of what appears to be an unusually conservative senior population (1.5:1).

Individualist

The individualists in the county sample possess special characteristics that may have inhibited them from forming tenant consciousness as defined in this study or from responding to the survey in as coherent a fashion as was required for scoring. The individualists were more heavily represented among Spanish-speaking Latinos (1.6:1), people over 60 years of age (1.4:1), and people with household incomes below $10,000 annually (1.2:1).

In this category women are marginally predominant (1.1:1). Elderly and Spanish-speaking women, who are likely to be working class (1.2:1) and to have stopped their education before entering high school (1.8:1) are especially visible in this group.

Defender

Defenders—those tenants who will join with other tenants in their building but will not work in the tenant movement—draw from the broadest possible cross-section of the tenant population. There is no demographic characteristic that seems to be correlated with a tenant's likelihood to be a defender.

Nevertheless, in this group there is a slight predominance of women with postgraduate educations in the professional-managerial class and a slight underrepresentation of men. Tenants who have family incomes over $30,000 are slightly overrepresented in the county sample, but this may be a result of the extreme underrepresentation of these tenants in higher-consciousness categories.

Consumer

Tenants under 30 years of age begin to be overrepresented at the first level of tenant movement consciousness, the consumer (1.2:1), although their numbers in this category are lower than we anticipated. It is also at the consumer level that a predominance of minorities, especially minority fathers, appears (1.2:1). English-speaking Latinos are only slightly overrepresented in this category, while blacks have higher representation at this level of consciousness than at any other group (1.4:1).

High-school-educated (1.3:1) and working-class men (1.1:1) as well as white women (1.2:1) are also overrepresented at the consumer level.

This is also true for women with postgraduate educations (1.2:1) and women who are members of the professional-managerial class (1.2:1).

Radicalized

In the county sample there is a greater overrepresentation of respondents under 30 years of age among the radicalized tenants than among consumers. It is interesting to note that men, who are substantially overrepresented at the lowest level of consciousness are also overrepresented at the top, although to a lesser degree (1.2:1). This was true among working-class (1.2:1) and professional-managerial class (1.3:1) men. It should be noted that there is a substantial overrepresentation of fathers (1.8:1) and especially minority fathers (2:1) in this category. It is also at this level that we find the substantial overrepresentation of English-speaking Latinos indicated in our earlier analysis (1.6:1).

NOTES

1. A discriminant analysis was also performed to see which characteristics significantly predicted tenant consciousness. In a step-wise analysis of the county using a "F" test of .05 (Nie et al. 1975, p. 447) age was entered first, followed in order by language preference (English or Spanish) gender, ethnicity, and class. In Santa Monica only, age and income were entered.

2. We see our data regarding levels of tenant consciousness as "categorical" data. We, therefore, employ a "nonparametric" test only in the analysis (Horowitz and Ferleger 1980, pp. 243–45).

3. Income was not introduced into the analysis. The introduction of gender, class, and ethnicity variables into the analysis removed the significance of the income data. Age was not originally significant. However, age became significant with the entry of the other variables and was entered fourth into the analysis.

4. Strong and very strong support of rent control: white women (308) 65 percent; white men (182) 47.5 percent; professional-managerial women (110) 71 percent; professional-managerial men (57) 54 percent; college women (186) 65 percent; college men (127) 51 percent; $20,000 to $30,000 women (43) 66 percent; $20,000 to $30,000 men (58) 47 percent.

5. Less than a fourth of the Santa Monica sample is married (23.4 percent N = 169). More of the Santa Monica respondents have never been married (SM 41.8 percent N = 302; LA 34.5 percent N = 499). Marital status was significantly related to tenant consciousness in the county sample; however, the relationship appeared to be more a product of age and income differences than a primary relationship. Marital status lost its significance and was not entered into the analysis of a step-wise discriminant analysis run on the demographic variables analyzed in this chapter.

6. In the county sample the economic differences are seen in the income figures: (196) 67 percent of Latinos and (117) 61 percent of blacks have annual household incomes of less than $10,000 compared to (280) 35 percent of whites, while (224) 28 percent of whites have incomes of $20,000 or more compared to (23) 12 percent of blacks and (23) 8 percent of Latinos. The breakdown regarding education and class shows similar variations.

7. Leggett found blacks to be more militant. His test for militance was the willingness to participate in a demonstration against landlords in the neighborhood who charge high rents and fail to maintain their property.

8. The consciousness of English-speaking Latinos and blacks did not vary significantly across other demographic variables. However, younger English-speaking Latino and black respondents have exceptionally high consciousness, with over 40 percent at the movement levels. This is particulary important in the case of English speakers because of their youth. White women's consciousness varied according to their age. Tenant consciousness of white women by age: Under 30—77 percent N = 162; 30–39—75 percent N = 98; 40–59—65 percent N = 94; 60 + over—59 percent N = 116. White men's consciousness varied by education and class. This will be discussed later in the chapter.

9. The significance level is .0899.

10. Individual action—English-speaking Latinos–86.4 percent (114); white women–84.4 percent (400); blacks 75.5 percent (157). Join with neighbors—English-Speaking Latinos–77.3 percent (102); white women–73.0 percent (346); blacks–64.9 percent (135).

11. Strong and very strong supporters of rent control: white women–65 percent; white men–45 percent. Against rent control: white women–10 percent; white men–24 percent.

12. For example, tenant voice: condominium conversion—white women–58 percent, white men–47 percent; renovation—white women–60 percent, white men–52 percent.

13. In Santa Monica English-speaking Latinos and blacks have higher consciousness than the whites. Spanish speakers again have the lowest consciousness. However, the number of minority group members in the Santa Monica sample is even smaller than in the county and prohibits further analysis.

14. The under $10,000 annual income: white men—LA 65 percent N = 88; SM 74 percent N = 62. The between $20,000 and $30,000 annual income: white women—LA 81 percent N = 53; SM 56 percent N = 55. Sixty years of age and older white women: LA 59% N = 116; SM 45 percent N = 65.

15. One of the first attempts in using class analysis in quantitative research was accomplished by Erik O. Wright and Luca Perrone. Their article, "Marxist Class Categories and Income Inequality" first appeared in 1977 and analyzed the returns from education realized through income by employers, managers, and workers. Their data base came from two random samples of approximately 1,500 adults (over 16) who were active in the labor force. However, their class typology differs from the one used in that study.

Wright's typology of five classes includes:

1. Employer: self-employed, has employees and subordinates
2. Manager: employed by others, has subordinates
3. Workers: employed by others without having subordinates
4. Petty bourgeois: self-employed (stockholders) and has neither employees or subordinates
5. Ambiguous: self-employed (consultants), have no employees, but have subordinates

We initially grouped the ambiguous class with the petty-bourgeois class because they too were self-employed. Then it was noticed that the employer category, which we called capitalist, comprised less than 1 percent of our sample population and that all respondents in this category had family incomes over $30,000. For purposes of practical analysis they are not employers, but petty bourgeois as well (Loren 1977). We also changed Wright's category of managers into a smaller grouping called professional. Wright used the criterion of supervision of other workers to delineate managers from workers. We found that this led to a conceptual difficulty where a large percentage of clerical workers were classified as managers. The question of supervision should not be authoritative alone, but should encompass supervision not just of others, but the production process as well. We go along with Braverman and others placing clerical workers in the working class, reserving the professional-managerial class for those with a large degree of autonomy in their labor. We included in this category not only those whose major function was supervision, but also those employed in the professions.

Wright and Perrone wrote their article as an exercise in pure and formal class analysis. This study attempts to use class analysis with an eye toward the attitudes of classes with respect to tenant consciousness. When Wright's categories were applied to our data base, they masked an important finding. For example, when clerical workers were classified as managers, nothing was revealed about the tenant consciousness of this group. But when we placed clerical workers in the working class and removed many of these workers from the professional-managerial class, we not only found that they behave like the rest of the working class, but that women in the professional-managerial class have high tenant consciousness.

16. It should be noted that the claimed lack of upward mobility among professional-managerial women has been a major issue in the women's movement (Deckard 1979, pp. 122-50).

17. The distribution is not statistically significant.

18. There is a sharp contrast between white women and white men in the groups (Under 30–69 percent N = 155; 30 to 39–56 percent; $20,000 to $30,000–58 percent N = 95). Women are the only group in which age is significantly related to tenant consciousness.

19. Level of education is also only significant with white men. Consciousness tends to decline with additional education among white men; the exception is with those who have not attended high school:

	Overall		Movement	
Elementary	(7)	35%	(2)	10%
High School	(77)	65	(35)	29
College	(107)	64	(31)	19
Post-Grad	(38)	51	(17)	23

20. The relationship is stronger than in the county (contingency coefficients: LA = .14029; SM = .22329).

5

Everyday Experience

As we discussed in the Introduction, Gramsci saw consciousness as an amalgam of everyday experience and ideological hegemony. Everyday experience tends to unite people with each other in "practical transformation of the real world," while ideological hegemony tends to create "political passivity" (Gramsci 1972, p. 333). The dominance of hegemony over everyday experience is not even across the population. Some groups, class strata, or individuals may be more or less free of hegemonic control. In part this may be an explanation for what has been found in the previous chapter. On the average, however, it should be expected that those people who have had negative experiences and recognize them as such have higher consciousness. Almost all the activists took this position.

In this chapter two aspects of the everyday experience of tenants are examined. In the first part of the chapter, the contemporary situation in which tenants found themselves when they were interviewed is explored. In the second part the tenants' history of negative experiences, including their knowledge of friends having had negative experiences, is added to the analysis. In this chapter reference is made to the demographic characteristics discussed in Chapter 4 to see if everyday experiences explain the earlier findings. Also, the issue of whether consciousness creates reality or reality generates consciousness is confronted. The solution to this riddle is very much a part of Gramsci's theory.

THE CONTEMPORARY SITUATION

Perhaps the central rule of most political organizing situations is that you must start your efforts from where the people to be organized "are at." This means, in many cases, their contemporary situation. The activists agreed, for example, that it would be very difficult to organize a tenant union in a building in which the tenants consider the rent fair and the conditions good and the landlord is liked. In this first part of our examination of the everyday experience of tenants, three aspects of the tenants' contemporary situatiton are examined: the rental characteristics of the tenants' situation at the time of the interview, the tenants' satisfaction with that situation, and the nature of the relationship between the tenants and their landlords.

Rental Characteristics

Eight rental characteristics were examined: 1) building type, 2) number of rooms in the rental unit, 3) number of persons in the household, 4) overcrowding, 5) whether the owner or a manager lived in the building, 6) building ownership, 7) length of residence at present address, and 8) sheltercost (the proportion of income expended in rent).

As is seen in the Table 5.1, the samples were generally similar with respect to the rental characteristics. Notable exceptions were the types of buildings, household size, and percentage of resident owners. More county tenants lived in either small or very large buildings and had large households. More Santa Monica tenants lived in owner-occupied, middle-sized buildings with five to 20 units and lived alone.[1]

There was little direct relationship between the rental characteristics and tenant consciousness. In the county only building ownership and building type proved to be statistically significant with respect to the tenant consciousness; in Santa Monica only the length of residence at the president address was statistically significant.[2] There were, however, some dramatic relationships between the demographic and rental characteristics that seemed indirectly to contribute to the formation of tenant consciousness.

Building Type and Ownership

Some of the activists who were interviewed stated that tenants in smaller buildings and those owned by individuals would have lower consciousness because of their closer relationships to the owners.[3] In the county it was found as was predicted; building size and the nature of the ownership were significantly related to tenant consciousness. Although the pattern was somewhat mixed, it can generally be said that tenants in larger buildings had higher consciousness.[4] Examining the impact of ownership, it was found that the highest consciousness was among those living in public housing (77 percent), followed by those living in

Table 5.1. *Rental Characteristics (Los Angeles County and Santa Monica Samples)*

	Los Angeles County		Santa Monica	
	Percent	*Number*	*Percent*	*Number*
Building Type				
Single family house	24.9%	(360)	7.7%	(56)
Duplex	5.9	(85)	2.1	(15)
3–4 unit apartment	11.4	(165)	11.6	(84)
5–9 unit apartment	14.9	(216)	26.8	(194)
10–20 unit apartment	17.4	(252)	31.2	(226)
21 units or more apartment	25.4	(367)	20.6	(149)
Number of Rooms in Unit (excluding bathrooms)				
1	3.9%	(57)	3.8%	(28)
2	10.9	(159)	11.0	(80)
3	27.6	(401)	32.1	(234)
4	29.4	(428)	28.1	(205)
5 or more	28.2	(410)	25.0	(182)
Number of Persons in Household				
1	38.2%	(556)	51.0%	(372)
2	29.7	(532)	30.2	(220)
3	13.3	(193)	11.0	(80)
4	10.3	(150)	5.5	(40)
5 or more	8.6	(125)	2.3	(17)
Overcrowding (Persons to rooms ratio)				
Less than 1.5 persons per room	94.7%	(1378)	97.3%	(709)
1.5 or more persons per room	5.3	(77)	2.7	(20)
Resident Owner or Manager				
Owner Resident	9.2%	(134)	16.2%	(118)
Manager Resident	35.7	(516)	37.0	(267)
Building Ownership				
Individually owned	76.0%	(1044)	79.9%	(545)
Company owned	21.3	(292)	19.8	(135)
Government owned	2.7	(37)	0.3	(2)
Length of residence at present address				
1 year or less	39.7%	(577)	36.4%	(264)
2–5 years	41.5	(603)	42.8	(311)
6 or more years	18.7	(272)	16.5	(90)
Sheltercost (% of income paid for rent)				
Under 25%	52.1%	(571)	49.9%	(256)
25%–50%	33.7	(370)	32.6	(167)
Over 50%	14.2	(156)	17.5	(90)

buildings owned by companies (69 percent), followed by those living in
buildings owned by individuals (63 percent).[5]

Length of Residence

Some of the activists also thought length of residence would relate to the
level of tenant consciousness. Length of residence was thought to be
related to general satisfaction with the rental situation. Satisfied tenants,
in turn, were thought to be either complacent about the problems of
tenants as a group or fearful that an aggressive position on tenant issues
would endanger their favorable rental situation.[6]

Length of residence at the present address was found to be significantly related to tenant consciousness in Santa Monica, but not in Los
Angeles County. In Santa Monica persons who had resided at their
present address for six or more years tended to be very low-
consciousness individuals, with over 50 percent below the defender
level of tenant consciousness and nearly 20 percent at the antagonist
level. Predominant among persons who had resided at their present
address for six or more years were the low-consciousness Santa Monica
seniors, discussed in the previous chapter. However, length of residence
of the seniors did not appear to explain their low consciousness. In both
Los Angeles and Santa Monica, approximately half of the persons who
reported that they had been living at their present address for more than
six years were seniors. In the county sample, consistent with the findings of Chapter 4, the long-residing seniors did not have particularly low
consciousness.

Overcrowding

As seen in Table 5.2, nearly one-third of the Spanish-speaking Latinos
lived in overcrowded conditions.[7] Less than 5 percent of any other group
was overcrowded. Particularly prominent among the county respondents who were overcrowded were the high-consciousness minority fathers. One-third of the minority fathers in the county reported that they

Table 5.2. *Percent Overcrowded Units by Ethnic Group*
(Los Angeles County Sample)

	Percent	Number
Whites	0.9%	(8)
Blacks	1.0	(2)
English-speaking Latinos	4.5	(6)
Spanish-speaking Latinos	30.6	(60)
Other	1.6	(1)

lived in singles or one-bedroom apartments, compared to only 7.5 percent of the white fathers. The overcrowding of the male-headed families, particularly the minorities, may have been a major factor in their high consciousness. It would certainly increase the pressure to escape tenancy into homeownership.

Sheltercost

Sheltercost is the percentage of income paid toward rent.[8] Again, certain demographic groups diverged from the total population distribution with respect to this variable. In both samples the high-consciousness tenants under 30 years of age and the low consciousness seniors had the highest sheltercosts, with over half in excess of 25 percent. Females, in general, and working-class women, in particular, spent more of their income on rent than their male counterparts. The low-consciousness groups and strata, white and professional-managerial men and the petty bourgeois had the lowest sheltercost, with two-thirds paying less than 25 percent of their income for rent.

Sheltercost was highly related to income. Lower-income tenants were much more likely to pay a high proportion of their income in rent than higher-income tenants. Because of this, it is interesting to note that Santa Monica tenants, who on the average had higher incomes than tenants in the county, actually were more likely to have higher sheltercost than county tenants. The comparison was most dramatic among tenants with annual family incomes below $20,000. Sheltercost by income is set forth for both data sets in Table 5.3.

Table 5.3. *Sheltercost by Annual Family Income (Los Angeles County and Santa Monica Samples)*

Income	Sheltercost					
	Less than 25%		25%–50%		Over 50%	
Under $10,000						
LA	(117)	22.2%	(260)	49.2%	(151)	28.6%
SM	(23)	13.1	(69)	39.4	(83)	47.4
$10,000 to $20,000						
LA	(276)	71.9%	(103)	26.3%	(5)	1.3%
SM	(121)	57.1	(84)	39.6	(7)	3.3
$20,000 to $29,999						
LA	(140)	95.2%	(7)	4.8%	—	—
SM	(90)	88.2	(12)	11.8	—	—
$30,000 and Above						
LA	(38)	100.0%	—	—	—	—
SM	(22)	91.7	(2)	8.3	—	—

Residential Satisfaction

Several questions in the survey asked respondents about their attitudes and perceptions toward their rental situation. Those that proved to be the most closely associated with tenant consciousness were: neighborhood satisfaction, satisfaction with rental unit, perceived condition of rental unit, and fairness of rent.[9] Table 5.4 shows the results of the survey with respect to these four variables.

Table 5.4. *Tenant Attitudes and Perceptions (Los Angeles County and Santa Monica Samples)*

	Los Angeles County		Santa Monica	
	Percent	Number	Percent	Number
Neighborhood Satisfaction				
Very satisfied	42.0%	(612)	60.9%	(443)
Somewhat satisfied	38.8	(565)	31.9	(232)
Not very satisfied	13.3	(193)	4.8	(35)
Not at all satisfied	5.9	(86)	2.5	(18)
Rental Unit Satisfaction				
Very satisfied	34.4%	(500)	45.1%	(328)
Quite satisfied	40.1	(583)	40.4	(264)
Not very satisfied	20.2	(294)	12.4	(90)
Not at all satisfied	5.4	(78)	2.2	(16)
Perceived Condition				
Very good	26.1%	(380)	29.4%	(214)
Good	32.7	(476)	39.6	(289)
Fair	30.2	(439)	25.1	(183)
Poor or very poor	11.0	(160)	5.9	(43)
Rent Fair?				
Yes	75.9%	(1103)	84.0%	(611)
No	24.1	(350)	16.0	(116)

Two findings stood out in this data. The first was that a majority of the respondents in both the county and Santa Monica were satisfied with their neighborhood and rental unit, the condition of their unit, and fairness of their rent. The second was that in each instance Santa Monica respondents were more satisfied than their county counterparts. Keeping this in mind, it should be noted that in each sample, there was a substantial proportion of tenants, although more so in the county, who held negative views with respect to these attitudinal variables. In the county one-fifth of the survey respondents were not satisfied with their neighborhoods, one-fourth were not satisfied with their rental units,[10] over 40 percent perceived their homes to be in less than good condition, and one-fourth felt their rent was unfair.

The most striking difference between responses in the county and Santa Monica was in neighborhood satisfaction. Sixty percent of Santa Monica tenants were very satisfied with their neighborhood, compared to just over forty percent in the county, and less than ten percent of the Santa Monicans were dissatisfied compared to nearly twenty percent of tenants in the county. Some people have observed that the Santa Monica tenant movement is based in large part on the desirability of living in that city and on the west side of Los Angeles. The findings of such overwhelming neighborhood satisfaction would seem to give credence to this observation.

Satisfaction with unit, perceived condition of the unit, and fairness of rent were significantly related to tenant consciousness in both Santa Monica and the county. Neighborhood satisfaction was significantly related to tenant consciousness only in the county due to the overwhelmingly positive response to this question in Santa Monica. Persons who were negatively disposed toward their rental situation tended to have higher tenant consciousness than persons holding positive attitudes and perceptions. However, the effect on consciousness was not generally dramatic.[11] Whether a respondent believed that the rent was unfair was an exception. Figure 5.1 sets out the data on the relationship between perceived fairness of rent in the county. The results in Santa Monica were similar.

Figure 5.1. *Tenant Consciousness by Fairness of Rent (Los Angeles County Sample)*

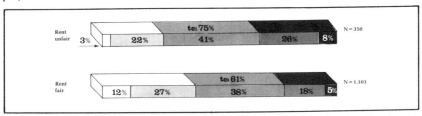

Note: *Please see Figure 4.1 for explanation of shaded bar codes. The classifications, in order, are: 1) Antagonist; 2) Individualist; 3) Defender; 4) Consumer; and 5) Radicalized.*

As would be expected, there was general consistency among the responses given to these attitudinal inquiries. Persons who reported that their homes were in poor or very poor condition, for example, were much less satisfied with them, and were much more likely to feel their rents were unfair, than were those persons who felt that their residences were in good or very good condition. Similarly, persons who expressed satisfaction with their rental units were more likely to express satisfaction with their neighborhoods and were more favorably disposed toward the fairness of their rents. In the county almost ninety percent of those who were very satisfied with their units, for example, felt that their rent was fair, compared with only 55 percent of those who were not satisfied with their units.

Demographic Difference

As discussed in Chapter 4, many of the activists suggested that minority and working-class tenants would have different attitudes and perceptions about their rental situation than whites and middle-class tenants. Whites and middle-class tenants were seen as perceiving their problem as almost entirely one of rising rents and were, therefore, primarily focused on the issue of rent control. Minority and working-class tenants

From *Coalition for Economic Survival, Los Angeles, CA. Reprinted by permission.*

Photo: Paul Gleye: Reprinted by permission.

were thought to already be paying more rent than they could afford and, in addition, facing the problem of poor conditions. While minority and working-class tenants were seen as supportive of rent control, it was not considered to be the entire answer to their problems.

The failure of the rent control effort to fully address the problem of conditions was said to be interfering with the formation of a unified tenant movement. In addition the feeling was that even on the issue of rents, the white and middle-class side of the problem was more tractable. The fear was that once their problem is ameliorated, white and middle-class tenants would leave the movement, leaving minorities and the working-class tenants with their more difficult and longstanding problems.

Table 5.5 shows how the different ethnicity/gender groups, classes, and ages in our Los Angeles County sample responded to our four residential satisfaction questions.[12]

The table indicates that the activists were largely correct in their predictions. In almost every case minority and working-class tenants were less satisfied than white and middle-class tenants. However, the activists also stated that they expected the ethnic groupings and classes to be closer on the question of rents than on the question of conditions. On this point the data did not entirely bear them out.[13] Instead, what was found was that only among the high-consciousness white and professional-managerial women did the activists' prediction prove to be true. Their attitudes were similar to those of minorities and the working

Table 5.5. *Satisfaction of Ethnicity/Gender Groupings, Classes and Age Groups (Los Angeles County Sample)*

	Not very or not at all satisfied with neighborhood		Not very or not at all satisfied with rental unit		Rental unit in very poor, poor, or fair condition		Rent not fair	
Ethnicity/Gender								
Blacks	29.7%	(62)	36.1%	(75)	45.2%	(94)	31.9%	(66)
Spanish-speaking Latinos	18.2	(36)	38.1	(75)	74.6	(147)*	27.4	(54)
English-speaking Latinos	20.0	(29)	28.0	(37)	44.7	(59)	27.3	(36)
White women	16.3	(77)	20.1	(95)	34.0	(161)	23.3	(110)
White men	16.2	(62)	19.6	(75)	29.3	(112)	17.2	(66)
Class								
Working-class women	20.3%	(11)	29.1%	(159)	44.9%	(246)	27.2%	(149)
Working-class men	19.8	(76)	27.1	(104)	43.3	(166)	22.7	(87)
Professional-Managerial women	13.6	(21)	20.0	(31)	31.8	(49)	24.5	(38)
Professional-Managerial men	17.0	(18)	17.0	(18)	27.3	(29)	18.1	(19)
Petty Bourgoise	16.7	(30)	20.0	(36)	32.8	(59)	18.3	(33)
Age								
Under 30	19.0%	(107)	26.3%	(148)	44.2%	(249)	30.4%	(171)
30–39	19.8	(71)	32.0	(115)	41.8	(150)	23.4	(84)
49–59	16.3	(48)	24.9	(73)	38.9	(114)	22.8	(67)
60 and older	22.4	(52)	14.6	(34)	36.1	(64)	12.0	(28)

Note: About one-half of the Spanish-speakers stated that their units were in fair condition.

class. The low-consciousness white male and professional-managerial and petty-bourgeois tenants were less dissatisfied than the other groups consistent with the gender and class differences found in Chapter 4.

It should be noted that the tenant movement in the more homogeneous city of Santa Monica did not, in the main, face this problem.[14] However, Santa Monica, with its higher sheltercost and more white middle-class character, almost seems a model of what the activists were worrying about vis-a-vis the broader movement. How the Santa Monica movement will relate to growing movements in other areas with the complexities of ethnic diversity remains an open question.

As noted, the findings with white and professional-managerial men and women with regard to residential satisfaction, were consistent with the finding in Chapter 4. The findings with regard to other ethnic groups and class strata were not. A partial explanation for this difference was found when the impact of residential dissatisfaction on tenant consciousness was examined in each of the demographic groups and classes. It was found that in the various groups or strata, as a general rule, perceptions about the condition of an apartment did not significantly affect tenant consciousness. The only group in which the effect was both significant and dramatic was white men, and this was not so much because dissatisfaction with conditions appeared to be related to very high consciousness but because satisfaction appeared to be related to low consciousness.[15] Perceptions of conditions were also significantly related to tenant consciousness among English-speaking Latinos. However, while dissatisfaction with conditions appeared to have been a source of their high consciousness, it was clearly not the dominant factor.[16] For example, 41 percent of the English-speaking Latinos who responded "very good" were at the movement levels.

In contrast the respondents' attitudes about the fairness of their rent did significantly affect consciousness among most groups and strata.[17] The exceptions were seniors, Spanish speakers, and surprisingly, professional-managerial women. The lack of significance with professional-managerial women did not result from low consciousness on the part of those who thought their rent was unfair (76 percent N = 54), but from the high consciousness of those who thought their rent was fair (77 percent N-117). This high consciousness of the professional-managerial women who thought their rent was fair also helped explain why white women had overall higher consciousness than blacks.[18] It was the white women who thought their rent was fair that pushed white women's consciousness to a higher level.[19] The solution to the findings with regards to English-speaking Latinos and conditions and professional-managerial women and fairness of rent appeared to be found in the difficulty of buying a home experienced by these tenants. The impact of this difficulty will be discussed in Chapter 7.

The most contradictory findings were with the Spanish speakers. Why their consciousness scores may be low has already been discussed. However, whatever the reason, the dissatisfaction level of the Spanish speakers seems to indicate that the tenant movement should look closely at ways to mobilize the dissatisfaction of this group. If language is the problem, the strategy now being employed in Los Angeles may be the answer. Further investigation of this effort seems to be warranted.

From Coalition for Economic Survival, Los Angeles, CA. Reprinted by permission.

Why Tenants Say the Rent is Unfair

What is fair rent to one person may not be seen as fair to another, and what are adequate conditions to one person may not be adequate to another. In this regard the impact of tenant consciousness itself on the responses to the satisfaction variables can not be ignored. A tenant with high consciousness should, in theory, be more critical of rent levels and conditions than someone with low consciousness. At the extremes of consciousness, most antagonists should believe that it is a landlord's right to charge whatever he or she likes, and most radicalized tenants should question the wisdom of continuing to tolerate private landlordism and rent in any form or at any level.

The uncertain interaction of experience and consciousness inherent in attitudinal questions such as those relating to residential satisfaction are not unique to this study. It is an expression of the classic philosophical question of whether consciousness reflects reality or reality generates consciousness. Gramsci's position was that there exists a dialectic unity of the two positions in the interaction of hegemony and everyday experi-ence (Adamson 1980, p. 136). At the root, however, Gramsci believes, was the driving force of experience. While experience itself would not create a radical transformation, it is from experience that the initial movement should spring.

The data in this study lend some credence to Gramsci's position. The response that the rent was unfair was significantly related to the material reality of the percentage of income paid in rent. As shown in Table 5.6, the larger the percentage of income paid in rent, the more likely the tenant was to think it was unfair.

Table 5.6.   *Unfairness of Rent by Sheltercost (Los Angeles County and Santa Monica Samples)*

	Los Angeles County		Santa Monica	
Under 25% of Income	(102)	18.7%	(27)	10.5%
25%–50% of Income	(118)	32.5	(31)	18.7
Over 50% of Income	(55)	35.3	(21)	23.3

The relationship between sheltercost and attitudes about the fair-ness of the rent helps explain the rise of the drive for rent control over the past decade. The decade of the seventies has been marked by a steady rise in the percentage of tenants' incomes taken in rent. In 1970 the nationwide average percentage of rent taken in income was 20 per-cent; by 1976 the figure had risen to 24 percent; and a figure approaching 30 percent can be expected in the 1980 census (Sternlieb and Hughes 1980, p. 262). The Los Angeles figures are quite similar, while the curve in Santa Monica would likely be considerably steeper up to the adoption of rent control.

Sheltercost did not directly relate to the other three measures of satisfaction. However, this does not mean it had no impact on these attitudes. When the tenants' other attitudes about residential satisfaction were controlled by their attitude about the fairness of rent, it was found that sheltercost did impact upon attitudes about the condition of the units and overall satisfaction. Table 5.7 presents a summary of this inter-action from the county data. Tenants, having decided that their rent was unfair, seemed to have become increasingly critical of the physical con-dition of the unit and less generally satisfied with the unit as their rent increased and consumed a larger percentage of their income. If present trends continue, this suggests the possibility of a geometric rather than arithmetic increase in rental dissatisfaction. Such a progression, if main-tained, would serve, over time, to reduce the gap between ethnic groups and class strata.

Table 5.7. *Residential Satisfaction Among Tenants Who Think Their Rent is Unfair by Sheltercost (Los Angeles County Sample)*

Satisfaction	Under 25% of Income		25%–50% of Income		Over 50% of Income	
Unit is very poor, poor, or fair condition	30.6%	(66)	40.7%	(70)	45.5%	(35)
Not at all or not very satisfied with unit	41.5	(47)	52.4	(54)	56.1	(23)

In Chapter 8 the issues of consciousness and experience will again be discussed. The question there is how general political identity interacts with experience, attitude, and tenant consciousness. So as to not overstate the problem, at present, it should be kept in mind that the majority of tenants did not hold extreme positions at either end of the spectrum that could dramatically affect the results of the analysis.

Relationship to Landlord

Like the variables just discussed, the relationship to the owner of the rental unit should reflect the respondents' attitudes about their contemporary rental situation. The tenants' relationship with their landlord would be expected to be related to residential satisfaction. Tenants who believed that their rent was unfair were not likely to have had a good relationship with the landlord who was demanding this unfair rent. However, the relationship with the landlord is more than a synonym for the residential satisfaction variables. It is a social relationship that involves more than questions of levels of rent and conditions. Theoretically, this relationship should be central to what is being examined.

Almost all the activists interviewed believed that the nature of the relationship between the landlords and tenants would be a central variable in this study. A bad relationship supposedly raises consciousness and, conversely, a good relationship lowers consciousness. Typical of the activists' position, one stated, "I think the strongest, best organizers in California . . . are landlords. The landlords literally drive people into tenant groupings. For every tenant that we actively organized, that is, went out and knocked on his door and said, 'This is an issue—are you interested?' we've had five find us because the landlords have driven them berserk. . . . The occasional very good one—that sweetheart landlord—he can hold people back."

The literature seems to confirm the activists' position. A study of landlord behavior in Columbus, Ohio, focused in on how the relation-ship between the landlord and tenant can inhibit any aggressive action by the tenant (Vaughan 1972). In particular the study noted that small landlords often form near familial relationships with their tenants and through this device control their tenants' behavior. Another article that contains a report of the Ann Arbor, Michigan, organizing effort of the late 1960s gives the nature of the landlord-tenant relationship special attention. According to the author of the article, the landlords went a long way in defeating a round in the organizing drive by launching a concerted "counteroffense" that consisted primarily of making repairs and being nice to the tenants. The result was that the tenants did not want to take action against "good" landlords (Jennings 1972, p. 59).

To find out about the relationship between the landlords and ten-ants, respondents were asked to describe their relationship with their landlord according to a fixed set of responses, including very good, good, fair, poor, or very poor. The answer that the respondent had no relationship with the landlord was also accepted. The results for each sample are set forth in Table 5.8.

Table 5.8. *Relationship to Owner (Los Angeles County and Santa Monica Samples)*

	Los Angeles County		Santa Monica	
Poor and very poor	(97)	9.8%	(54)	7.4%
Fair	(181)	13.5	(87)	11.9
Good	(287)	21.4	(128)	17.6
Very good	(421)	31.4	(229)	31.4
No relationship	(355)	26.5	(231)	31.7

The first finding of interest was that a substantial number of tenants in each sample had no relationship with their landlord.[20] The second finding of importance was that approximately three-quarters of the ten-ants in both samples who had relationships with their landlords had good or very good relationships.[21] If a poor relationship with a landlord is a prerequisite to tenant organizing, we would have to wonder at this point about the ability of the tenant movement to sustain itself or grow.

This conclusion was partially tempered by the finding of a strong connection between the relationship to the landlord and age. The youn-ger the tenant, the poorer the relationship. Substantially fewer young tenants had very good relationships with their landlords,[22] particularly in contrast to seniors.[23] Only time will tell whether the young tenant of

Figure 5.2. *Tenant Consciousness by Relationship to Owner (Los Angeles County Sample)*

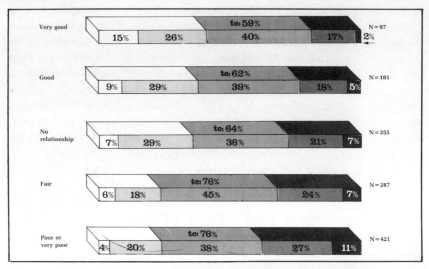

Note: *Please see Figure 4.1 for explanation of shaded bar codes. The classifications, in order are: 1) Antagonist; 2) Individualist; 3) Defender; 4) Consumer; and 5) Radicalized.*

Figure 5.3. *Tenant Consciousness by Relationship to Owner (Santa Monica Sample)*

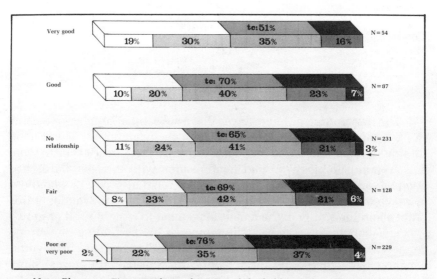

Note: *Please see Figure 4.1 for explanation of shaded bar codes. The classifications, in order, are: 1) Antagonist; 2) Individualist; 3) Defender; 4) Consumer; and 5) Radicalized.*

today is a new cohort experiencing a particularly difficult time for tenants that will, with its consciousness raised, continue to support a tenant movement over the years, or whether the young tenant of today will mellow with years and find a way to have a better relationship with future landlords.

When the tenant consciousness of tenants, according to their relationship with their landlords, was examined, it was found, as shown in Figures 5.2 and 5.3, that the quality of the relationship significantly affected tenant consciousness. In the county this relationship was as predicted: the worse the relationship, the higher the consciousness. Those respondents with no relationship were in the neutral position between the respondents who answered ''good'' and those who answered ''fair.''

In Santa Monica the findings only match those predicted results at the extremes. There was a major divergence in consciousness between those with poor or very poor relationships and those with very good relationships, but the remainder of the population seemed relatively unaffected by their relationship with the landlord. This makes sense if Santa Monica's population is viewed as having existed in a very politicized environment.

As will be seen later, in a politicized environment, problems become more collective and less individual. In such a situation only extreme personal experiences, whether good or bad, would be expected to have a significant effect. In the less politicized county the day-to-day experience of an individual, as crystalized in that tenant's relationship with his or her landlord, would be expected to have a more significant effect.

The relative importance of the quality of the relationship between landlord and tenant in the two samples can be seen in the proportion of radicalized tenants in each sample. Eleven percent of the tenants in the county with poor or very poor relationships with their landlords were in the radicalized category, compared to 4 percent in Santa Monica. This resulted, in large part, from the pattern of responses in the two samples to the question regarding nationalization or cooperatization of the rental housing stock. In the county 28 percent of the respondents who had poor or very poor relationships with their owner supported this proposition, compared to 15 percent of those with good relationships. In Santa Monica the figures for these two groups were nearly identical, 19 percent and 18 percent respectively.

The finding that the present day-to-day experience appeared to have this dramatic effect on county respondents raises the question of whether their responses are transitory or represent a serious conversion to antilandlordism principles. Some authors have criticized studies such as this one that attempt to measure political consciousness because of the transitory nature of such opinions (McCarney 1980). The responses of the Santa Monica tenants, which appear to result less from a moment of anger, may be less transitory. Of course, the opposite might also be true. Anger might lead to permanent change, where calmer reflection might not.

The relationship to the owner was, as expected, related significantly to the residential satisfaction variables. For example, nearly 90 percent of the respondents in the county who stated that they had very good relationships with their landlords also stated that their rent was fair, while only about half of the respondents who said they had poor or very poor relationships with their landlords felt their rent was fair. Nearly half of the respondents with very good relationships with their owners stated their apartments were in very good condition (75 percent in good or very good condition), compared to less than 5 percent (25 percent in good or very good condition) of those with poor or very poor relationships with their owners.

At the same time it is clear that there were other interactions between the landlords and tenants that may have resulted in a poor relationship. In Santa Monica, for example, one-third of the tenants who reported poor or very poor relationships with their landlords did not complain either about the unfairness of their rent or the condition of their apartment. There are many issues around which landlord and tenant may clash. These can range from arguments about the tenant having a pet to arguments about when, if ever, the landlord can come into the apartment.

The quality of the relationship between landlord and tenant was significantly related to ethnicity in the county. Minority respondents (regardless of group) were more likely to have had a relationship with their landlord and more likely to have had a poorer quality relationship than whites (regardless of gender).[24] When the analysis was limited to those respondents with a relationship with the owner of their apartment, the difference became substantial.[25] This was likely the product of the minorities' lower residential satisfaction. However, as in the case of residential satisfaction, the minority tenants' consciousness was not significantly affected by the quality of their relationships with their landlords.

Among the minorities consciousness dropped off only with those who had a very good relationship with their landlords and then only at the movement levels. In contrast both white men and women seem to have been significantly affected. The drop in consciousness between those with a fair relationship and those with a good relationship among white men and women was substantial.[26] White women with very poor, poor, and fair relationships with their landlords had very high consciousness. White men with good and very good relationships with their landlords had particularly low consciousness in the county. It can only be surmised that the overall low material quality of minority tenants' lives and the general low quality of interactions with figures in society such as landlords, may have drowned out some of the impact of their reactions to the quality of their apartments and their relationships with their landlords (Ermer and Strange 1972). This may also be the reason that more minority tenants have not focused on tenant issues and become active in the tenant movement.

LANDLORD-TENANT PROBLEMS—PAST AND PRESENT

The relationships uncovered in the first part of this chapter between tenant consciousness, rental characteristics, residential satisfaction, and the relationship to the landlord all pertain to the tenants' situation at the time of the interview. Tenants may have a satisfactory rental situation at present, but they may have had problems in the past that left a permanent impression on their consciousness. In this section the discussion broadens to consider the problems the respondents have had over the entire course of being tenants. Two types of problems are covered: problems with landlords and forced moves. Of necessity both of these were self-defined by the respondents. In addition the impact of knowing about friends' problems on consciousness is examined.

Most of the activists who were interviewed suggested that such negative experiences would raise the consciousness of the tenants involved. Interestingly, the minority of activists who did not believe negative experiences would necessarily raise consciousness had never had a problem themselves. Those activists who had experienced problems themselves were unanimous about their consciousness-raising impact.

Disputes

Looking first at problems with landlords, about one-third of the respondents in both samples responded "yes" to the question "have you ever had any problems or disputes with a landlord?" Of the respondents who responded affirmatively, one-third reported only one problem or dispute in their entire history as a tenant. The remaining two-thirds reported having two or more problems or disputes.[27]

The respondents were also asked about the nature of their problems or disputes with landlords. They were given a fixed set of items, including conditions and rents, and could add others. As is seen from the data presented in Table 5.9, problems and disputes about conditions were the

Table 5.9. *Types of Disputes (Los Angeles County and Santa Monica Samples)*

	1 dispute		2 + disputes		total pop.	
			Los Angeles County			
Condition of Unit	43.6%	(13)	79.3%	(214)	19.6%	(285)
Other Disputes	37.6	(62)	43.0	(116)	12.2	(178)
Rent Increase	8.0	(13)	37.8	(102)	7.9	(115)
Security Deposit	9.9	(16)	34.9	(94)	7.6	(110)
Condo Conversion	0.0	(0)	6.7	(18)	1.2	(18)
			Santa Monica			
Condition of Unit	44.4%	(40)	75.2%	(112)	21.0%	(152)
Other Disputes	28.9	(26)	38.3	(57)	11.5	(83)
Rent Increases	15.6	(14)	41.5	(61)	10.4	(75)
Security Deposit	8.9	(8)	28.4	(42)	6.9	(50)
Condo Conversion	2.2	(2)	8.7	(13)	2.1	(15)

Note: Respondents were assigned to more than one category.

most commonly mentioned, followed in order of frequency by 'others,' rent increases, security deposits, and condominium conversions. The results in the two samples were quite similar, with the exception that more tenants in the county mention problems or disputes not on our list, while more tenants in Santa Monica mentioned problems with rents, particulary those who had experienced only one problem or dispute.

The analysis of the effect of these landlord-tenant conflicts on tenant consciousness was two dimensional. We wanted to know both whether the number of conflicts was related to consciousness and whether the nature of the dispute had an independent effect. In the county the consciousness of tenants experiencing a single problem or dispute with a landlord was not distinguishable from tenants who had never had a problem or dispute, but tenants who reported multiple disputes had markedly higher consciousness.[28] In Santa Monica the findings were different. A significant increase in consciousness was noted with the first conflict, and a further increase accompanied multiple conflicts.[29] It is important to note, however, that in both samples increased consciousness at the movement levels only occurred with multiple disputes.[30] The increased consciousness in Santa Monica with one dispute was limited to an increase in the proportion of tenants at the defender level.

The nature of the problem or dispute also significantly related to the level of consciousness. In both samples tenants with disputes about rents had the highest consciousness.[31] In the county the increased consciousness among those with multiple disputes seemed to be independent of the combination of the disputes experienced. In Santa Monica the increased consciousness both with one dispute and with multiple disputes seemed to be related to the greater incidence of conflicts over rent levels. This is consistent with the strength of the rent control movement in Santa Monica and worries about its middle-class character.

In both samples the more types of problems a person had experienced, the higher the consciousness. Needless to say, those few tenants who had faced unsatisfactory conditions, unfair rent increases, security deposit problems, condominium conversions, and other problems had been extraordinarily radicalized.

As with the relationship to the landlord, having a history of disputes with landlords was significantly related to age. It was also related to the ethnicity/gender groupings. The older the tenants were, the less likely they were to report having experienced a problem or dispute. Seniors were again the most extreme case. Only about 10 percent of the seniors reported such a history. The relationship with ethnicity/gender appeared to be a manifestation of age and not an independent variable. The class/gender strata were not significantly related.

Friends' Disputes

In addition to asking whether the respondents had experienced a landlord-tenant conflict, the tenants were also asked whether they knew if friends of theirs had ever had a negative experience with a landlord. More tenants in Santa Monica knew of friends who had had problems or disputes (SM–41.5 percent; LA–31.7 percent). This was likely a product of the intense activity in Santa Monica that made tenant issues a primary topic of conversation and brought many people together to work toward solutions to the problems. In both samples those who knew that their friends had had negative experiences had higher consciousness than those who either said their friends had not had negative experiences or said they did not know.[32]

Knowledge of friends' problems was strong enough in both samples to cause the relationship to the landlord to lose its statistically significant impact on tenant consciousness. The relationship to the landlord remained significant among tenants who were unaware of friends' problems.

Knowing that a friend had experienced landlord-tenant problems was particularly significant for tenants who reported no problems of their own. In both samples tenants who did not report any problems had significantly higher consciousness if they knew of friends' problems.

They were more likely to be defenders and consumers and less likely to be either antagonists or individualists than tenants who had no problems of their own and had no knowldge of their friends having had such problems.

This finding, together with the finding of broader knowledge of friends having had problems in Santa Monica, helps explain the weaker association between the relationship to the landlord and tenant consciousness in that city. In both samples there was a significant difference in the level of consciousness of tenants with good and very good relationships with their landlords, depending on whether they knew of friends' problems. The difference was sharpest among tenants with good relationships. In the county 30 percent of the tenants with good relationships with their landlords knew of friends' problems; in Santa Monica 44 percent knew of friends' problems. In both samples the difference was expressed at the movement levels. In the county nearly twice as many tenants who knew friends who had problems were at the movement levels (17 percent to 35 percent); in Santa Monica the percentage nearly tripled (17 percent to 47 percent).

It is important to note that knowing friends have had problems with a landlord also seemed to impact the consciousness of people who have had their own problems.[33] An acknowledged commonality of experience seemed to play a role in moving tenants to the radicalized level of consciousness. In some ways this is more important from a movement point of view than the finding that people without problems of their own have their consciousness raised by knowledge of friends' problems. It makes it clear how vitally important it is to bring tenants with problems together, to organize, so that they can learn that they are not alone. Without this awareness of common experiences, even multiple negative experiences can have a limited effect. Full development of all of the elements of tenant consciousness, a perceived common problem, group identity and sophistication, as well as the willingness to work in the movement all seem related to experiencing the problem in a collective way.

The finding regarding the importance of knowing about friends' problems provided additional information about why the Spanish-speaking Latinos had low consciousness. Only 17 percent (33) of the Spanish speakers knew of friends having had problems, in comparison with a consistent 34 percent (1192) of the remainder of the county sample. This is consistent wih the findings of other studies regarding the isolation of immigrants and the Spanish speakers' concentration in this study at the individualist level of consciousness (Rex and Moore 1967, p. 277). In Santa Monica white tenants were more likely than any of the minority groups to be aware of friends' problems. This is consistent with the primary white character of the tenant movement in that city.

Not surprisingly, in both samples the older the tenants, the less likely they were to know of friends' disputes. In both samples middle-class tenants, the professional-managerial and petty bourgeois, were also more likely to know of friends' problems. In the county this may be, in part, explained by the isolation of the Spanish speakers. However, as will be seen in Chapter 8, this may also be a product of more direct involvement in the tenant movement of such middle-class tenants. This was particularly the case in Santa Monica.

Forced Move

The second type of problem analyzed was the forced move. The investigations into this realm of tenant experience yielded information on two types of moves: 1) evictions as a result of landlord-tenant dispute; and 2) forced moves that were not identified with a landlord-tenant dispute. About one-third of the Los Angeles County sample had experienced one of these two types of forced moves, with a slightly higher percentage found in the Santa Monica sample. A few individuals had experienced both an eviction and a forced move unrelated to a dispute.

In gathering information on forced moves, respondents were asked whether they had ever been forced to move for one of four reasons: 1) a rent increase; 2) poor condition of the rental unit; 3) condominium conversion; or 4) renovation of the unit by the landlord. Consistent with the demographic differences in the two populations, county respondents were more likely to mention poor conditions as the basis of their forced moves, while Santa Monica respondents were more likely to mention rents and condominium conversions. Table 5.10 shows the percentage of our two sample populations that experienced each type of forced move.

There was no statistically significant difference between the tenant consciousness of respondents who had been evicted as a result of a

Table 5.10. *Types of Forced Moves (Los Angeles County and Santa Monica Samples) (Percentage of sample population experiencing)*

Type of Forced Move	Los Angeles County		Santa Monica	
Evictions	3.6%	(53)	5.5%	(40)
Forced moves not associated with a landlord–tenant dispute (all types)	28.7	(417)	30.7	(224)
Rent Increase	11.6	(169)	14.9	(108)
Poor Condition of Unit	19.3	(281)	14.6	(106)
Condo Conversion	2.7	(40)	4.7	(34)
Renovation of Unit	6.6	(96)	6.7	(49)

dispute and those who had not been evicted in either sample. However, tenants in both samples who had been forced to move for reasons unrelated to a dispute did prove to have significantly higher consciousness than those who had never had such an experience. This impact of a forced move was found to exist regardless of whether or not the respondents had reported a landlord-tenant conflict. Those people who had experienced both multiple landlord-tenant conflicts and a forced move, needless to say, had exceptionally high consciousness. Figure 5.4 shows the relationship between problems, whether disputes and/or forced moves, and tenant consciousness in the county.[34]

Figure 5.4. *Tenant Problem by Tenant Consciousness (Los Angeles County Sample)*

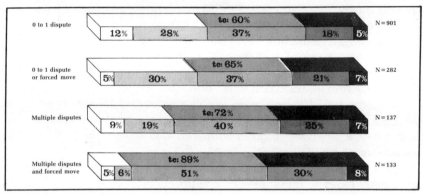

Note: *Please see Figure 4.1 for explanation of shaded bar codes. The classifications, in order, are: 1) Antagonist; 2) Individualist; 3) Defender; 4) Consumer; and 5) Radicalized.*

In Santa Monica the pattern at the movement levels was very similar. However, the overall relationship was again less dramatic. Ten percent more of the Santa Monica tenants who experienced one problem and a forced move were found among the defenders rather than among the individualists, and more than twice the percentage of Santa Monica tenants who experienced multiple problems and a forced move remained at the individualist level rather than joining the ranks of the defenders.

In the analysis of rental satisfaction and the relationship between landlords and tenants, it was found that the consciousness level of minority tenants was not significantly affected by perceptions of the condition of the apartment or the quality of the relationship with the landlord. This was not the case with blacks and tenant problems. Blacks with multiple problems (problem or problems and forced moves) had significantly higher consciousness than blacks with one problem or no problems. In the three categories of multiple problems, more than 40 percent of the blacks were at the movement levels. The level of consciousness of blacks ranged from 70 percent to over 90 percent with increasing numbers of multiple problems. Blacks with multiple problems had higher consciousness than white women with multiple problems.[35] The overall high consciousness of the white women in the county comes from the higher consciousness of white women who reported no or just one dispute and no forced moves.

The earlier finding again held true, however, with Latinos, whether English- or Spanish-speaking. The English-speaking Latinos' consciousness was raised by negative experience, but the baseline of consciousness of this group was so high that the added increment was not sufficient to make a statistical difference. For example, among English-speaking Latinos with no or one tenant problem, 72 percent (N = 84) had tenant consciousness. Negative experiences express themselves in even higher consciousness. For example, 15 percent (N = 47) of English-speaking Latinos with multiple problems were found at the radicalized level of consciousness, compared to 6 percent of those with no or one problem. Why the baseline was so high will await further investigation.

Once again, whether or not the tenant knew of friends having had problems appeared to contribute to dramatic differences in the level of consciousness. Statistically, the difference was significant in both samples only with tenants who had experienced no or one dispute and a forced move.[36] However, the impact at the important radicalized level remained apparent among those with multiple problems and those with multiple problems and a forced move. Instead of 2 or 3 percent at the radicalized level among those who did not know of others' problems, 10 and 11 percent were found among those who also had friends with negative experiences.

Whether or not a tenant had experienced a forced move was not generally related to the demographics. However, age was again a significant factor. Seniors experienced the lowest percentage of forced moves.

Cumulative Effects of Problems

Earlier it was noted that relatively few tenants were dissatisfied with their present rental situation or not getting along with their landlords and that this certainly did not appear to bode well for the future of the tenant movement. However, when the entire history of tenants' negative experiences, both direct and indirect, through knowledge of friends' problems, is considered, the findings were much more positive, from a movement organizer's point of view. In the county over half (55 percent) of the tenants interviewed had a history of direct or indirect negative experiences with landlords, and in Santa Monica this figure was nearly two-thirds (64 percent).

As with the earlier findings, the likelihood of having a history of negative experiences was related to the age of the tenant.[37] Table 5.11 sets out this relationship. What is seen is that tenants under 30 years of age were nearly twice as likely as seniors to have had such a history.

Table 5.11. *Tenants Who Have or Do Not Have a Direct or Indirect–Tenant Conflict History of Landlords by Age (Los Angeles County and Santa Monica Samples)*

	Los Angeles County		Santa Monica	
	Have	Have Not	Have	Have Not
Under 30 years old	(401) 65.2%	(214) 34.8%	(170) 75.6%	(55) 24.4%
30 to 39 years old	(231) 64.3	(128) 35.7	(146) 70.5	(61) 29.5
40 to 59 years old	(167) 56.8	(127) 43.2	(98) 63.6	(56) 36.4
60 years of age and older	(79) 33.9	(154) 66.1	(57) 41.3	(81) 58.7

This finding, seen together with seniors' greater residential satisfaction and better relations with their present landlords, would seem to argue against the proposition stated in Chapter 4 that seniors' lower consciousness was a product of the limitations of action that come with age. It may be that a substantial proportion of seniors who entered the rental market some years ago when the rental situation was more favorable to tenants and who have lived in their present apartments for a long period of time had been somewhat isolated from the intense conflict of recent years.

It should be remembered, however, that these findings regarding lack of problems and complaints must be seen against the finding that a high proportion of seniors were under considerable financial pressure, paying over 25 percent of their income in rent and that they heavily supported rent control. It may be that the seniors saw their problems, in large part, as being related to the decline in their income-stream with retirement, rather than to landlord behavior. Their support for rent control may have come out of necessity rather than from anger or ideology.

A high proportion of tenants under 30 also paid more than 25 percent of their income in rent. In contrast to the seniors, the young tenants appeared to blame the landlords for this problem. They were the least satisfied and had the poorest relationships with the landlords and the greatest history of problems. The difference is that they were presumably working hard and, in Skidmore's terms, their labor was being "extracted" in the form of rent. This population also faced all the problems of petty accumulation necessary for upward mobility and future security, including buying a home. Rent can get in the way of saving for a home. If, as will be discussed in Chapter 7, an increasing proportion of this population is having difficulty moving up, buying a home, the consciousness of the tenant population of the future could be far more radicalized.

In Santa Monica the incomes of the respondents also related to the combination variable. Fewer tenants with under $10,000 annual family income and $30,000 or more annual family income have histories of negative experiences than those with incomes between $10,000 and $30,000.

Not surprisingly, tenants who had no negative experiences and had no knowledge of friends having had negative experiences had significantly lower consciousness than those who had had negative experiences or had friends who had had negative experiences. As with the knowledge of friends' problems, the impact of this composite experience measure was most telling in Santa Monica. Those tenants untouched by tenant problems in Santa Monica tended to have exceptionally low consciousness. Only 45 percent of these tenants had tenant consciousness, with 21 percent at the antagonist level. Santa Monica seniors again had the lowest consciousness; only 35 percent of these seniors with no histories of problems had tenant consciousness. In contrast among Santa Monica senior tenants who have had a history of problems, the percentage with consciousness increased to 60 percent.

It is important to note that the findings of low consciousness did not hold for the county. In particular tenants 40 years of age or older with no direct or indirect history of negative experiences did not seem as dramatically affected. While those who had histories of negative experiences had higher consciousness than those who did not, the difference was not statistically significant. The difference between the two data sets was not explained by demographics or other factors examined to this point. Additional explanations for what might be causing the difference will be discussed in Chapter 8.

SUMMARY

This chapter contains an examination of the impact of everyday experience on tenant consciousness. In the first part of the chapter, tenants' contemporary situation was examined. It was found that few rental characterastics related significantly to tenant consciousness, although they seemed to contribute in an indirect way to later findings. Only the size of the building and the nature of the ownership in the county and the length of residency in Santa Monica related significantly to tenant consciousness. This was true even though other variables such as over-crowding and sheltercost related significantly to the demographics ex-amined in Chapter 4.

Four dimensions of residential satisfaction were measured: condi-tions, rent levels, overall, and neighborhood. In each case the more satisfied the tenant, the lower the consciousness. Only in the case of the fairness of the rent was the relationship dramatic. Santa Monica's ten-ants were more satisfied with their rental situation, particularly when it came to neighborhood satisfaction. This appeared to be evidence of the placed-base nature of the Santa Monica movement.

Some of the activists had predicted that minority and working-class tenants would be most dissatisfied with both rent levels and conditions, but that white and middle-class tenants would score close to the minor-ity and working-class tenants on the question of rents. The findings varied from those predicted in that *only* the white and professional-managerial women were close to the minorities on the question of rents. This finding was taken as evidence of the validity of the position that there is a danger that if the problem of "high" rents can be solved to the satisfaction of the white and middle-class tenants, these tenants might abandon the tenant movement.

While the findings regarding residential satisfaction generally matched those of Chapter 4 regarding demographics, minority tenants seemed less sensitive to residential satisfaction than whites. Except for the issue of rent, the minority's level of consciousness was not signifi-cantly affected by dissatisfaction. This again proved true when examin-ing the impact of a poor relationship with a landlord on consciousness. This was taken as evidence of the greater overall difficulty of minority tenants' lives that would make tenant issues just another point of friction rather than the central area of concern. This could explain the lower involvement of minority tenants in the tenant movement.

An investigation of the causal relationship between consciousness and experience disclosed that experience appeared to play a major role in the formation of consciousness. It was found that the material factor of the percentage of income paid in rent related significantly to the tenants' attitudes about the fairness of the rent. The higher the sheltercost, the more likely the tenant was to think that the rent was unfair, and among those who thought that the rent was unfair, the higher the sheltercost, the more likely they were to think the apartment was also in poor condition. More on this issue is presented in Chapter 8.

The tenants' relationships with their landlords also related significantly to their level of tenant consciousness. However, the relationship was much more regular in the county, with the poorer the relationship, the higher the consciousness. In Santa Monica only at the extremes were the levels of consciousness dramatically different. The reason for this difference is largely explained in the second portion of the chapter.

In both the case of residential satisfaction and relationship to the landlord, age proved to be significantly related to the tenants' responses. The younger the tenants, the less satisfied they were and the poorer their relationships with the landlords. This finding, along with similar findings in the second part of the chapter, appeared to be important in explaining the lower consciousness of seniors.

In the second part of the chapter, the impact of having a history of negative experiences was examined. As a general rule, the more conflicts and forced moves tenants had experienced over their lives as tenants, the higher their consciousness, although again the relationship was more regular in the county sample. Disputes about rents seemed to generate higher consciousness than other disputes, including those about conditions. This was particularly true in Santa Monica.

The differences between the county and Santa Monica findings, with regards to the impact of such a history on consciousness, as well as problems with the present landlords, appeared to be explained by the impact on consciousness of knowledge of friends' problems. Substantially more tenants in the politically active Santa Monica tenant population were aware of friends having had problems with landlords. This had a particularly significant impact on the consciousness of those who had no problems of their own. This seemed to demonstrate what is gained when a movement is formed and an environment politicized. Those tenants without either a personal history of problems or knowledge of friends having had problems had exceptionally low consciousness in Santa Monica. These tenants were totally isolated from the experiential base of the movement.

Overall, about a half of the county population and two-thirds of the Santa Monica population had direct or indirect histories of tenant problems. This seems to indicate that although tenants may be relatively happy with their present rental situations and landlords and not immediately organizable at their buildings, they may still be potential supporters of the tenant movement.

As in the first portion of the chapter, it was found that having a history of problems was significantly related to age. This seems to be explained by the different nature of tenants' situations across age groups. With seniors, in particular, the problem is not so much the landlord's choice of rent level as the lack of income. Although seniors supported rent control out of necessity, the desire for broad reform was lacking. Young tenants, in contrast, are working and trying to engage in the process of petty accumulation. In this context Skidmore's analysis seemed more relevant. The landlord can be seen as expropriating the product of the tenants' labor in the competition for accumulation. This hypothesis will be reexamined in Chapter 7, when the desire for homeownership is considered.

NOTES

1. The difference in household size between the samples resulted largely from the presence of a larger percentage of tenants under 40 living alone in Santa Monica.

2. It was anticipated that resident ownership would be a significant factor.It did prove to significantly affect the relationship with the landlord (better with resident landlords), but not tenant consciousness. See Chapter 5, Note 21 for discussion.

3. In the county the larger the building the more likely the tenant was to believe the rent was unfair. For a comparison of the behavior of different types of landlords, see Krohn et al. (1977). For a discussion of impact of ownership on relationship to the landlord, see Chapter 5, Note 20.

4. *Tenant Consciousness:* One unit–63 percent; two units 66 percent; three-four units–57 percent; five-nine units–64 percent; ten-twenty units–64 percent; twenty-one or more units–69 percent.

5. The finding is somewhat more dramatic at the movement levels. *Movement levels:* public-owned–46 percent; company-owned–33 percent; indivdual-owned–23 percent.

6. For example, the longer the tenants had resided in the apartment, the more likely they were to believe the rent was fair. This is likely because such tenants receive "tenure discounts." For a discussion of tenure discounts, see Clark and Heskin (1982).

7. Our measure of overcrowding was calculated by dividing the total number of persons in the household by the number of rooms in the rental unit, excluding bathrooms. Cases with a person-per-room ratio of 1.5 or more were considered to be overcrowded; those with fewer than 1.5 persons per room were not. For a discussion of this and other methods of measuring overcrowding, see R.J. Greenfield and F. Lewis (1980). The authors state that "Generally the person-per-room ratio uses 1.5 persons or more per room as evidence of overcrowding" (p. 174). They caution, however, that this measure has certain shortcomings because it does not take into account "the living-space needs for adequate socialization nor . . . mate-sex configurations in sleeping room arrangements that are culturally acceptable and culturally unacceptable," (p. 176). They advocate the use of their own method of measuring overcrowding, which attempts to take all the aforementioned factors into consideration. For simplicity's sake we have used the crude person-per-room ratio, which according to Greenfield and Lewis, if anything, underestimates the amount of overcrowding in a given population.

8. Three-fourths of the respondents reported both income and rent figures.

9. The four questions were as follows: 1) How satisfied are you with the neighborhood you now live in? 2) How satisfied are you with the apartment or house you are now living in? 3) How would you describe the condition of your house or apartment? and 4) Do you feel that your present rent is fair?

10. Persons who answered either "not at all satisfied' or "not very satisfied" with their rental unit or neighborhood were considered to be not satisfied with their present rental situation.

11. The most dramatic was perception of conditions: poor–70 percent, fair–67 percent, good–61 percent, very good–63 percent. At the movement level the difference was slight, from 28 percent to 25 percent.

12. All four variables also relate significantly to income. When we control the ethnicity/gender categories by income, there are still significant variations among the groups with the overall finding.

13. The nature of the interaction between ethnicity and class as discussed in Chapter 4 was again demonstrated when we control for one against the other. With regards to conditions within each class, for example, ethnicity is a significant factor, but it was only with whites that class comes into play. Among working-class tenants, white men and women were the least dissatisfied with the conditions in which they live (poor or fair–whites 33.7 percent; minorities 55.1 percent), but among white tenants, working-class male and female tenants were the most dissatisfied. Among professional-managerial tenants, whites were again less dissatisfied (Poor or fair–whites 25.6 percent; minorities 44.2 percent), and among whites, the professional-manageral tenants were the least dissatisfied. The image that was created was one that matches empirical reality. Urban minority tenants tend to be segregated into the poorest housing regardless of class (Mandelker et al. 1981, p. 19). In addition among whites the classes are segregated so that the white working-class tenant has the poorest housing among the whites.

14. Similar patterns exist in Santa Monica data, but the percentage of minorities is not sufficient to create a movement-threatening conflict. The primary minority neighborhood in Santa Monica is now organizing with support from the city. It will be interesting to see how this potential conflict is handled. As with tenant consciousness, there is no difference in satisfaction between white men and women in Santa Monica.

15. White men: good condition–53 percent N-152; very good condition–56 percent N = 119.

16. The following chart sets out the data:

Perception of Conditions	Tenant Consciousness	
Poor or very poor	79%	N = 14
Fair	89	N = 45
Good	64	N = 39
Very good	70	N = 34

17. The importance of this factor is demonstrated by the finding that in no instance was the tenants' perception regarding conditions significant in relation to tenant consciousness if they believed the rent was unfair.

18. The respondents who think the rent was unfair had a pattern like the overall finding. Movement levels: blacks–44 percent; white women–39 percent. Individualist: blacks–33 percent; white women–25 percent.

19. Movement: blacks 23 percent–white women 26 percent. Defender: blacks 37 percent–white women 41 percent. Individualist: blacks 33 percent–white women 25 percent.

20. In the county sample 5.2 percent (76) of the respondents did not know who their landlord was. In Santa Monica the figure was 6.2 percent (45). Well over half of the tenants in buildings owned by companies had no relationship with the landlord, compared to less than 20 percent of the cases where individuals own the property; and only about a third of the tenants who lived in buildings owned by companies had good or very good relation-

ships with their landlords, compared to almost two-thirds of those in buildings owned by individuals.

21. Many of the activists mentioned the difficulty of organizing tenants when the owner lived in the building. While this may pose tactical problems of organizing, residency of landlords in their buildings did not significantly relate to tenant consciousness. However, tenants in the county did report better relationships with resident landlords. In the county over 85 percent of the tenants who lived in the same building with the owner reported good or very good relationships with that owner, compared to 70 percent of those whose landlords did not live in the building. In Santa Monica, where there were more such resident owners, the difference was significant but smaller. Seventy-five percent of those with resident landlords had good or very good relationships, compared to 70 percent of the respondents with nonresident landlords. For a discussion of the practices of resident landlords, see Vaughan (1972).

22. County (136) 26.1 percent; Santa Monica (46) 20.1 percent.

23. County (95) 46.1 percent; Santa Monica (63) 45.7 percent.

24. No relationship: minorities (99) 20.9 percent; whites (233) 25.2 percent.

25. Very poor, poor, and fair relationship: minorities (127) 34.1 percent; whites (144) 25 percent.

26. Poor or very poor relationship: white men 73 percent; white women 84.6 percent. Fair relationship: white men 76 percent; white women 88 percent. Good relationship: white men 55 percent; white women 66 percent. Very good relationship: white men 51 percent; white women 65 percent.

27. No differentiation was made between present or past problems or whether there were multiple disputes with one landlord or a single dispute with multiple landlords.

28. No dispute–60 percent; one dispute–60 percent; multiple disputes–81 percent.

29. No dispute–57 percent; one dispute–69 percent; multiple disputes–79 percent.

30. County: No dispute–24 percent; one dispute–22 percent; multiple disputes–35 percent. Santa Monica: No dispute–21 percent; one dispute–21 percent; multiple disputes–36 percent.

31. Rents: LA–85 percent; SM–81 percent; Conditions: LA–78 percent; SM–77 percent.

32. Tenant Consciousness—Friend had Dispute: LA–(460) 76 percent; SM–(300) 76 percent. No, or Don't Know: LA–(991) 59 percent; SM–(426) 54 percent.

33. The number of such tenants is relatively small in the samples. In part because of this, the difference was short of being statistically significant. The difference was more dramatic in Santa Monica. The chi-square score was .08.

34. We formed the groupings based on the consistency in the county data. In Santa Monica the consciousness of tenants with good and very good relationships with their landlords was significantly affected by their past negative experiences. In the county the consciousness of tenants with good relationships with their landlords was raised by past negative experiences, but the consciousness of those with very good relationships was not. This is consistent with differences between the level of tenant movement activity in the two cities. In Santa Monica the powerful movement could build off past negative experience even if the tenants' present situations were very good. In the county a very good present experience seemed to take the edge off the impact of past problems.

35. Blacks with multiple problems: 78 percent tenant consciousness; 45 percent Movement levels (N = 73). White women with multiple problems: 76 percent tenant consciousness; 34 percent movement levels (N = 167). Blacks with no or one problem: 57 percent (N = 134). White women with no or one problem: 60 percent (N = 306).

36. Part of the reason for the loss of statistical significance. was that tenants with negative experiences were much more likely to know of friends' problems. For example,

two-thirds of those in the county and three-quarters of those in Santa Monica who had multiple problems and a forced move had friends who had had problems with a landlord.

37. Age seemed to be central. Ethnicity and gender are statistically related, but this is a product of age. Class was not significantly related.

6

Action Begets Action

While a worsening rental housing situation and landlord-tenant conflict of one form or another are necessary first elements in the emergence of a tenant movement, they are not the only essential elements necessary for the development of that movement. In Gramsci's conceptualization all they do is create a "terrain more favorable" for the movement to form (Adamson 1980, p. 141). The reason Gramsci gave for this was that hegemony, with its dominance in the society, tends to suppress *action*. However, Gramsci went on to state that it is action that is required for higher consciousness to develop (p. 160).[1]

While the activists interviewed for this study did not speak in terms of hegemony, they did agree with Gramsci that it is the initial taking of action by the tenant that is key to the formation of higher consciousness and the building of a movement. Their position was that the impact that the negative experiences of tenancy has on tenant consciousness depends on the action tenants take "against the landlord." The more aggressive and collective the action, the higher the consciousness that will result. The activists saw their job as assisting the tenants in taking that first aggressive and collective action leading to higher consciousness.

The activists believed that more than the tenants' present level of consciousness, that is, the degree of hegemonic domination, determines whether they can be motivated to actively resist landlords' actions. Of primary importance in the activists' concept of the problem was fear—what they called "fear of eviction." This is, of course, not the only factor external to consciousness that can suppress action. Bertell Ollman (1972) in his article, "Towards Class Consciousness Next Time," lists a number of such factors, but Ollman, like the activists, lists fear as the last and most difficult such factor to overcome.

In this chapter an analysis of tenant actions in response to landlord-tenant conflicts discussed in Chapter 5 will be conducted. The question is whether the theories of Gramsci and the activists are supported by the data. The third of the sample that had such problems will be the focus of this investigation. In addition the role of fear of eviction will be examined. It should be noted here, however, that some of the activists stated that the level of this fear of eviction appeared to lessen after the passage of Proposition 13. They said that the passage of the proposition seemed to turn what had been fear into rage. In tones of amazement, several activists told of receiving phone calls after the passage of the proposition in which tenants they had never met stated, "Hello! We are organized and on strike. Now what do we do next?"

THE TENANTS' RESPONSES TO PROBLEMS WITH A LANDLORD

To determine what actions the tenants interviewed took when they had problems with landlords, they were asked a series of questions similar to those asked in the hypothetical rent increase case. They were asked if they simply moved, just talked to the landlord, took some individual action, or joined with their neighbors.[2] In both samples about two-thirds of the tenants took either individual or collective action. As Table 6.1 shows, the major difference between the two samples was that more Santa Monica tenants joined with their neighbors, that is, organized.

Table 6.1. *Response to Landlord-Tenant Conflicts (Los Angeles County and Santa Monica Samples)*

	Los Angeles County		Santa Monica	
Moved	(16)	3.8%	(5)	2.2%
Talked to Landlord	(139)	33.3	(65)	28.1
Took Individual Action	(175)	41.9	(98)	42.2
Organized	(88)	21.1	(63)	27.3

In examining the two major categories of conflict, conditions and rents, it was found that the responses to disputes involving rents generate substantially more aggressive tenant action than disputes regarding conditions, particularly in Santa Monica. Table 6.2 sets out the responses to both types of conflict. In Santa Monica organizing against a rent increase actually has been the most common response reported.

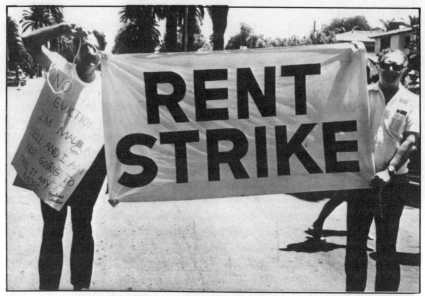

Photos: Paul Gleye. Reprinted by permission.

Although the tenants did not organize against rent increases in the same percentages as the populations indicated they would in response to the hypothetical, they did act aggressively, considering both individual and collective actions, in proportions that rival or exceed the stated intentions of the samples. Eighty percent of both samples said they would consider taking individual or collective action or both. In the county this was the same percentage that took such action. In Santa Monica the actual response was greater than indicated by the responses to the hypothetical case. The shortfall in collective action may be be-

Table 6.2. *Responses to Landlord–Tenant Conflicts Involving Conditions and Rents (Los Angeles County and Santa Monica Samples)*

| | Los Angeles County | | Santa Monica | |
	Conditions	Rents	Conditions	Rents
Moved	(10) 3.6%	(3) 2.7%	(1) .7%	(1) 1.4%
Talked to Landlord	(80) 28.8	(21) 18.6	(39) 25.8	(7) 9.5
Took Individual Action	(119) 42.8	(56) 49.6	(67) 44.4	(30) 40.5
Organized	(69) 24.8	(33) 29.2	(44) 29.1	(36) 48.6

cause the opportunity to take such action did not present itself. The tenants who faced objectionable rent increases may have lived in single-family houses, or the dispute may have been resolved short of collective action.

In instances where those involved met with their neighbors about the problem (LA (64) 50.2 percent; SM (58) 77.3 percent), the incidence of collective action was higher. In Santa Monica it is the same as the stated intention. Two-thirds of the tenants who met with their neighbors in Santa Monica organized to resist a rent increase. In the county just over one-half of these tenants did the same. Table 6.3 sets out these data.

Table 6.3. *Responses to Landlord–Tenant Conflicts Compared to Intentions of Organizing in a Hypothetical Future Situation (Los Angeles County and Santa Monica Samples)*

	Los Angeles County Will Organize		Santa Monica Will Organize	
Moved	(9)	56.3%	(2)	40.0%
Talked to Landlord	(87)	62.6	(43)	66.2
Took Individual Action	(140)	80.0	(76)	77.6
Organized	(79)	89.9	(60)	95.2

In addition to creating an inference that there may be a great deal of reality in the findings regarding the potential for aggressive tenant action in the future, this data comparison also seems to indicate that, as hypothesized, taking aggressive action encourages further aggressive action. Tenants who have organized seem very willing to do it again, and tenants who had taken the step of individual resistance seem prime candidates for organizing in a future situation.

Although most of the activists interviewed believe action begets action, it should be noted that not all activists ascribe to this position without qualification (Burghardt, S. 1967). It is said that activism that ends poorly can be a tremendous drain of energy rather than consciousness raising.

While the general finding was that action begets action, it was found in some situations that how the tenant fared in past actions affects future intentions. In particular those tenants in the county who took individual or collective action and who ended up evicted in their past conflicts were significantly less interested in trying collective action in the future. Interestingly, in Santa Monica this was not true. Table 6.4 sets out the data on this point.

Table 6.4. *Responses to Landlord–Tenant Conflicts Compared to Intentions of Organizing in a Hypothetical Future Situation of Evicted and Not Evicted Tenants (Los Angeles County and Santa Monica Samples)*

| | Los Angeles County Will Organize | | Santa Monica Will Organize | |
	Evicted	Not Evicted	Evicted	Not Evicted
Individual Action	(18) 66.7%	(122) 82.4%	(17) 85.6%	(58) 76.3%
Organized	(10) 71.4	(69) 93.2	(12) 92.3	(47) 95.9

The difference between the county and Santa Monica was likely explained by the presence of a visible citywide movement in Santa Monica. In the county aggressive but evicted tenants could feel very alone in their new apartments without the support of tenants with whom they previously joined. In Santa Monica, evicted or not, they were still part of the movement. This seems to be very important in understanding the effect of having a recognized, successful movement and how such a movement renews and sustains itself even in the face of individual crises.

In both samples, as predicted, there was a strong relationship between the action taken and tenant consciousness. Those tenants who limited their responses to moving or talking to the landlord did not have high consciousness. In fact their consciousness was less than the overall average in each data set. The highest-consciousness group was made up of those who had joined with their neighbors. These tenants were followed closely by those who took individual action. Figure 6.1 set out the results for Santa Monica. The county results were similar.

In each sample, more than 40 percent of the tenants who had organized were at the movement levels and few had less than defender consciousness. When the outcome of the landlord-tenant conflict was controlled for, it was found that the outcome had no significant effect on the overall consciousness of those who took individual or collective action, even though those who were evicted in the county said they would take less action in the future. This indicated that although an eviction dissuaded a portion of the county population from action, it did not reduce their support for the other elements of tenant consciousness.

Figure 6.1.   *Tenant Consciousness by Response to Landlord-Tenant Conflict (Santa Monica Sample)*

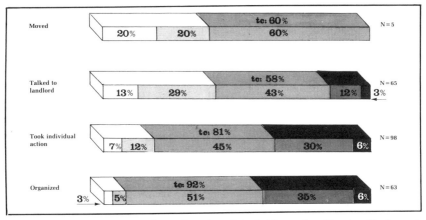

Note: *Please see Figure 4.1 for explanation of shaded bar codes. The classifications, in order, are; 1) Antagonist; 2) Individualist; 3) Defender; 4) Consumer; and 5) Radicalized.*

The actions the tenants took, as a general proposition, had no relationship to the demographics. However, it must be remembered that much of variance of age was factored out by limiting the analysis to tenants who stated they had experienced a landlord-tenant conflict. In spite of this, age was significantly related to the responses in Santa Monica. Tenants under 30 years of age were most likely to take individual or collective action, while the seniors were the most likely to have moved or talked to the landlord.

Several other observations are worth note from the data on tenant responses to problems. In about a quarter of the cases involving rent or conditions disputes, the tenants withheld all or part of the rent,[3] less than 10 percent of the disputes resulted in legal action against the landlord[4] and, not surprisingly, Santa Monica tenants complained to their increasingly protenant government 50 percent more often in the case of rent disputes than in the county, as a whole.

FEAR OF EVICTION

The findings in the first portion of this chapter are, with regards to the
willingness to act, consistent with what the activists reported. Since the
passage of Proposition 13, organizers said they had found a much more
aggressive tenant population than they had experienced in the past.
Previous to the passage of Proposition 13, the activists stated that a "fear
of eviction" significantly restrained tenant organization.

In terms of this study, this change can be seen in the large number of
tenants at the defender level of consciousness. The activists would have
predicted a much larger percentage of individualists and fewer defenders had this study been done a few years earlier. They stated that
their problem today is more moving tenants from the defender level to
the movement levels. Previously they had to move tenants from the
individualist to the defender category.

As was seen in the previous section, there were still tenants who
were very afraid of being evicted. The activists said that even high-
consciousness tenants involved in movement activity sometimes asked
to be assigned to work in another part of town than the one in which they
lived so that their landlords would not know what they were doing. In
particular the activists stated that aged and disabled people, the people
who couldn't physically move, were still very afraid of being forced to
move. Further, they said that not all tenants who were not afraid were
now willing to stand and fight. The activists made special note of tenants with high mobility, in particular, the higher-income tenants, who
they stated would rather move than fight.

One of the reasons that the fear of eviction may have decreased was
that recently passed rent control laws provided eviction protection. As a
result, tenants in rent controlled jurisdictions had a great deal more to
fight with and about when threatened with an eviction than they had
previously. California state law provides that a tenant without a lease
may be evicted with 30 days notice without cause. However, when there
is rent control, under local law, tenants may be evicted only with "just
cause." As was stated in Chapter 2, disagreements over the definition
and enforcement of these eviction protections have occurred in all rent
controlled areas. However, regardless of what "just cause" protection
means, its presence in the law gives organizers a way to respond to
questions about the possibility of strong action against a landlord leading to an eviction and, in the process, quell the fears of tenants in a
manner not available in California in earlier periods.

In all Southern California cases except Santa Monica, the local rent
control ordinances contain vacancy decontrol provisions. This means
that if a tenant moves, he or she, in effect, loses much of the benefits of

"No," said Sally. "It won't help to move because rents are going up everywhere. And I don't even know who to talk to.
It just says here the tree-owner is MoneyTree Corp."
"Oh no!" cried the kids. "Not another giant Corp!"
"But I'm so mad," said Sally. "I'm going to find this MoneyTree Corp anyway, and tear it limb from limb!"

Downtown she found MoneyTree Corp.
"Uncle Greedy! What are you doing in here?"
"I run this branch of MoneyTree Corp. Aren't you proud of me?"
"No I'm not!" said Sally. "You should be ashamed of yourself -- raising our rent!"
"I'm sorry, but our profits must be protected."
"But my home and **children** must be protected!" she said angrily.
"You should be glad **I even let** children live there. Most tree-owners don't anymore. Besides you're lucky I haven't made your tree into Condos yet."

"You wouldn't dare," she yelled. "And who gave you the right to own my tree anyway? It just grew there. You didn't have anything to do with it."
"But your home in the tree had to be built by someone."
"Did you build it with your own hands Uncle Greedy?"
"No, of course not. But I'm buying it."
"With my rent money, right?" shouted Sally.
"Right," smiled Uncle Greedy. "You see the law says every tree is owned by somebody. I own your tree, and the law lets me charge whatever I want for your beautiful home."
"200 acorns for that hole?" said Sally. "Nuts to you!"

Illustrations by Lance Jordan, from the Coloring Book Tale, "Can Sally Pay the Rent?" Copyright 1979 by William A. Eddy. Ocean Beach Community School, P.O. Box 7423, San Diego, CA 92107. Reprinted by permission.

rent control. The new landlord may charge the moving tenant whatever the market will bear. In a study of the effect of rent control with vacancy decontrol in the City of Los Angeles, a sharp drop in mobility was noted, particularly among the moderate-income and minority tenants (Clark and Heskin 1981). Only the unsettled, single, low-income tenant and the relatively wealthy and white tenants seemed substantially unaffected. The study indicated that tenants who moved could expect about a 25 percent increase in rent in the year in which they moved. A tenant who had been in a one-bedroom apartment for three years would have to pay about $800 more a year in rent. A tenant who had spent the same length of time in a two-bedroom apartment would have to pay about $1,200 more a year. In either case the rent control ordinance had structured in a considerable inducement to stand and fight if possession was threatened.

In Santa Monica this inducement could be even greater. The law in that city has no vacancy decontrol provision, and the rent board in Santa Monica has granted lower annual increases than those granted in the other cities and in the county. Moving meant assuming the risk of having to leave the city and the protection of Santa Monica's law.

To test for the tenants' fear of eviction, two questions were asked. They were placed in the survey instrument after the questions on how the tenant would respond to an unfair rent increase. The first question asked whether the respondents would take more or less action in their choice of action by a threat of eviction by the landlord as opposed to a rent increase. The answer "unaffected" was also accepted. This question was followed by an open-ended question about what problems an eviction would cause.

Because fear of eviction should result in a retreat from action rather than willingness to fight, the "more action" response was interpreted as indicative of lack of fear of eviction. Consistent with this approach, the "less action" response was taken as indicative of fear of eviction. The "no effect" response was interpreted as representing a lack of concern and high mobility. The answers regarding the problems of moving were to serve as a check to our interpretation.

As predicted, the overwhelming response of the tenants in both samples was that they would take more action if threatened with eviction. In the county sample, for example, nearly 80 percent of the tenants responded that they would take more action. The second most prominent response was that the threat of eviction would have no effect. Approximately 15 percent gave this response. The smallest group of responses, at about 5 percent, was that the tenant would be inclined to take less action. The mix of responses was similar in Santa Monica.

The general appropriateness of the measure of fear of eviction was established by its strong relationship with the scores on the action scale.[5] The action scale included both the measures of what actions a tenant would take in response to an unfair rent increase and whether he or she would do movement work. As shown in Table 6.5, the higher the score on the action scale, the more likely a tenant was to answer that he or she would likely take more action if threatened with an eviction. The lower the score on the action scale, the more likely a tenant was to reply that he or she would not be affected either way. The third response, less likely to take action, was, appropriately, less coherently related to the action scale. These were the tenants who would shy away from the actions they indicated they would take in response to an unfair rent increase.

Table 6.5. *Action Scale by Effect of Threat of Eviction on Choice of Action (Los Angeles County Sample)*

Action Scale	More Likely		Less Likely		No Effect	
1 No Action	(96)	53.0%	(17)	9.4%	(68)	37.6%
2 Individual	(164)	71.0	(13)	5.7	(52)	22.7
3 Tenant Union						
Member	(297)	77.5	(26)	6.8	(60)	15.7
4 Movement Worker	(280)	90.6	(7)	2.3	(22)	7.1
5 Organizer	(253)	90.4	(9)	3.2	(18)	6.4

With this strong relationship between responses to the threat of eviction question and the action scale, it is not surprising that the responses also related significantly to tenant consciousness. Those who would take more action (little fear of eviction) tend to have high consciousness, with 71 percent at the defender level or above, and those who would not be affected (no fear of eviction–high mobility) tend to have low consciousness, with 61 percent below the defender level. The tenants who stated a threat of eviction would result in less action (fear of eviction or no mobility) were in the middle. This group probably contains some of the people the activists feared would move down a notch in consciousness if the going got too difficult. The results were similar in Santa Monica, with the exception that tenants who would not be affected have even lower consciousness (about 7 percent less, with 7 percent more antagonists). Figure 6.2 illustrates the county data on this point.

In general the responses to this question were not related to the demographics. The only exception was age. The older the respondent, the less likely he or she was to take more action. For example, 86 percent

Figure 6.2. *Tenant Consciousness of Respondents to Threat of Eviction Question (Los Angeles County Sample)*

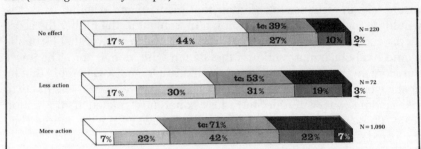

Note: *Please see Figure 4.1 for explanation of shaded bar codes. The classifications, in order, are; 1) Antagonist; 2) Individualist; 3) Defender; 4) Consumer; and 5) Radicalized.*

of the tenants under 30 years of age would take more action as a result of a threat of eviction, compared to 63 percent of the seniors. Conversely, 28 percent of the seniors would be unaffected by a threat, compared to 11 percent of the under 30 groups, and 8 percent of the seniors would take less action, compared to 4 percent of the tenants under 30 years of age.

Age, of course, related to the question of taking action in general. However, age also relates strongly to mobility. The study of the impact of rent control on the City of Los Angeles found that 46 percent of the tenants under 26 years of age moved in the year of the study, compared to 9 percent of those 65 years of age or older. Whether what was being measured was what was referred to as the infirmities of age, or in fact a greater fear of eviction, becomes an issue here. More information on this question will be available when the responses to the second question in this section are examined.

There was one other characteristic that also related to the responses to the threat of eviction question. Respondents who were parents, particularly the fathers, were significantly more likely to say they would take more action. In Chapter 4, fathers were identified as a high-consciousness group, but parents, in general, did not have significantly higher consciousness. Here, however, the impact of discrimination against children, which makes this group considerably less mobile than others, may be expressing itself.

The fact that ethnicity, gender, class, and income were not significantly related to the response to this question indicated the very broad and consistent pattern of responses. This seemed to argue against the activists' prediction that the response of high-income tenants, particularly the mobile, would be different from that of the other respondents. However, when the demographics were held constant, it was found that the mobile did have a different response pattern. The only groups with which fear of eviction did not significantly affect consciousness were white men, professional-managerial men, and respondents with $30,000 or more family income, the most mobile groups in our society. Their apparent lack of concern may be representative of what the activists referred to.

While the responses to the threat of eviction question did not generally relate to the demographics, they did relate to all the variables discussed in the last chapter. Tenants were more likely to give an aggressive response to the threat of eviction question if their apartment was in less than satisfactory condition, they did not have a good relationship with their landlord, or they had experienced a problem with a landlord, been forced to move, or had friends that had such problems. The relationship between the responses to the question at hand and these variables seemed to reaffirm the position of the activists that tenants were more willing to fight for possession of their homes.

The responses to the second question regarding the problems an eviction would cause were coded and clustered.[6] Nine discernible clusters of responses were identified. As seen in Table 6.6, the most common response, consistent with the effect of moving under rent control with vacancy decontrol, was that an eviction would result in higher costs.

Table 6.6.   *Problems an Eviction Would Cause (Los Angeles County and Santa Monica Samples)*

	Los Angeles County		Santa Monica	
Cost	(513)	36.3%	(215)	30.8%
Looking	(234)	16.5	(112)	16.0
No Place	(149)	10.5	(72)	10.3
Attached	(129)	9.1	(80)	11.4
Child	(126)	8.9	(38)	5.4
Inconvenience	(124)	8.8	(117)	16.7
None	(66)	4.7	(36)	5.2
Aged or Disabled	(49)	3.5	(21)	3.0
Pet	(25)	1.8	(8)	1.1

The next was needing to look for a new place, which can either be taken as a statement of the obvious or a recognition of Los Angeles' tight housing market. This response, in turn, was followed by the serious concern that the tenant would not be able to find another place to live or that the tenant would have to move away from an apartment or neighborhood to which he or whe was attached. Next came concern with finding a place that would take a child, and the general category that covers a variety of minor annoyances under the title of inconvenience. Inconvenience was a more common answer in Santa Monica than in the county. Finally, there were a few respondents who felt it would present no problem, who were aged or disabled and could not move, or who had a pet and were concerned that they would not find a new place that would take their pet.

The responses to this question related significantly to the answers to the threat of eviction question in both samples. Table 6.7 sets out the county sample results.[7] The pattern in Santa Monica was quite similar.

Table 6.7. *Overrepresented Responses About Problems and Eviction Would Cause by Response to a Threat of Eviction (Los Angeles County Sample)*

	More Likely to Take Action		Less Likely to Take Action		No Effect	
Child	(106)	10.0%	—		—	
Attached	(103)	9.7	—		—	
Cost	(407)	38.3	—		—	
No Place	(115)	10.8	—		—	
Inconvenient	—		(9)	12.9%	—	
Aged or Disabled	—		(7)	10.0	(10)	4.7%
None	—		(5)	7.1	(24)	11.4
Looking	—		(12)	17.1	(46)	21.8
Pet	—		—		(5)	2.4

Tenants who said they would take more aggressive action tended to give the more serious responses, such as having to encounter discrimination against children, having no place to which to move, or being attached to their apartment or neighborhood. In contrast the people who would not take more action against a threat of eviction than against a rent increase tended to give the least serious responses. They tended to respond that they would be inconvenienced, have to look for another place to live, or that an eviction wouldn't create any problems. The sole exceptions to this clear division were the tenants who gave the very serious response that they were aged or disabled. These tenants were inclined to say they would take less action or that they would not be affected. This group, however, is the group the activists mentioned as having no mobility and great fear of eviction.

The picture that emerges from the data shows that tenants caught in the tight Los Angeles housing market with limited mobility were the tenants most willing to fight for possession of their homes. Those who were most likely to shy from such a fight were the tenants with no mobility or those who had relatively high mobility. This was consistent with the activists' position. If tenants' new, increased aggressiveness is related to this limited mobility, there is every reason to believe that tenant activism is here for some years to come. A tight housing market seems to be likely for some time (Sternlieb and Hughes 1981).

The responses to the question about what problem an eviction would cause also significantly related to tenant consciousness in the county. The relationship was similar to that between the problems an eviction would cause and the action that would result from a threat of eviction. Movement-level tenants, whether radicalized or consumer, tended to give the responses indicating restricted mobility, including having a child, there being no place to which to move and cost. In addition the consumers tended to respond that they were attached to the apartment or neighborhood. Defenders gave a mixed set of responses, including costs, attachment, having a pet, and inconvenience. Individualists and antagonists tended to give the responses indicating high mobility or no mobility, including looking, none, or aged, and disabled. Table 6.8 sets out the findings on this point.

Table 6.8. *Overrepresented Responses About Problems an Eviction Would Cause by Tenant Consciousness* *(Los Angeles County Sample)*

	Radicalized		Consumer		Defender		Individualist		Antagonist	
Child	(14)	17.9%	(26)	9.4%	—		—		—	
No Place	(11)	14.1	(34)	12.3	—		(42)	11.3%	—	
Cost	(29)	37.2	(110)	39.7	(202)	39.4%	—		(51)	36.7%
Attached	—		(29)	22.5	(64)	11.7	—		—	
Pet	—		—		(15)	2.7	—		—	
Inconvenience	—		—		(52)	9.5	—		(16)	11.5
Aged or Disabled	—		—		—		(21)	5.6	(8)	5.8
Looking	—		—		—		(82)	22.0	(28)	20.1
None	—		—		—		(18)	4.8	(10)	7.2

Two exceptions to a consistent pattern existed in the data. Individualists were overrepresented among those who responded that there would be no place to go to if they were evicted; and antagonists were overrepresented among those who stated an eviction would mean increased costs. The response of the individualists may be, in part, an expression of the remaining hard core of the fear of eviction. This group was primarily low-income and elderly. The antagonists who responded that an eviction would mean increased costs, however, were more middle-aged and higher-income. Increased cost, while mentioned, may not have been a serious problem for this group. Also, two-thirds of that group of antagonists had never had a negative experience, nor did they know anyone who had. It may be that while they knew an eviction would mean increased costs, they did not think an eviction was likely. Perhaps, for this same reason, they were also more likely to say they would not be affected by a threat of eviction or that they would be less likely to take action.

The responses to the problems that an eviction would cause in the county also related significantly to all the demographic characteristics. Tenants overrepresented among those who indicated an eviction would have serious consequences, such as increased costs or that they would have no place to go, tended to be young or middle-aged, have incomes under $20,000 a year, be working-class and Latino or white women. Those tenants who indicated less serious or no problems, including inconvenience or having to look for a new place, tended to be between 30 and 59, have more than $20,000 annual family income, to be a working-class or professional-managerial man or petty bourgeois, and be either a white man or black. The respondents who indicated they were attached to their apartments are more distinguishable by who they were not than by who they were. They were not likely to be senior, to have less than $10,000 a year income, be a working-class man or black. The tenants who indicated having a child would be a problem were heavily between 30 and 39, with under $10,000 a year income, working-class, and minority. The tenants who indicated age or disability as a problem, in addition to being seniors, tended to have less than $10,000 annual income, and be women, regardless of class, and white.

These results are consistent with much of what was found in Chapter 4 about the relationship between demographics and tenant consciousness. Age, gender, ethnicity, and income all were factors in how an eviction would affect a tenant, in much the same way as they related to tenant consciousness. The similarity of the relationship seemed to indicate that tenants' perceptions of their mobility may have been a very important component in determining their level of consciousness in the county. This is consistent with the conclusion that tenants' day-to-day experiences were the major factors determining tenant consciousness in the county.

The finding that blacks were overrepresented in those stating relatively minor problems was surprising. However, it may help explain the apparent inconsistency in the earlier findings. In Chapter 4 white women were found to have higher overall consciousness than blacks, with a heavy concentration of blacks at the individualist level. This was true even though in Chapter 5, it was found that blacks were, across the board, less satisfied with their apartments than white women. Here, the difference in consciousness of blacks and white women appeared to be highly related to the two groups' perceptions of what problems an eviction would cause. In particular the response "looking," was given by nearly a quarter of blacks, compared to 15 percent of the rest of the population, and 71 percent of the blacks who gave this answer were in the individualist category.

This response also seemed to contribute to understanding the findings in the next chapter regarding consciousness and expectations about buying a home among blacks. Blacks who were apparently frustrated about not being able to buy a home were again unusually concentrated at the individualist level. When the intersection between expectations about buying a home and problems an eviction would cause was examined, it was found that among tenants stating disappointment about not being able to buy, the response "looking" was again much more common among blacks.

In general tenants who expected to buy in the next few years tended not to be very concerned with problems of eviction, while tenants who said they could not buy tended to be very concerned about such an eventuality. It was as though the inability to escape tenancy through buying a home increased the concern about being evicted. With a portion of the black population, this did not appear to be true. It may be that with this group, a high sense of mobility among apartments lessened the impact of not being able to buy a home.

An alternative explanation is also possible. The finding with regards to this portion of the black population is reminiscent of the findings of such studies as *Black Rage* (1968). In that study William Grier and Price Cobbs discuss how generation after generation of blacks, starting with slavery, have been taught to suppress their anger in order to survive in this society. Blacks' experiences, in this regard, are unique among the populations studied. It is possible to interpret the response "looking" in this passive sense. However, it should be remembered, so as to not overstate what has been found, that blacks were also quite prominent at the movement levels of consciousness.

Three additional groups of respondents deserve special attention in this portion of the study: the people who mentioned having children as a problem, the aged and disabled, and those living in unsatisfactory conditions.

Children

The problem of discrimination against children in the rental industry is well-documented. A recently published survey conducted by the United States Department of Housing and Urban Development (1980) found that, nationwide, one out of four rental units were not available to families with children. A study by the Fair Housing Project (1979) found the problem in the City of Los Angeles to be even more severe. An analysis of advertised rental units disclosed that over 70 percent would not accept children.

In this study just over a quarter of the renters with children in the county sample specifically mentioned the problem of finding a place that would take children. An additional 8 percent of the renters with children stated that they would not be able to find another place to rent. This categorization of their responses may be, in part, a difference in recording or coding the responses. If it is assumed that the reason this group anticipated it would not be able to locate another place was because of having a child, this would mean a third of the respondents with children indicated fear of discrimination against having a child.

Photo: Ralph Mechur, Ocean Park Perspective. *Reprinted by permission.*

When the demographics of the tenants in the county who reported this problem were examined, it was found that lower-income minority women were most likely to give this response. This finding is in contrast with the HUD conclusion that minorities do not encounter this problem more than others.[8] The HUD report also stated that single women did not have the problem more than married couples. The findings here were again somewhat different. Married and never-married parents gave similar respones, but divorced or separated parents were significantly more concerned. The difference was between about a quarter of the first group and a third of the second.

The lower percentage of concerned married respondents resulted in large part from the inclusion of a significant percentage of men among the married respondents. About 20 percent of the married men gave the response of being concerned with children. Almost stereotypically, the men with children tended to give the response of increased costs rather than having children. Working-class men gave both the child and cost responses more often than professional-managerial fathers.

Earlier it was noted that tenants with children did not, in general, have higher consciousness than others. The exception was with men who had children. The findings were very similar here. While tenants with children had a higher percentage at the movement levels than other groups, thanks largely to the high consciousness of fathers who reported having children as a possible problem in moving,[9] they did not have particularly high consciousness overall.[10] The pattern of responses of these tenants was very much like the pattern of the other tenants facing difficult problems.[11] The highest overall consciousness was actually found among those attached to their homes and those with pets, because of heavy concentration at the defender level.[12]

Aged and Disabled

The aged and disabled were a group the activists singled out as particularly lacking in mobility and justifiably afraid of eviction. Their problem was not just finding another place to live, but physically moving. About 15 percent of the respondents 60 years of age or older stated that their age or disability would make an eviction a problem. When this group was examined in greater detail, it was found that with increasing age, the percentage of tenants who state this problem increased. The increase was from 13 percent of the 60 to 69 group to 23 percent of those 80 and older.

This group of tenants, as a whole, have very low consciousness and scored particularly low on the action scale.[13] When seniors, such as these, try to resist a landlord, it can be very frightening. A Santa Monica activist related a story of trying to organize a group of seniors that illustrates the point. He told the story, having to pause as his voice broke several times.

The activist was helping to organize a 16-unit building occupied largely by seniors. The landlord of this property had been giving 10 percent rent increases every two months for six months and had done no maintenance at all on the building during this period. The combination of rent increases and very serious maintenance problems that were increasing drove the tenants to organize. The landlord attempted to intimidate those who were organizing by observing the tenants' meetings and writing down the names of the tenants who attended. At one meeting, the landlord waited outside the apartment at which the meeting was taking place. When the meeting ended and the tenants began to file out, the landlord served 30-day eviction notices on all the tenants in attendance. The shock of this action caused one of the tenants, a 84-year-old-man, to sink to his knees and beg the landlord not to evict him. The overall effect of the landlord's action was to end the organizing effort.

The activist's spirits rose as he reported, with a smile, that two of the senior tenants, unbeknownst to the landlord, joined the tenant movement and worked in the successful effort to bring rent control and security of tenure to the city.

Tenants Living in Poor Conditions

The last group worthy of note were the tenants who stated they were less than satisfied with the conditions in which they lived. As was seen in the last chapter, these tenants tend to have high consciousness. It was also true that they tended to believe that an eviction would have more serious consequences than those tenants living in units they said were in good or very good condition. The tenants who stated they lived in poor or very poor conditions were overrepresented in the groups that stated that there would be no place to go to, that it would be hard to find a place that would take a child, or that they were either aged or disabled. The tenants living in units that they stated were in fair condition were also overrepresented in the "no place to go" and "child" categories, and, in addition, they were overrepresented among tenants who stated increased cost would accrue. Taken as a group, the "poor" and "fair" conditions respondents gave the more serious responses in two-thirds of the cases, compared to one-half of the cases involving tenants living in conditions they felt were good or very good. This seems at least a partial answer to why they remain in units that they consider less than satisfactory and how this lack of mobility contributes to increased frustration and higher consciousness.

As was stated, the variables that identified the problems an eviction would cause did not have a significant relationship to tenant consciousness in Santa Monica. The reason for this was that movement-level consciousness tenants were overrepresented both among those who stated they would be inconvenienced and that an eviction would not cause any problem. This appeared to be a product of the breadth of the tenant movement in Santa Monica. It was the white men and the professional-managerial men and petty bourgeois that were responsible for the "inconvenience" and "no problem" scores among movement level tenants. However, these were the people, who, as will be seen in the next chapter, felt cut off from being able to buy a home.

SUMMARY

This chapter examined the impact of engaging in resistance to landlord actions had on tenant consciousness and the extent to which fear of eviction had restrained that resistance. In theory it is the taking of action that raises consciousness. Through collective action, in particular, the domination of hegemony is thought to be weakened. Regardless of the extent of this domination, material condition can also prevent action. Fear of eviction is such a constraint.

A significant relationship between resistance to landlord actions, as those examined in the previous chapter, and tenant consciousness was found. Importantly, those who engaged in action in the past were quite willing to do it again. An exception to this general rule was found in the county. Tenants who were evicted as a result of their previous resistance were less willing to try it again than those who were not evicted. In Santa Monica this exception did not exist. In fact tenants who took individual action against their landlords and were evicted seemed more willing to take collective action in the future. The difference between the two samples was explained by the strong presence of the tenant movement in Santa Monica. Tenants evicted in the county likely became isolated from their previous organizing partners. In Santa Monica the movement provided a continuing collective presence.

The activists interviewed in this study stated that the fear of eviction had been a major constraint on tenant resistance to landlord actions. With the passage of Proposition 13, tenants became quite willing to organize at the building level and often moved ahead of the activists. The findings were consistent with these statements. Most tenants stated that they would be more likely to take action against a landlord who threatened them with an eviction than one who just gave an unfair rent increase. Responses to this question seemed to be an extension of the already discussed aggressive responses of the tenant interviewed. The more aggressive the action the tenant stated he or she would take to a proposed "unfair" rent increase, the more aggressive the response would be to a threatened eviction. Consistent with this, the more aggressive the response, the higher the consciousness of the respondent.

The responses to the threat of eviction question were significantly related to the tenants' sense of mobility. As a general rule, the less mobile the tenants believed they were, the more aggressive the response. The primary exception to this rule was with the aged and disabled, who had no mobility. They seemed to have great fear of eviction and were not at all aggressive. Aside from the rage generated by landlords' failure to respond to the passage of Proposition 13, it was noted that the present rent control laws contain both protection from eviction and inducements to resist eviction not present earlier. Just cause to evict laws give tenants a way to resist landlord action and vacancy decontrol creates the financial incentive to resist.

The responses to the mobility question generally matched the distribution of consciousness among the various demographic groups examined in Chapter 4. This created the impression that a tenant's sense of mobility is very much of the everyday experience that contributes to the formation of tenant consciousness. Interestingly, white men, professional-managerial men, and higher-income tenants in the county, that is, the most mobile tenants, were the only groups that did not seem to be affected by the mobility issue. In Santa Monica mobility was not significantly related to aggressiveness or tenant consciousness. However, the type of mobility examined in this chapter was interapartment mobility. In the next chapter it is seen that intertenure moves, that is, homebuying, were more important in Santa Monica with these more mobile groups than in the county and helps explain the difference between the two samples.

NOTES

1. It should be noted that this is only the next step in the process and not enough for the counter-hegemonic movement that Gramsci writes about. This will be discussed later in the book.

2. We should keep in mind in this analysis that we are reporting on a subset of tenants who defined one or more interactions with a landlord as a problem. Low-consciousness tenants may have had similar situations, but not defined them as problems. We cannot know how often this has occurred.

3. In the county, younger tenants and English-speaking Latinos and blacks were significantly more likely to refuse to pay their rent in response to a problem than others, and no seniors, at all, chose this tactic.

4. In the county it is worth noting that legal action was primarily the tool of the wealthiest tenants, with $30,000 or more income. They reported taking legal action three times as often as other tenants.

5. See Chapter 3 for a detailed discussion of the action scale.

6. About 40 percent of the respondents gave multiple answers. In these instances, the most serious and most specific responses were selected.

7. Only the overrepresented responses are set out for emphasis.

8. It was found that professional-managerial women (41.4 percent) were more often concerned with the problem than working-class women (30.9 percent). It should be noted that working-class women make up an overwhelming majority of women with children (88 percent) in the county sample.

9. Forty-eight percent (23) of the working-class fathers who reported having children as a problem were at the movement levels. Only two professional-managerial fathers reported this problem.

10. Sixty-eight percent overall consciousness; movement levels 33 percent.

11. No place to go–66 percent; costs–67 percent.

12. Attached–77 percent, defender–50 percent; pets–76 percent, defender–60 percent.

13. Forty-three percent individualists: 59 percent below defender.

CHAPTER

7

The American Dream

Landlord-tenant conflict, while definitely intrusive into a tenant's every-day life, would not be expected to be the only source of tenant consciousness. In the historical review in Chapter 1, this did not appear to be the case, and it would not be expected to be the case today. In that chapter it was theorized that a struggle for petty accumulation underlies landlord-tenant conflict and that homeownership is very much a part of that accumulation process. Any interruption in the expected process of accumulation should have its impact on tenant consciousness.

The organizers interviewed in this study believed that the difficulty tenants were having in buying homes played a role in the emergence of the tenant movement as a political force in the later 1970s. Many of them theorized that a "new, permanent, tenant under-class" was being formed that would fill the ranks of the tenant movement for years to come.

While there is little doubt about the validity of some of the observations of the organizers, the question of the relative importance of this current "home-buying crisis" is unknown. Not all tenants are involved in the accumulation process, and not all tenants who fail to attain homeownership may gain increased consciousness. Indeed, some may, under hegemonic domination, rather adopt the "failed yeoman" characterization presented in Chapter 2 and actually become less conscious.

Little is known about the interaction of problems in buying homes and landlord-tenant conflict, as described in Chapter 5. Certainly the tenants having difficulty escaping tenancy for economic reasons could see landlords as a source of this difficulty. Tenants frustrated in their efforts to buy might also look beyond the landlord-tenant relationship to a more systemic cause of their problems and begin to make demands other than those necessary to reform the landlord-tenant relationship on the state. In this sense these tenants could have higher consciousness, but take the movement in the direction feared by the organizers who worried about the current tenant movement becoming a middle-class movement. As will be discussed in the last chapter, here is where it is determined whether the tenant movement will become "counter-hegemonic" or drift into "reactionary populism."

In this chapter after investigating the situation the tenants interviewed in this study faced in trying to buy a home, the impact on consciousness of tenants' desires and expectations regarding the American dream will be examined. The analysis is divided into three parts. First, the analysis revolves around determining how broadly the dream is held and the consciousness of those who no longer want to become homeowners. The analysis turns to examine the expectations of those who desire to buy. Here, the focus is on the consciousness of the permanent, involuntary tenant. Finally, the analysis examines the expectations of those who expect to be able to buy someday. Here, the differences in the levels of consciousness of those who expect to buy in the near future and those who would like to buy soon, but do not believe they will be able to buy is compared. These findings are then integrated with the findings made in Chapter 5 with regards to landlord-tenant conflict. Finally, the impact of former homeownership is examined both in its relationship to present desires and expectations and tenant consciousness.

BUYING A HOME

In mid-1981, the time of this writing, interest rates soared beyond heights imagined only a few years before. Real estate activity has slowed, with at least a one-third decline in the number of home sales, and prices have stabilized (*LAT*, July 18, 1981, Part 1). The fixed-rate mortgage that made paying almost any price within the realm of possibility reasonable is virtually gone, and there is great concern about what must be done to keep open the option to buy (*LAT*, Aug. 1, 1981, p. VIII-19).

At the time this study was conducted, late 1979 to mid-1980, the situation was somewhat different. Interest rates were high, but the level of activity and increase in the price of housing was such as to compensate any buyer who could manage the costs (Grebler and Mittelbach 1979). There was almost a panic to get onto the inflationary spiral that had resulted, as one article estimated, in $1.5 trillion in "unearned increments" (Legates and Murphy 1981, p. 265). Increasing sacrifices had to be made to buy, and, importantly, by all reports, tenants in large numbers were making them. They devoted greater proportions of their incomes to buying. Wives went to work, and homes were purchased in less desirable areas. In addition the condominium or mobile home sometimes had to be substituted for the detached single-family house.

As early as 1972, authors began to note trends in the increasing cost of housing construction and sluggishness in income growth that could, in time, endanger the ability of segments of the population to purchase a home (Sternlieb 1972). By 1976 interest rate increases, along with taxes and costs of maintenance, were added to the cost problem (Lockwood 1976). Experts estimated that 85 percent of U.S. families were then priced out of the market for new homes (p. 76). New home prices, in the period between 1970 and 1976, had increased by nearly 90 percent and first-time buyers began to shy away from new homes and look toward the existing single-family market where the increase was less, at just over 65 percent (Downs 1978).

The problems of 1976 were only an introduction for the rest of the decade. Prices and interest rates took off from that point with a 14.8 percent nationwide annual increase in the medium-priced home between 1977 and 1979 and an annual inflation rate in the cost of ownership in this period of 17.3 percent (United States League of Savings Associations 1980). Increasingly, people spoke about "creative financing," as prospective first-time buyers could not qualify for even liberalized terms at financial institutions. Even though the requirement of the loan payment to income ratio was raised from 25 percent of income to a third, the percentage of first-time buyers using conventional financing dropped from 36 percent of the market in 1977 to 18 percent in 1979. Creative financing is a euphemism for sellers financing the sale. This form of financing has long been common in low-income minority communities where conventional financing has always been difficult. Its spread across the population was something new.

At this point it is uncertain how many people who would have purchased a home under other circumstances have found it impossible in the present circumstances. Through 1977 there was no dropoff in the percentage of owner-occupied units in the United States. However, it can be said without a doubt that it has become more difficult for those who have purchased to buy, and that whatever the magnitude of the problem nationwide, it has been more extreme in Southern California.

Southern California

Starting in 1975, house prices in Southern California started to soar. The rate of increase in prices in Southern California was nearly double that in the rest of the nation. By 1980 the gap between the average home price in Southern California and that in the nation approached $50,000, with an average home price of $124,100 in Southern California versus $77,000 in the nation (*LAT*, Nov. 23, 1980, p. IX-21). In some areas of Los Angeles County, the price rise was even more dramatic. In West Los Angeles, where Santa Monica is located, the average home price reached $200,000, five times the 1967 average price for the area (Real Estate Research Council of Southern California 1979). In Beverly Hills the average home price was $550,000. Condominiums did not escape the inflation in prices. A one-bedroom condominium in Santa Monica for example, rose $30,000, from $80,000 to $110,000, in 1978 alone (Sternberg 1978).

A United States League of Savings Associations (1980) study described the market within which the respondents in this study had to seek a home to buy. In Los Angeles in 1979, only 1.1 percent of the homes sold for under $30,000, and only 6.9 percent sold for under $50,000. About a third sold in the $50,000 to $80,000 range, while more than half sold for more than $80,000. Looking at the monthly housing expense, they reported that less than 1 percent of the purchasers in 1979 paid $300 or less monthly expenses, 18 percent paid monthly expenses of between $300 and $600, and the remainder, over 80 percent, had to pay more than $600 each month to buy a home.

The 1980 price increases further lessened the percentage of relatively low-cost housing available. A survey by the Federal Home Loan Bank Board indicated that homes selling for $50,000 or less accounted for only 3 percent of the 1980 real estate transactions in California (*Daily News*, Feb. 17, 1981, p. 1). These units were primarily available in minority and low-income areas. For example, in South Central Los Angeles, the primarily low-income black area in Los Angeles, the average unit in 1980 sold for $41,662, twice the 1976 price (Watts Labor Community Action Committee n.d.)

Knowledge of the nature of the market the Los Angeles tenants have faced reinforces the expectation that the difficulty in buying a home has been a major factor in the development of tenant consciousness. To see if this is true, a series of questions were asked about home-buying expectations. The tenants were asked whether they wanted to buy a home, and if they did, whether they expected to be able to buy one some day. Those respondents who both wanted and expected to be able to buy a home were asked whether they expected to buy a home within the next three years. Those who answered "no" to any of these questions were asked why they either did not want or expect to be able to buy a home.

DREAMING THE AMERICAN DREAM

It is clear from the findings of this study that the changing economic realities of home buying in the United States have not yet seriously

Table 7.1.   *Desire to Buy a Home by Age (Los Angeles County Sample)*

Age	Want Home		Don't Want Because Can't Afford Home		Don't Want Home	
Under 30	(544)	96.6%	(13)	2.3%	(6)	1.1%
Between 30–39	(329)	92.4	(13)	3.7	(14)	3.9
Between 49–59	(200)	68.7	(44)	15.1	(47)	16.2
60 and Older	(52)	22.6	(44)	19.1	(134)	58.3

dampened the American dream of home ownership. Among tenants interviewed in this study under 40 years of age, the desire to buy was nearly universal. It was only with increasing years that the desire lessened. In all, three-fourths of the responsdents wanted to buy. Table 7.1 sets out the data on desire to buy and age in the county.

Even among respondents aged 40 and older the desire to buy may have been greater than indicated at first. Among those respondents a substantial number answered that they did not want to buy a home anymore because the cost of purchasing a home was more than they would ever be able to afford. If these responses are interpreted as the residue of a desire to buy, albeit abandoned in the face of economic reality, the desire to buy was substantial, even among seniors. When age was controlled for, the desire to buy a home remained constant over ethnicity, gender, class, and income.

There was a significant relationship between the desire to buy a home and tenant consciousness in the county sample. Tenants who wanted to buy a home had higher consciousness than those who did not.[1] Table 7.2 shows the relationship between desire to buy and tenant consciousness.

Table 7.2.   *The Desire to Buy a Home by Tenant Consciousness (Los Angeles County Sample)*

Level of Consciousness	Want Home		Don't Want Home		Can't Afford Home	
Radicalized	(73)	90.1%	(4)	4.9%	(4)	4.9%
Consumer	(234)	79.6	(25)	8.5	(35)	11.9
Defender	(454)	79.5	(35)	6.1	(82)	14.4
Individualist	(264)	68.9	(35)	9.1	(84)	21.9
Antagonist	(101)	71.6	(15)	10.7	(25)	17.7

The very strong association between age and the desire to buy and the significant association between the desire to buy a home and tenant consciousness appear to be evidence that the desire to buy is a key factor in explaining why age is so important in this analysis. Younger tenants may have higher consciousness because they see the landlords as taking the product of their labor power in competition with their own desire to use their labor power to accumulate property. This competition between the young and landlords is one in which seniors, in the main, do not participate.

As noted earlier, the Santa Monica figures about the desire to buy are quite similar to those in the county. The only exception is with the 40 to 59 age group. Thirteen percent fewer of the tenants in this age group wanted to buy. The difference results from the lack of the desire to buy among single men with $25,000 or more annual family income.[2] This group was more common in the more affluent city of Santa Monica.

The desire to buy was also significantly related to tenant consciousness in Santa Monica. Tenants in Santa Monica who did not want to buy had even lower consciousness than their county counterparts.[3] However, the relatively wealthy 40 to 59 age group was not the source of the difference. The difference was in the consciousness of seniors, particularly those seniors with more than $15,000 annual income.

This group of low-consciousness seniors is the same low-consciousness group that had no history or knowledge of negative tenant experiences, discussed in Chapter 5. Among the Santa Monica seniors who did not want to buy and who claimed to be unaware of any tenant they knew having had negative experiences with landlords, only 34 percent (N = 53) had tenant consciousness. In the county 51 percent (92) of this group of seniors had tenant consciousness.

EXPECTING TO REALIZE THE DREAM

The overwhelming desire to own expressed by the tenants interviewed in this study is testimony to how deeply the drive to own one's home is lodged in the American psyche. Given the strength of this dream of ownership, it is not surprising that a few years of high prices and high interest rates have not caused the dream to fade. However, the continuing predominance of a preference for homeownership also supports the hypothesis that the collision of desires and reality contributed to the increased tenant activity of the late 1970s.

Having identified who wants to buy a home, the next question was who believed they would be able to buy. In the county two-thirds (743) of tenants who want to buy believed that they would be able to buy a home someday. Here again, younger tenants had greater expectations than older tenants. Table 7.3 sets out this data by age group.

Table 7.3. Expectation of Buying a Home Someday by Age (Los Angeles County Sample)

| | Of Those Who Want To Buy | | Of the Whole Population | |
| | Expect to Buy | Never Expect to Be Able to Buy | Expect to Buy | Never Expect to Be Able to Buy |
Age				
Under 30	(376) 76.1%	(121) 23.9%	(376) 72.5%	(121) 22.7%
Between 30–39	(237) 75.0	(79) 25.0	(237) 68.5	(79) 22.8
Between 40–59	(99) 54.4	(83) 45.6	(99) 35.2	(83) 29.5
60 and Older	(21) 47.7	(22) 52.3	(21) 9.2	(22) 9.6
Total	(733) 72.0%	(305) 20.0%	(733) 60.0%	(305) 22.2%

Table 7.4. Expectation of Being Able to Purchase a Home of Those Who Wanted to Buy a Home by Age and Income (Los Angeles County Sample)

Age	Under $15,000	$15,000–$24,999	$25,000 and up
Under 30	(243) 75.9%	(95) 77.2%	(29) 80.6%
Between 30–39	(107) 68.2	(73) 80.2	(46) 90.2
Between 49–59	(42) 44.6	(25) 55.6	(22) 67.7
60 and older	(13) 44.8	(5) 71.4	(1) 50.0

Unlike the case of tenants' desire to buy, expectations about being able to buy appeared to be influenced by the demographic characteristics. Income appeared to be a particularly important factor with tenants who were 30 years of age or older. It was as though youth carried with it a hopefulness that faded with age and recognition of the difficulty of buying a home. Table 7.4 shows this relationship between expectations of buying, age, and income.

Income was not the only factor related to the expectation of buying. In the county women had significantly lower expectations than men.[4] Only two-thirds of the professional-managerial and working-class women in the county who want to buy expected to be able to do so, compared to 75 percent of the working-class men, more than 80 percent of the professional-managerial men, and 100 percent of the petty bourgeois.

In Santa Monica the percentage of respondents expecting to buy someday, among those who want to buy, was the same as in the county. However, the expectations were higher (82.2 percent) among the under 30 group, regardless of income, and lower (73.3 percent) among the 30 to 39 age group, particularly in the $15,000 to $25,000 income group (69.6 percent). In Santa Monica among the class strata, working-class women stood out from the rest. Less than two-thirds of these women who wanted to buy expect to be able to buy someday, compared to about three-quarters of the rest of the population. It is interesting to note that more Santa Monica professional-managerial women and fewer Santa Monica professional-managerial men and petty bourgeois expected to be able to buy than in the county.

In the county as shown in Table 7.5, the expectation that a respondent would be able to buy appeared to have a positive effect on tenant consciousness, while the belief that a respondent would never be able to buy appeared to have an opposite, negative effect. Only 62 percent (N = 306) of the tenants who stated they would like to buy, but believe they will never be able to buy, had tenant consciousness, compared to 70 percent (N = 743) of those who expect to be able to buy.[5]

It is important to note that this negative relationship between tenant consciousness and one's belief that it will be impossible to purchase a home was consistent with few exceptions across categories of age, income, ethnic/gender, and education in the county.[6] It is as though, rather than becoming enraged by the vision of a deprived future, a portion of these tenants had sunk into the depression of propertiless citizens observed by the nineteenth-century missionary and reported in Chapter 1.

Women of the professional-managerial class were the primary exception to this general rule. The professional-managerial women in the county who felt permanently frozen out of the homeownership market had a level of consciousness (82 percent N = 39) even higher than the overall high consciousness (77 percent) of their class strata. The uniqueness of this group in this regard points again to the particular problems of upward mobility faced by professional-managerial women and the role these problems play in the high consciousness of this group. The only other exception of note was the few fathers who felt that they would never be able to buy a home.

Importantly, the general rule of the county did not hold in Santa Monica. The tenants who felt permanently shut out of the housing market in Santa Monica had high consciousness relative to other Santa Monica tenants (39 percent movement levels; 70 percent defender, or higher). The differences between the two samples result from the higher consciousness of Santa Monica white men, professional-managerial men, and the petty bourgeois who wanted to buy, but believed they would never be able to do so. It was noted in Chapter 4 that white men and these class strata had higher consciousness in Santa Monica than in the county.

Two mutually reinforcing reasons appeared in the data to help explain the difference between the two samples. Both of them seemed to be the expression of the active tenant movement in Santa Monica and demonstrated the importance such a movement can play in the formation of tenant consciousness. The first was the higher proportion of Santa Monica tenants who knew of others' landlord-tenant problems, and the second was the more common identification in Santa Monica of speculation as a primary cause of the rising rents. The Santa Monica respondents who felt permanently cut off from buying (55 percent) were more likely than the average Santa Monica respondent (45 percent) or county permanent tenant (30 percent) to have known of friends' problems with landlords.

Santa Monica tenants who felt permanently cut off from buying a home also blamed speculators for increasing rents significantly more than any other group. Approximately 70 percent of the tenants who believed they would never be able to buy stated that speculators were a very important cause of rents increasing. This compared to 60 percent or less of any other group in Santa Monica and approximately 40 percent of those tenants who felt permanently cut off from homeownership in the county.

These two variables, knowledge of friends' problems and speculation, were significantly related to one another. If respondents know of friends' problems, they were more likely to believe speculation was a very important cause of rent increases (LA 45 percent; SM 77 percent). The impact of this knowledge and belief in consciousness was very significant, particularly in Santa Monica. An extraordinary 51 percent of the involuntary tenants in Santa Monica who knew of friends' problems and who believed speculation was an important cause of increasing rents had movement level consciousness, and 90 percent had tenant consciousness.[7] Just the belief that speculation was a problem was not adequate to raise consciousness in either sample. In Santa Monica, for example, only 55 percent of these involuntary tenants had tenant consciousness, and 34 percent were, appropriately, in the individualist category.[8]

The overwhelming impression this data created was that interpreting the inability to buy, to move up in this society, was very dependent on the presence or absence of supportive social relations.

A substantial percentage of the isolated people appeared to feel personally defeated and depressed, as it was put in the Introduction, for being a "failing yeoman." In contrast taking the position of being an "exploited yeoman" and developing a systematic analysis of the problem, appeared to be, in part, dependent on the type of interactions with other people who shared their problems. Collective consciousness, in this case tenant consciousness, appeared to come from the knowledge that the individual was not alone. This analysis seems to indicate that a growing housing crisis can provide "fertile ground" for organizing the involuntary permanent tenant. It also seems to suggest that a deeper home-buying crisis will not, as Gransci pointed out, necessarily lead to a spontaneous increase in consciousness and a tenant revolt.

It is important to note that this avenue of analysis was only significant for the involuntary permanent tenant.[9] Tenants who did not want to buy did not face the issue. Those who expected to buy, although perhaps not when they wanted to, appeared to be too individually caught up in the pursuit of their goals for social relationships and questions of why there were problems to have had a major impact on their consciousness.

SHORT-TERM EXPECTATIONS

Respondents who stated that they expected to be able to buy a home someday were asked whether they expected to make their purchase within the next three years. Tenants who answered that they did not expect to buy within the next three years were asked why to determine whether this was because they did not want to buy or because they could not afford to buy. Most of the activists felt that tenants who expected to buy a home within the next three years would have lower consciousness than those who did not. The activists believed that people who saw their tenancy as a temporary situation which they would soon escape would not have as much concern for the problems that tenants face.

Table 7.5. Expectation of Being Able to Purchase a Home by Tenant Consciousness (Los Angeles County Sample)

Level of Consciousness	Of Those Who Want To Buy		Of the Whole Sample	
	Expect to Buy	Want, but Never Expect to be Able to Buy	Expect to Buy	Want, but Never Expect to be Able to Buy
Radicalized	(57) 81.4%	(13) 18.6%	(57) 73.1%	(13) 16.7%
Consumer	(162) 72.3	(62) 27.7	(162) 57.1	(62) 21.8
Defender	(303) 72.4	(115) 27.5	(303) 56.6	(115) 21.5
Individualist	(157) 64.6	(186) 35.4	(157) 43.3	(86) 23.8
Antagonist	(64) 68.4	(30) 31.6	(64) 47.7	(30) 22.4

Table 7.6. Expectation of Being Able to Buy in Three Years by Age (Los Angeles County Sample)

	Of Those Who Want To Buy in the Next Three Years		Of Those Who Want To Buy		Of Whole Population	
	Will Buy	Can't Afford	Will Buy	Can't Afford	Will Buy	Can't Afford
Under 30	(22) 61.7%	(138) 38.5%	(222) 43.8%	(138) 27.2%	(222) 41.7%	(138) 25.9%
Between 30–39	(155) 67.1	(76) 32.9	(155) 49.1	(76) 24.1	(155) 44.8	(76) 22.2
Between 40–59	(76) 80.0	(19) 20.0	(76) 41.8	(19) 10.4	(76) 27.0	(19) 6.8
60 and older	(14) 77.8	(4) 22.2	(14) 31.8	(4) 9.1	(14) 6.1	(4) 1.8
Total	(467) 66.3%	(237) 33.7%	(467) 44.6%	(237) 22.6%	(467) 33.7%	(237) 17.1%

A minority of the activists took the position that short-term expectations would not make a dramatic difference in the level of consciousness. They believed that most tenants who anticipate buying a home today would have such financial difficulty in doing so that they would be very sensitive to the everyday problems of tenants—especially rent increases that might jeopardize their opportunities to save towards a home. A few of the activists stated that tenants who anticipated buying a home would be the most aggressive. They reasoned that renters who know that soon they will escape tenancy would be more aggressive because they would feel that they could avoid any negative consequences of their actions.

Just over a half (704) of the tenants interviewed in the county sample believed they would be able to buy someday and wanted to buy in the next three years.[10] Among these respondents, about two-thirds (467) expected to buy in this period. Most of the remainder (237) stated that they would like to buy in the next three years but that they could not afford to buy.

Several demographic characteristics were significantly related to both the desire to buy in the next three years and the belief that the respondents would actually purchase in this period. The most striking was, of course, age. Because far fewer middle-aged and senior tenants want or expect to be able to buy, the question of the impact of short-term expectations on consciousness was a much more important issue with those under 40 years of age than with those above this age. The difference was dramatic, with two-thirds of the tenants under 40 in the county sample wanting to buy in the next three years, compared to a third of those between 40 and 59 years of age and less than 10 percent of the seniors.

Limiting the analysis to those who want to buy in the next three years, age was again a factor. This time, however, as shown in Table 7.6, the older the tenants were, the more likely they were to believe they would be able to buy.

Earlier it was found that while income generally affects long-term expectations about buying a home, tenants under 30 years of age with low incomes had nearly the same long-term expectations as other young tenants with high incomes. This time, regardless of age, as shown in Table 7.7, the higher the tenant's income, the more likely it was that he or she expected to be able to buy within the next three years. Over 80 percent of the respondents with annual family incomes of $25,000 or more expect to be able to buy in the next three years, compared to about three-quarters of the respondents in the $15,000 to $25,000 bracket and just over a half of those with incomes under $15,000.

Table 7.7. Expectation of Being Able to Buy a Home in the Next Three Years of Those Who Wanted to Buy a Home in the Next Three Years by Age and Income (Los Angeles County Sample)

	Under $15,000	$15,000–$24,999	$25,000 & Up
Under 30	(123) 54.9%	(68) 76.4%	(20) 71.4%
Between 30–39	(65) 61.9	(45) 64.3	(36) 80.0
Between 40–59	(27) 65.9	(20) 87.0	(22) 100.0
60 and older	(9) 75.0	(3) 100.0	(1) 100.0
Total	(224) 51.0%	(136) 73.0%	(79) 84.0%

Table 7.8. Respondents Who Anticipated Purchasing a Home in the Next Three Years by Ethnicity/Gender and Income (Los Angeles County Sample)

Income	English-Speaking Latinos	White Women	Blacks	White Men	Spanish-Speaking Latinos
Under $15,000	(26) 61.9%	(43) 42.1%	(50) 66.7%	(34) 25.4%	(62) 93.4%
$15,000–$24,999	(14) 33.3	(38) 37.3	(17) 22.7	(56) 41.8	(3) 4.6
$25,000 and up	(2) 4.8	(21) 20.6	(8) 10.7	(44) 32.8	(1) 1.5
Total	(42) 100.0%	(102) 100.0%	(75) 100.0%	(134) 100.0%	(66) 100.0%

Although the lower-income respondents express lower expectations of buying within the next three years than those with higher incomes, their expectations still appear overly optimistic when they are compared with actual buying power indicated in the U.S. League of Savings Associations study (1980) results.

Just over one-half of the respondents in the county sample who believe that they would buy a home in the next three years had less than $15,000 annual family income, while only 10 percent of first-time buyers who purchased a home with institutional financing in 1979 had incomes that low. In contrast only 30 percent of the respondents in the county sample who believed they would buy a home in the next three years had annual family incomes between $15,000 and $25,000, compared to 70 percent of 1979 first-time buyers. Only among those with incomes over $25,000 was the percent of those who intend to buy and those who actually bought in 1979 similar.

Of course, it is possible that the lower-income tenants anticipated substantial increases in family incomes within the next three years through promotion, additional family members entering the workforce, or marriage. Fifty-five percent (N = 276) of those who stated they would buy in the next three years were single, compared to 30.7 percent of the first-time buyers in 1979 reported by the United States League of Savings Associations (1980, p. 13).

It is also possible that the high percentage of respondents with low incomes who expected to buy in the next three years was a function of the demographic makeup of the tenant population sampled in the county. As was discussed earlier in this chapter, low-income people, particularly low-income minorities, often use noninstitutional means of financing a home purchase. The contract of sale in which the seller, in effect, finances the sale is common. In addition the prices of homes in minority neighborhoods where whites will not go are still substantially below those in white areas, making the anticipation of homeownership among some lower-income minority tenants more realistic than such expectations would appear to be among all lower-income tenants taken as a whole.

Support for these explanations being factors in the results in this study was found in the breakdown of the ethnicity and gender of the respondents who believed they would be able to buy in the next three years set forth in Table 7.8. In the county 64 percent of the respondents who planned to purchase a home in the next three years were members of minority groups. Almost all of the respondents in the county sample who were Spanish-speaking Latinos and who expected to buy within the next three years had annual family incomes under $15,000. In addition over 60 percent of the blacks and English-speaking Latinos who believed they would buy had annual family incomes under $15,000. This compared to 40 percent of white women and 25 percent of white men.

Table 7.9 shows the expectations of the respondents in the county by tenant-counsciousness categories. A pattern was found that appeared to be consistent with the feelings of the majority of activists. As a general proposition, it can be said that the movement-level tenants who wanted to buy within the next three years had the lowest expectation of being able to do so and that the antagonist tenants had the highest expectation of having the ability to buy. However, this pattern was, importantly, not statistically significant—supporting the position of the minority of activists that buying may be as hard as not being able to buy is frustrating.

Table 7.9. *Expectation of Buying a Home Within the Next Three Years of Those Who Wanted to Buy in the Next Three Years by Tenant Consciousness (Los Angeles County Sample)*

Level of Consciousness	Expect to Buy		Can't Afford to Buy	
Radicalized	(34)	60.7%	(22)	39.3%
Consumer	(95)	62.1	(58)	37.9
Defender	(191)	66.3	(97)	33.7
Individualist	(99)	67.8	(47)	32.2
Antagonist	(48)	78.7	(13)	21.3

When income was controlled for as set forth in Table 7.10, it was found that virtually no difference in expectations existed across levels of consciousness among those in the $15,000 to $25,000 income group. It is in this group that hopes may have been high, but very vulnerable. Any unexpected problem could make buying out of the question. Additional support for this interpretation of the data and the minority hypothesis was found in the strong relationship between the percentage of the tenant's income devoted to rent and the tenant's attitude about the fairness

Table 7.10. *Expectation of Buying a Home in the Next Three Years as a Percentage of Those Who Wanted to Buy a Home in the Next Three Years by Annual Family Income by Tenant Consciousness (Los Angeles County Sample)*

Level of Consciousness	Under $15,000		$15,000–$25,000		$25,000 and Above	
Radicalized	(19)	54.3%	(13)	75.0%	(1)	33.3%
Consumer	(45)	51.7	(34)	72.3	(13)	100.0
Defender	(86)	58.1	(55)	74.3	(38)	77.6
Individualist	(56)	64.6	(20)	74.1	(14)	77.8
Antagonist	(18)	72.0	(15)	71.4	(13)	100.0

of his or her rent in this group. Forty-four percent (64) of the tenants who expected to buy and who paid over 25 percent of their income for rent believed that their rent was unfair, compared to 20 percent (41) of those paying 25 percent or less.

The short-term expectations of the respondents in the county were significantly related to the ethnicity/gender groups. As seen in Table 7.11, the high-consciousness white women and English-speaking Latinos were the least likely to believe they would be fulfilled. Looking at the whole ethnicity/gender groups, it is again seen that English-speaking Latinos and white women had the highest percentage of short-term disappointed tenants, and Spanish-speaking Latinos had the least. Also notable was the low percentage of white women in the expect-to-buy category. In part this was due to the proportion of seniors in the white female population.[11]

The impact of short-term expectations on tenant consciousness is set forth graphically in Figure 7.1. The findings were again, in the main, consistent with the hypothesis of the minority of the activists. The only group that had significantly higher consciousness among those disappointed about not being able to buy were the white men.

In the case of the English-speaking Latinos and blacks, the tenants who believed they were about to buy actually had higher overall consciousness than those who felt shut out. In both cases the percentage of tenants at the movement levels was greater with those who believed they would not be able to buy, with an extraordinary 21 percent of the English-speaking Latinos at the radicalized level, but this higher movement-level consciousness was more than offset by a higher percentage of respondents at the defender level. This heavy concentration at the defender level is what would be expected of tenants struggling to save money to buy. The unusually high percentage of blacks in the individualist category was as noted in the last chapter.

The finding that the anticipation of purchasing a home did not appear to statistically lower the consciousness of the three high-consciousness groups, English-speaking Latinos, white women, and blacks, may be an expression not only of the difficulty of buying a home among these groups, but also the reduced symbolism of the purchase of a home among groups facing other quite significant problems in upward mobility.

As with earlier findings among white men, statistically significant variation among white men came not so much from the particularly high consciousness of the disappointed white men, but rather from the particularly low consciousness of those who expected to buy. This finding of low consciousness among white men who expect to buy is consistent with the fears of the activists who saw the support of the middle class as

Table 7.11. Expectation of Buying a Home Within the Next Three Years by Ethnicity/Gender Group (Los Angeles County Sample)

	Wanted to Buy in the Next Three Years		Whole Sample	
	Expect to Buy	Can't Afford to Buy	Expect to Buy	Can't Afford to Buy
English-speaking Latinos	(45) 61.6%	(28) 38.4%	(45) 36.0%	(28) 22.4%
White women	(108) 56.5	(83) 43.5	(108) 23.6	(23) 18.1
Blacks	(78) 70.3	(33) 29.7	(78) 38.0	(33) 16.1
White men	(140) 68.6	(64) 31.4	(140) 38.7	(64) 17.7
Spanish speakers	(75) 81.5	(17) 18.5	(75) 40.8	(17) 9.2

Table 7.12. Expectation of Buying a Home Within the Next Three Years by Class/Gender Group (Los Angeles County Sample)

	Wanted to Buy in the Next Three Years		Whole Sample	
	Expect to Buy	Can't Afford to Buy	Expect to Buy	Can't Afford to Buy
Professional-Managerial Women	(41) 55.4%	(33) 44.6%	(41) 27.0%	(33) 21.7%
Working-Class Men	(139) 69.5	(61) 31.5	(139) 38.6	(61) 16.9
Working-Class Women	(143) 61.4	(90) 38.6	(145) 27.2	(90) 17.1
Professional-Managerial Men	(47) 73.4	(17) 26.6	(47) 46.5	(17) 16.8
Petty bourgeois	(73) 74.4	(25) 26.6	(73) 42.2	(25) 14.5

Figure 7.1. *Tenant Consciousness of Those Who Expected to be Able to Purchase a Home, and Those Who Believed They Could Not Afford to Purchase a Home in the Next Three Years by Ethnicity/Gender (Los Angeles County Sample)*

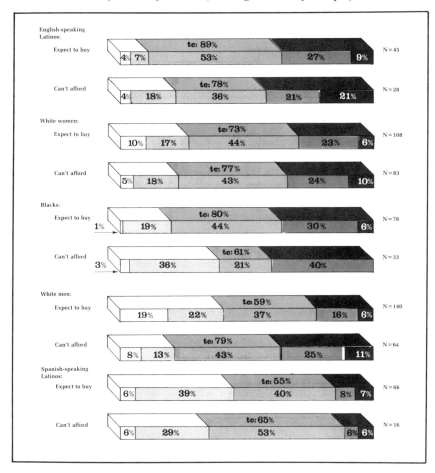

Note: *Please see Figure 4.1 for explanation of shaded bar codes. The classifications, in order, are: 1) Antagonist; 2) Individualist; 3) Defender; 4) Consumer; and 5) Radicalized.*

being transitory. White men, who have already indicated fewer overall problems as tenants, may become less prominent in the movement if the homebuying problem is resolved. Class will be examined in the next section.

The short-term expectations of the respondents in the county were also significantly related to the class/gender strata. As shown in Table 7.12, consistent with the theory that frustration over a lack of upward mobility was a particularly important factor in the high consciousness of professional-managerial women, professional-managerial women who wanted to buy in the next three years were the most likely to believe they would not be able to buy. The professional-managerial men and the petty bourgeois, who were seen as highly upwardly mobile, were the most likely to believe that they could buy a home. Taken as a whole, the difference among these strata remained dramatic, although more so in the percentage of each population that expects to buy. Among the professional-managerial and petty-bourgeois populations, a figure approaching one-half expect to buy in the next three years, with the percentage among the professional-managerial women being just over a quarter.

The impact of short-term expectations on tenant consciousness is set forth graphically in Figure 7.2. In contrast to the analysis of ethnicity/gender groups, the pattern anticipated by the majority of the activists exists in every class/gender strata. However, as in the previous instance, the differences were not generally statistically significant. The only group in which the difference was significant was among the professional-managerial men. In part this was because an extraordinary 29 percent of the professional-managerial men who believed they could not buy in the next three years were in the radicalized category. This seems to be further evidence that the fear of possible transitory support for the tenant movement among the middle class may be valid.

There was additional evidence in the data for the position of the minority of activists who stated that whether one could buy may not always be of central importance. Among both professional-managerial women and men, for example, a substantial proportion of the tenants who were about to buy with under $15,000 incomes were at the movement levels (43 percent Women, N = 15; 43 percent Men, N = 16). In both groups the percentage of respondents at the movement levels drops precipitiously with increasing income ($15,000 to $25,000–Women–25 percent, N = 16; Men–22 percent, N = 18; Over $25,000–Women–11 percent, N = 9; Men–17 percent, N = 12). The overall difference between the two strata was primarily found in the percentage of professional-managerial women was greater in the defender categories at all income levels and increased more rapidly with higher income.[12] This difference between the two groups may be related to the sex-role differences discussed in Chapter 4.

It is worth noting that the problems of buying also seem to weight more heavily upon working-class tenants who had lower incomes.[13] Nearly two-thirds of the working-class tenants who believed they would buy in the next three years reported less than $15,000 annual family incomes. This tended to reduce the gap between those expecting to buy

Figure 7.2. *Tenant Consciousness of Those Who Expected to be Able to Purchase a Home, and Those Who Believed They Could Not Afford to Purchase a Home in the Next Three Years by Class/Gender (Los Angeles County Sample)*

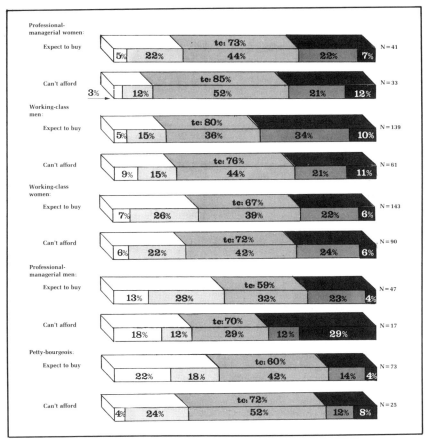

Note: *Please see figure 4.1 for explanation of shaded bar codes. The classifications, in order, are: 1) Antagonist; 2) Individualist; 3) Defender; 4) Consumer; and 5) Radicalized.*

and those disappointed about not being able to buy. The result was the relatively similar levels of consciousness in the two groups. Among the professional-managerial tenants, only about a third of those who believe they will buy had less than $15,000 annual family incomes.

The short-term expectations of tenants in Santa Monica were less hopeful than those in the county. The same percentage of Santa Monica tenants as in the county wanted to buy in the next three years, but only about 55 percent (184) of Santa Monica tenants who wanted to buy in the next three years expected to be able to do so, compared to two-thirds in the county. The difference cut across all income groups. Table 7.13 sets forth the short-term expectations of county and Santa Monica tenants by income group. The difference in the two samples expressed itself with

Table 7.13. *Expectation of Buying in the Next Three Years Among Respondents Who Wanted to Buy in the Next Three Years by Income (Los Angeles County and Santa Monica Samples)*

	Under $15,000	$15,000-$24,999	$25,000 & Above	Total
Los Angeles County (225)	58.6% (136)	73.5% (79)	82.3% (440)	67.5%
Santa Monica (67)	43.5 (63)	63.6 (41)	69.5 (171)	57.1

white men and blacks as well as in all class strata except professional-managerial women, where there was a greater expectation of buying in the next three years than in the county. There were also lower expectations among white women in Santa Monica, but this difference was not great because of the higher expectations of the professional-managerial women.

When the relationship between short-term expectations and tenant consciousness was examined in Santa Monica, the pattern anticipated by the majority of activists was found. Over 70 percent of the radicalized tenants stated they would not be able to buy in the next three years, and the figure drops steadily with consciousness to the antagonist level, where only just over 20 percent of the respondents stated they would not be able to buy. Table 7.14 sets out the finding on this point.

Table 7.14. *Expectation of Buying a Home Within the Next Three Years of Those Who Wanted to Buy a Home in the Next Three Years by Tenant Consciousness (Santa Monica Sample)*

Level of Consciousness	Expect to Buy		Can't Afford to Buy	
Radicalized	(4)	28.6%	(10)	71.4%
Consumer	(37)	44.6	(46)	55.4
Defender	(72)	54.1	(61)	45.9
Individualist	(41)	64.1	(23)	35.9
Antagonist	(30)	79.9	(8)	21.1

The impact of short-term frustration on consciousness was again felt significantly by the white male population, with the difference in consciousness between those who expected to buy and those frustrated about not being able to buy very similar to that in the county. In Santa

Monica the impact of this pattern was greater because white men make up a substantially larger proportion of the Santa monica population that wanted to buy in the next three years (41.2 percent in Santa Monica to 28.4 percent in the county).

As in the county, the differences between the two groups of white men was, again, the only significant differnce among the ethnicity/gender categories. However, the differences between these two portions of the Santa Monica white female population were substantial (Buy 63 percent, N = 71; Can't 80 percent, N = 65).[14] Much of the gap between the white women who thought they would buy and those who believed they would not be able to buy was found among the professional-managerial women. However, this difference (Buy 62 percent, N = 45; Can't 82 percent, N = 28) was also not statistically significant.[15] Even though these differences were not statistically significant, the higher proportion of white women, and especially professional-managerial women, in Santa Monica who believed they could buy seemed to be an important factor in their having lower consciousness than in the county.

When the other class/strata were examined, a partial explanation for the higher consciousness of the Santa Monica petty bourgeois was also identified. In Santa Monica this was the only strata in which the difference between the likely and frustrated purchaser was statistically significant (Buy 65 percent, N = 37; Can't 78 percent, N = 27). An extraordinary percentage of the petty-bourgeois tenants who could not buy were at the movement levels (52 percent). Like the professional-managerial women, the difference between the two groups of professional-managerial men was substantial (Buy 64 percent, N = 28; Can't 80 percent, N = 15), but not statistically significant.[16]

The Santa Monica results also differed from the county results in another important way. Only 46 percent (N = 41) of Santa Monica's high-income, soon-to-be-homeowning respondents had tenant consciousness, compared to 66 percent (N = 79) of the high-income county respondents who expect to buy.[17] Like the finding regarding white men, the overall impact of the variation between county and Santa Monica high-income respondents was increased by the higher incomes of the Santa Monica residents buying homes. The respondents having an annual income of $25,000 and up made up 24 percent of the Santa Monica respondents buying homes, compared to 18 percent of those in the county.

As with the Santa Monica low-consciousness seniors, the low consciousness of the high-income tenants appeared to be associated with being unaffected by negative tenant experiences. Only 39 percent (N = 51) of the tenants who were about to buy in Santa Monica and had never had a negative experience with a landlord and had no friends who had had such an experience had tenant consciousness. This alone, however, does not explain the low consciousness of the seniors or high-income tenants. Both groups' consciousness was substantially lower consciousness than that of tenants with a similar history in the county.[18] In contrast tenants who expected to buy and had negative experience in the two samples had almost identical levels of consciousness.[19]

It may be that the low consciousness of the high-income Santa Monica respondents who were about to buy, like the low consciousness of the Santa Monica seniors, was a product of political polarization in Santa Monica.

THE AMERICAN DREAM AND EVERYDAY EXPERIENCE

The effect of the tenants' positions vis-a-vis the American dream cannot be seen in isolation from the tenants' everyday experiences examined in Chapter 5. When the interaction between the two—the American dream or everyday experience—was examined, it was found that problems in either area could independently significantly raise tenant consciousness. However, when one or the other problem was present, the addition of the other did not have a significant impact on the level of consciousness. For example, in both samples the tenants' desires and expectations regarding homeownership significantly affected the level of tenant consciousness of tenants who had little or no (0 to 1) history of disputes with landlords.[20] Again, in both samples when tenants reported they had experienced multiple problems with landlords (2 or more or 1 or more and a forced move), then their situation regarding homeownership did not appear to significantly affect their level of consciousness.[21] The same finding was made when the analysis was reversed.[22]

While this general finding was true in both samples, there was a very interesting twist in the Santa Monica findings that again appeared to demonstrate the effect of the tenant movement in that city. When the variable that indicated whether the tenants knew of friends' problems was added to the analysis, the findings in Santa Monica regarding the impact of tenants' desires and expectations regarding homeownership were the reverse of the general finding. Whether or not the Santa Monica tenants desired or expected to be able to buy did not significantly affect the level of consciousness of those who had no direct history of negative experience or indirect history through knowledge of friends having had such experiences. However, if the tenants had either any direct or indirect history of problems, whether or not they wanted to buy or expected to buy, their level of consciousness was significantly affected.

This variable, likely indicative of a connection to the tenant movement in Santa Monica, seemed to accentuate the impact of the tenants' relationship to the American dream. Knowledge of friends' problems in the county, where the tenant movement was much weaker, did not have as dramatic an effect. For example, among those tenants who did not want to buy and had no direct or indirect history of landlord-tenant problems, only 35 percent (N = 77) had tenant consciousness in Santa Monica while 55 percent (N = 138) had tenant consciousness in the county. The same held true for those who expected to buy in the next three years. Only 39 percent (N = 51) of those with such a history had tenant consciousness, compared to 63 percent (N = 172) in the county. Among those who were frustrated with regards to the American dream, the impact of the tenant movement in Santa Monica could also be seen, although it was less dramatic. Among the permanent, involuntary tenants with a direct or indirect history of landlord-tenant problems, tenant consciousness was found among 87 percent (N = 61) of the Santa Monica tenants and only 79 percent (N = 92) of the county tenants. Among those who wanted to buy in the next three years, but couldn't, the finding was 84 percent (N = 68) with tenant consciousness in Santa Monica and 76 percent (N = 96) in the county.[23]

Before concluding, one further variable with regard to homeownership is worthy of investigation. The next section will focus on this variable, former homeownership.

FORMER HOMEOWNERSHIP

In both samples a substantial proportion of the respondents once owned their own homes. As a general proposition, the older and wealthier the tenant, the more likely he or she was to have once been a homeowner. In the county sample about 10 percent (58) of those under 30, 25 percent (89) of those between 30 and 39 years of age, just over 50 percent (157) of those between 40 and 59 years of age, and about 60 percent (138) of those 60 years of age or older once owned a home. In both samples income was a major factor indicative of home ownership with those over 40 years of age. In the county, for example, about one-half (170) of the respondents 40 to 59 years of age and 60 and older with less than $15,000 annual income once owned a home, compared to two-thirds of those between 40 and 59 years of age and 90 percent of those 60 years of age and older with more than $15,000 annual income.

As a general proposition, fewer former homeowners wanted to buy a home than those who had never owned, but those former owners who did want to buy were more likely to believe they would be able to buy in the next three years. Having the proceeds of the sale of the formerly owned property may have been a major factor in facilitating the new purchase.

For the most part a tenant who once owned a home had less tenant consciousness than one who had never owned a home. This was found to be true in both the county and Santa Monica samples. However, in the county sample, when the demographic differences were controlled for, most of the significance in the variance disappeared. Former homeownership remained a factor only for those under 30 years of age and professional-managerial women. In both cases, however, the consciousness differences appeared as much an artifact of present income differences as former ownership.

The fact that a tenant once owned a home appeared to be a more important factor in the wealthier Santa Monica sample. Figure 7.3 shows graphically that former owners had lower consciousness. Former ownership seemed to lower tenant consciousness among white and working-class tenants. In the over $25,000 annual family income group, 72

Figure 7.3.   *Tenant Consciousness of Those Who Have and Have Not Owned a Home (Santa Monica Sample)*

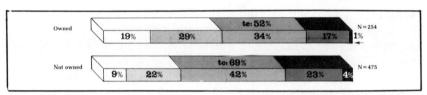

Note: *Please see figure 4.1 for explanation of shaded bar codes. The classifications, in order, are: 1) Antagonist; 2) Individualist; 3) Defender; 4) Consumer; and 5) Radicalized.*

percent (N = 35) of those who had never owned a home had tenant consciousness, compared to only 33 percent (N = 39) of the former home owners. Previous homeownership also appeared to be a major factor in the very low-consciousness level of Santa Monica seniors. For example, only 30 percent (N = 33) of the white women 60 or older who had formerly owned a home had tenant consciousness.

Consistent with this last finding and the earlier finding regarding higher-income seniors, former homeownership also appeared to be a factor in the very low consciousness of the Santa Monica respondents who did not want to buy a home.[24] In Santa Monica two-thirds (100) of the predominantly senior respondents who stated they did not want to buy a home were former homeowners. In this group only 44 percent had tenant consciousness. This alone, however, does not tell the story. In the county where former homeowners made up a half (118) of those who did not want to buy, 55 percent of these former homeowners had tenant consciousness. As with the finding regarding all high-income respondent homebuyers in Santa Monica, why former homeownership should have a more dramatic effect in Santa Monica seems again to have been a product of the intense tenant activity in the city.

SUMMARY

Table 7.15 summarizes the data in this chapter with regards to the desire and expectation of buying a home, and Figures 7.4 and 7.5 present the relationship between tenant consciousness and these desires and expectations. The results in Santa Monica regarding tenant consciousness fit the predicted pattern. The county results do not.

Two primary factors seem to have determined the base findings in Santa Monica. One was the tenants' relationship to property—have they had it or were they about to buy it; and the other is the tenants' sense of upward mobility—did they believe they were upwardly mobile or that their upward mobility was blocked. Tenants who had no interest in buying a home or upward mobility had the lowest consciousness, particularly if they were former homeowners. They were followed by the tenants who were about to buy, particularly those who have the greatest upward mobility, white men.

Figure 7.4. *Tenant Consciousness by Desires and Expectations of Home Ownership (Santa Monica Sample Sample)*

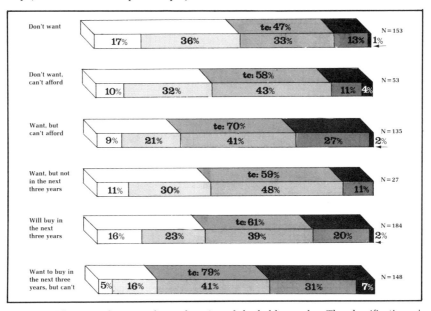

Note: *Please see figure 4.1 for explanation of shaded bar codes. The classifications, in order, are: 1) Antagonist; 2) Individualist; 3) Defender; 4) Consumer; and 5) Radicalized.*

Table 7.15. Comparison of Desires and Expectations Regarding Home Ownership (Los Angeles County and Santa Monica Samples)

	Total		Those Who Want to Buy		Those Who Expect to Buy		Those Who Want to Buy In Three Years	
	LA	SM	LA	SM	LA	SM	LA	SM
Don't Want	(230) 16.5%	(153) 21.8%	—	—	—	—	—	—
Don't Want Because Can't Afford	(114) 8.2	(53) 7.6	—	—	—	—	—	—
Subtotal	(344) 24.7	(206) 29.4	—	—	—	—	—	—
Want, but Can't Afford	(306) 22.0	(135) 19.3	(306) 29.2%	(135) 27.3%	—	—	—	—
Want, but not in the Next Three Years	(39) 2.8	(27) 3.9	(39) 3.7	(27) 5.5	(39) 5.2%	(27) 7.5%	—	—
Will Buy in Three Years	(467) 33.5	(184) 26.3	(467) 44.5	(184) 37.2	(467) 62.9	(184) 51.3	(467) 66.3%	(184) 55.4%
Want to Buy in Three Years, but Can't Afford	(237) 17.0	(148) 21.1	(237) 22.6	(148) 30.0	(237) 31.9	(148) 41.2	(237) 33.7	(148) 44.6
Subtotal	(1,049) 75.3	(494) 70.6	(1,049) 100.0%	(494) 100.0%	(743) 100.0%	(359) 100.0%	(704) 100.0%	(332) 100.0%
Total	(1,393) 100.0%	(700) 100.0%						

Figure 7.5. *Tenant Consciousness by Desires and Expectations of Home Owner-ship (Los Angeles County Sample)*

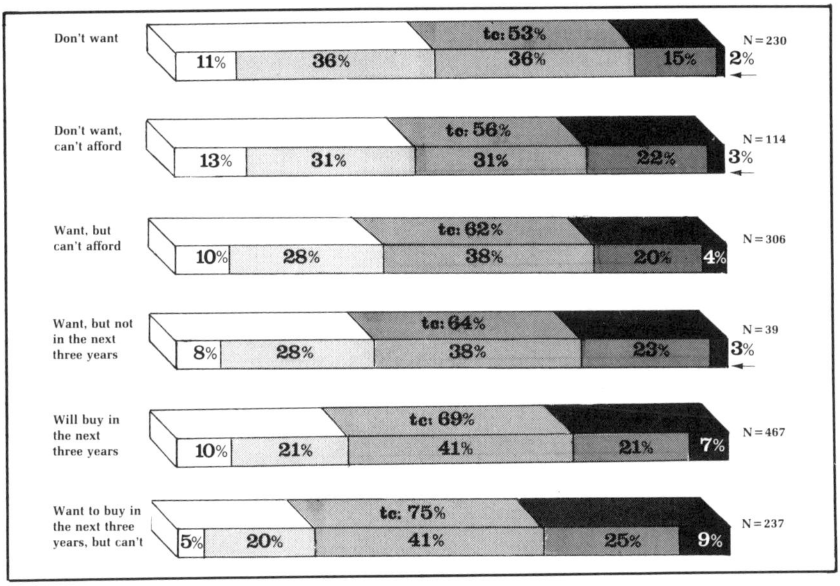

Note: *Please see figure 4.1 for explanation of shaded bar codes. The classifications, in order, are: 1) Antagonist; 2) Individualist; 3) Defender; 4) Consumer; and 5) Radicalized.*

The tenants with the highest consciousness in Santa Monica were those who were frustrated about not being able to buy. The highest-consciousness tenants, as a group, were the respondents who believed they would be able to buy someday or wanted to buy in the next three years, but did not believe they would be able to afford it. The tenants who couldn't buy in the next three years were followed closely in Santa Monica by the tenants who wanted to buy but believed they are forever shut out from buying.

The results in the county were somewhat different and did not obviously fit the mold. The tenants no longer interested in buying and upward mobility did have the lowest consciousness but not as low as in Santa Monica. The tenants frustrated by not being able to buy in the next three years had the highest consciousness but not as high as in Santa Monica. The difference appears to be the product of the political polar-ization in Santa Monica that will be discussed in the next chapter.

This did not explain, however, the remainder of the findings. The two samples varied in the consciousness of those about to buy. In the county this group had higher consciousness. When the findings were examined, controlling the results by the ethnicity/gender categories, an apparent explantion was found. The groups least affected by buying were the groups with the least upward mobility, minorities and women, particularly working-class women. These groups face great difficulties in realizing the goal of homeownership, and even if achieved, it did not appear to be the ticket up or the symbol of success to these groups that it is to the more upwardly mobile portions of the population.

Finally, while the involuntary, permanent tenants of Santa Monica had relatively high consciousness, the tenants in the county permanently cut off from ownership had relatively low consciousness. This may very well have been indicative of an element of defeat in this population in the county, rather than the defiance that appeared to be be associated with this loss of upward mobility in Santa Monica. Importantly, this difference appeared to be an expression of the organizing that has taken place in Santa Monica, and suggests that further organizing could raise the consciousness of tenants who find themselves in this situation.

NOTES

1. Those who do not want to buy–52 percent tenant consciousness N = 230; those who can't afford to buy–56 percent tenant consciousness N – 114; those who want to buy–68 percent tenant consciousness N = 1126.

2. We will use different income groups in this section to match housing data.

3. Those who do not want to buy–47 percent tenant consciousness N = 153; those who can't afford to buy–55 percent tenant consciousness N = 53; those who want to buy–72 percent tenant consciousness N = 494.

4. Ethnicity was also a factor. In particular Spanish-speaking Latinos stood out with 33.7 percent in this category, followed by white women (24.0 percent), English-speaking Latinos (20 percent), white men (18 percent), and blacks (17.1 percent).

5. The white women and Spanish speakers also are overrepresented in the group of tenants in the county who want to buy, but never believe they will be able to do so. Only 60 percent of the very low-income Spanish speakers think they will be able to buy, compared to about two-thirds of the white women and three-quarters of the other ethnicity/gender groups.

6. This does not mean all these groups had low consciousness. For example, 76 percent (N = 26) of English-speaking Latinos have tenant consciousness. Young, low-income minorities and white men who felt shut out had relatively high consciousness, but again not as high as those who expected to buy someday.

7. In the county 36 percent (N = 43) of these respondents are at the movement levels, and 83 percent have tenant consciousness.

8. In the county 51 percent (N = 71) of these respondents have tenant consciousness, and 42 percent are individualists.

9. In Santa Monica the analysis is also significant with tenants who say they no longer want to buy because they will never be able to buy.

10. A small percentage (under 6 percent) in each stated they expected to buy but did not want to in the next three years.

11. The percentage was 24.7 percent (116). The next highest group was white men–14.4 percent (55). The low was the English-speaking Latinos–8.3 percent (11).

12. The overall consciousness of professional-managerial women drops from a high of 80 percent in the under $15,000 group to a low of 67 percent in the over $30,000 group. Among the professional-managerial men, the drop is from 69 percent among the under $15,000 group to 50 percent with the over $30,000 group. In these two strata the defender level figures go from 34 percent to 56 percent among the women with increasing income and from 25 percent to 33 percent among the men. The percentage of professional-managerial women and men in each income group was almost identical.

13. A British study found that working-class homeowners with below average incomes were approximately twice as likely to vote for Conservative candidates as working-class tenants or working-class homeowners with average or above average incomes (McKenzie and Silver 1968, p. 96).

14. Chi square of .0761

15. Chi square of .1577

16. Chi square .0662

17. The pattern of consciousness for the respondents who expect to buy in the next three years with less than $25,000 annual income is very similar in the two samples.

18. The percentage is 63 percent, (N = 172).

19. The percentages are LA–72 percent, (N = 205); SM–70 percent, (N = 133).

20. High consciousness was present only among those disappointed in the short term (LA–72 percent, N = 144; SM–75 percent, N = 79). Consistent with earlier findings, the consciousness of those expecting to buy was also relatively high in the county (LA–66 percent, N = 255; SM–52 percent, N = 103). The lowest consciousness was again among those who did not want to buy (LA–50 percent, N = 172; SM–41 percent, N = 107).

21. For example, the consciousness level of those with multiple problems who believed they would buy (LA–72 percent, N = 212; SM–74 percent, N = 81) was about as high as those without multiple problems who wanted to buy in the next three years but coulld not (LA–72 percent, N = 144; SM–75 percent, N = 79). The most striking increase in consciousness was among the permanent, involuntary tenants (LA–73 percent, N = 73 from 55 percent N = 187; SM–86 percent, N = 57 from 58 percent, N = 78). The tenants who could not buy in the short term had the highest consciousness (LA–89 percent, N = 93; SM–85 percent, N = 69).

22. The number of problems was significantly related to tenant consciousness in both samples among those who did not want to buy and those who believed they would never be able to buy. It was also significant among those who expected to buy in the next three years in the county. When the tenants' knowledge of friends' problems was added to the analysis, the presence or absence of a direct or indirect history of problems was also significant in Santa Monica among those expecting to buy in the next three years. In neither case was there a significant variation in the level of consciousness of those who wanted to buy in the next three years but could not.

23. It should be noted that direct or indirect history of landlord-tenant problems did not significantly increase the consciousness of those who wanted to buy in the next three years and could not. In the county the difference was nil—no problems 74 percent, (N = 90); history of problems 75 percent, (N = 147). In Santa Monica, although not significant, there was a substantial difference—no problems 68 percent, (N = 41); history of problems 83 percent, (N = 107).

24. Former homeowners have lower consciousness across the board in the home-ownership desire and expectation categories. Among former homeowners the desires and expectations do not significantly affect consciousness. Only the few such respondents with short-term frustration have relatively high consciousness. However, in none of the categories does former homeownership make a statistically significant difference in the level of consciousness.

PART 3

The Political Potential of the Tenant Movement

8

Political Identity, Mobilization, and Hegemony

Many tenant activists believe that permanent, building-level tenant unions should be the base unit of the tenant movement, just as union locals are the base unit of labor organizations. Importantly, Santa Monica was not organized in this fashion. The substantial building-level activity that took place in Santa Monica was aimed rather at winning the support of as many tenants as possible and mobilizing them temporarily, as needed, for the electoral drives.

The Santa Monica strategy was extraordinarily successful. In successive elections, an activated tenant community totally revamped the political establishment of the city. The conservative business-homeowner clique that once dominated the political life of the city was all but demolished as a political force and was replaced by a tenant-based, liberal, labor, Democratic Party coalition. The intense political activity, not surprisingly, politically polarized the city. The results of that polarization were seen in earlier chapters. In this chapter the nature of the polarization will be examined by comparing the relationship between tenant consciousness and political identity in the two samples.

Understanding both the nature of the polarization and the underlying relationship between tenant consciousness and political identity is central in the determination of the political potential of the tenant movement. Henry George argued that landlordism, as a political issue, should be separated from the general flow of politics because of landlordism's precapitalist content. However, as was seen, he did not succeed in convincing a majority of the people that this was the case. If tenant consciousness and political identity are strongly related, as George's failure seems to indicate, there may be a constraint on the movement that could be removed only by political changes beyond the boundaries of the tenant movement.

The tenant movement itself, however, may be a vehicle for such broader changes. The activists stated that tenants can be "radicalized" by their experiences as tenants. To some of the activists, the term radicalized meant a shift left in political perspective. To examine the process of radicalization, the relationship between tenant experience, expectation of homeownership, tenant consciousness, and political identity will be analyzed. While the process of radicalization is a dynamic one that cannot be seen in full by employing the data available in this study, what might be acting as a catalyst to begin and encourage such a process can be identified.

After this discussion the potential for mobilizing tenant consciousness will be examined. To do this, the focus will be on the movement successes that have occurred in Santa Monica. The first concern is with the sense of political efficacy, allegiance, and activism that has been developed in Santa Monica in comparison to that developed in the county. Then, to understand both the dynamics of the situation and its potential contribution to greater social change, the interrelationship of building-level activity, movement activism, and general social and political activism will be explored.

The chapter concludes with a discussion of the implications of this potential mobilization for the future of housing policy and this country's system of private property. In this discussion the question becomes whether the movement shows signs of escaping the hegemonic limits of its past that have had individual accumulation of property through enterprise at the center. Without this the tenant movement of today, whatever its potential for mobilization, cannot be seen, in Gramsci's terms, as counter-hegemonic.

POLITICAL IDENTITY

The activists were divided on the question of the relationship between tenant consciousness and overall political identity. At one extreme were those activists who took the position that tenant consciousness was not an independent phenomenon but rather a subset of general political consciousness. They believe the further left a tenant is, the higher their tenant consciousness will be. At the other extreme were those who saw tenant consciousness as related primarily to tenant experience, as part of what was often referred to as "single-issue" politics. In the middle were those who saw tenant consciousness as an extreme form of "consumer" consciousness with likely liberal overtones. This debate resulted in the split over the nature of the radicalized tenant discussed in Chapter 3: the economic and political radical, the tenantist, and the extreme consumer.

To gain perspective on the relationship between tenant consciousness and overall political identity, the respondents were asked two questions: one that called for the respondent's party affiliation, if any; and another that asked the respondents to self-identify their political perspective from a fixed set as a conservative, moderate, liberal, or progressive. A review of the political science literature on the question of identifying political identity indicated that party affiliation alone was no longer sufficient (Dolbeare and Edelman 1979). This was believed true, first, because many respondents do not have a party affiliation and second, because party affiliation no longer represents a consistent political position. Today, there is a tendency to use labels such as conservative and moderate to represent clusters of positions on social issues in place of party.

Political Party

Examining responses to the question regarding party affiliation, it was found that somewhat more of the respondents in both samples were identified with a party than was anticipated.[1] As seen in Table 8.1, in both samples, about two-thirds of the respondents stated a party affiliation. In both samples there were also about twice as many Democrats as

Table 8.1. *Party Identification (Los Angeles County and Santa Monica Samples)*

	Los Angeles County		Santa Monica	
Republican	(277)	19.0%	(153)	21.0%
Democrat	(627)	43.1	(319)	43.8
Other Party	(29)	2.0	(23)	2.5
Independent	(87)	6.0	(92)	12.6
Unaffiliated	(436)	29.9	(147)	20.2

Republicans. Less than 3 percent of the respondents in each sample identified with some other party. More Santa Monica respondents were independents and more county respondents were unaffiliated.

Political Perspective

Although the party breakdown was similar, the political perspectives of the two samples were not. In comparing the two samples, it was found that Santa Monica's respondents were more liberal and the county's respondents were more moderate. At the polar extremes, the proportions of progressives and conservatives were quite similar, with only a slightly higher proportion of progressives in the Santa Monica sample and a slightly higher proportion of conservatives in the county sample. Table 8.2 sets out the data on this point.

Table 8.2. *Political Perspectives (Los Angeles County and Santa Monica Samples)*

	Los Angeles County	Santa Monica
Progressive	11.4%	12.5%
Liberal	19.6	25.9
Moderate	41.3	35.6
Conservative	27.7	25.9

Political Identity—Composite

To investigate which form of political identity was most useful for this study, the party affiliation of the respondents was modified by their political perspective and the tenant consciousness of these composite categories was examined. The results of this analysis indicated that neither categorization of political identity alone was sufficient and that composite categories would better serve the purposes of this analysis.[2] The labels of political perspective categories are continued as identifiers of the composite political identity categories. From here on, whenever these political terms are used, they will represent the composite categories. The contents of the composite categories are shown in Table 8.3

The result of the reclassification of the categories is that Santa Monica respondents were more often at the political extremes, while county respondents tended to be clustered in the center. More of the Santa Monica tenants who were interviewed are progressive, liberal, or conservative, and more of the county tenants are moderate or unaffiliated.

POLITICAL IDENTITY AND TENANT CONSCIOUSNESS

In each sample, as seen in Figures 8.1 and 8.2, political identity was significantly related to tenant consciousness. As was predicted by one group of activists, the further left the political identity, the higher the consciousness. The relationship was stronger in the more politicized Santa Monica environment. As a general proposition, the Santa Monica progressives and liberals had higher consciousness than county progressives and liberals, while the Santa Monica moderates and conservatives had lower consciousness than county moderates and conservatives. The

Table 8.3. *Makeup of Composite Political Identity Categories (Los Angeles County and Santa Monica Samples)*

	Los Angeles County			Santa Monica		
Progressive						
Progressive Democrats	(62)	80.5		(36)	59.0	
Progressive Other Party	(06)	7.8		(09)	14.8	
Progressive Independent	(09)	11.7		(16)	26.2	
	(77)	100.0	5.5%	(61)	100.0	8.8%
Liberal						
Progressive Republican	(22)	10.0		(04)	2.7	
Liberal Republican	(23)	10.5		(08)	5.3	
Liberal Democrat	(149)	67.7		(114)	76.0	
Liberal Other Party	(07)	3.2		(01)	.7	
Liberal Independent	(19)	8.6		(23)	15.3	
	(220)	100.0	15.6	(150)	100.0	21.7
Moderate						
Moderate Democrat	(269)	62.6		(110)	61.1	
Conservative Democrat	(127)	29.5		(43)	23.9	
Moderate Independent	(34)	7.9		(27)	15.0	
	(430)	100.0	30.5	(180)	100.0	26.0
Unaffiliated						
Progressive No Party	(53)	14.9		(18)	15.3	
Liberal No Party	(63)	17.8		(26)	22.0	
Moderate No Party	(152)	42.8		(42)	35.6	
Conservative No Party	(87)	24.5		(32)	27.1	
	(355)	100.0	30.9	(118)	100.0	21.2
Conservative						
Moderate Republican	(89)	35.8		(83)	53.9	
Moderate Other Party	(05)	2.0		(02)	1.3	
Conservative Republican	(128)	51.4		(55)	35.7	
Conservative Other Party	(07)	2.8		(01)	.7	
Conservative Independent	(20)	8.0		(13)	8.4	
	(249)	100.0	17.6	(154)	100.0	22.3

consciousness level of the unaffiliated in both samples was quite similar.

The difference between the Santa Monica and county findings was indicative of the polarization previously observed. The fact that in Santa Monica, at the left end of the political spectrum, consciousness was

Figure 8.1. *Tenant Consciousness by Political Identity (Los Angeles County Sample)*

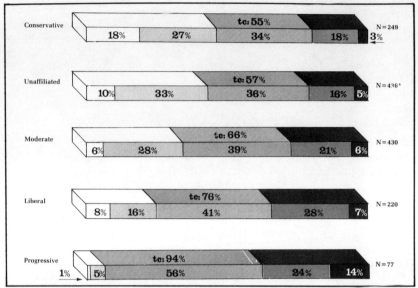

Note: *Please see Figure 4.1 for explanation of shaded bar codes. The classifications, in order, are: 1) Antagonist; 2) Individualist; 3) Defender; 4) Consumer; and 5) Radicalized.*
Includes unaffiliated with no professed political perspective.

higher and at the right end of the spectrum, it was lower than in the county suggested the "choosing of sides" became necessary only when issues are presented as strongly as they have been in Santa Monica. Tenants have had four chances to vote on the issue of rent control, had two elections for seats on a rent control board, and tenants' rights have been an issue in three city council elections. Questions, which in parts of the County of Los Angeles were hypothetical, were real issues in Santa Monica. Support or opposition in Santa Monica could make a difference.

To see the nature of the polarization—taking the county findings as a baseline—the levels of consciousness in the two samples were compared. Starting with the progressives, it was found that there appeared to have been a substantial shift in consciousness from the defender level of consciousness (LA–56 percent; SM–34 percent) to the movement levels (LA–37 percent; SM–57 percent) among Santa Monica progressives. This is encouraging to those interested in an effective tenant movement because it seems to portend the ability to mobilize a significant cadre of progressives around which a larger movement might be built. However, it seems important to note that the shift was primarily to the consumer level (LA–23 percent; SM–45 percent) rather than to the radicalized level (LA–14 percent; SM–16 percent), indicating a reform rather than radical movement nucleus.

Among liberals there was no such increase in the percentage of tenants at the movement levels. The figures at these levels were almost identical. The shift was rather entirely from individualist (LA–16 percent; SM–13 percent) and antagonist levels (LA–8 percent; SM–3 percent) to the defender level (LA–41 percent; SM–51 percent). This shift seems to indicate increased support for the movement, but little additional energy to fuel its growth. If the Santa Monica defenders were true to form, it also indicates a limited, self-interested commitment that should theoretically be very vulnerable to marginal improvement in the liberal tenants' personal situations.

Among moderates and conservatives the shift to lower consciousness was represented by a drop at the movement levels (Moderates: LA–27 percent, SM–18 percent; Conservatives: LA–21 percent, SM–14 percent) and an approximately equal increase at the antagonist level (Moderates: LA–6 percent, SM–12 percent; Conservatives: LA–18 percent, SM–24 percent), the segement of the tenant population that op-

Figure 8.2. *Tenant Consciousness by Political Identity (Santa Monica County Sample)*

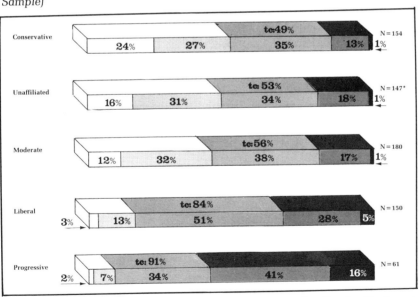

Note: *Please see Figure 4.1 for explanation of shaded bar codes. The classifications, in order, are: 1) Antagonist; 2) Individualist; 3) Defender; 4) Consumer; and 5) Radicalized.*
*Includes unaffiliated with no professed political perspective.

poses the movement effort. There are many historical examples of segments of U.S. society withdrawing support from what seemed, in abstract, to be a good idea, when that idea appeared likely to become a reality.

If the apparent shift to lower consciousness among the larger moderate and conservative categories is indicative of such a withdrawal of support, it portends a real break on how far the tenant movement might go without a major shift in the political identity of the population. It is also a reminder to organizers that their efforts may result not only in increased action but reaction as well.

Demographic Characteristics

Although examples of polarization were noted in earlier detailed findings, the data sets were examined to make sure that those earlier findings were not exceptions and that what was being measured was not primarily a product of the demographic differences between the samples. The general conclusion was that the earlier findings were not exceptions. While political identity, like tenant consciousness, was heavily related to demographic characteristics, the differences generally repeated themselves across these demographic lines. When the key levels of tenant consciousness indicated above[3] were examined, it was found that the differences were consistent with the polarization hypothesis in about 80 percent of the cases (65 out of 84 cases with two additional cases with no data in Santa Monica).[4] This does not mean that the demographic differences did not play a role in enlarging the differences. For example, white conservatives in Santa Monica had lower consciousness than white conservatives in the county, and, in addition, there were proportionally more white conservatives in Santa Monica than in the county.

The data regarding the relationship between tenant consciousness and political identity provided additional information regarding two of the demographic groups of which special note was made earlier, the Spanish-speaking Latinos and the seniors. The Spanish speakers again stood out from the rest of the ethnicity/gender groupings. Seventy percent of this group was in the unaffiliated category, more than twice the percentage in any other group. This reaffirms the Spanish speaker's lack of involvement in political activity. It may also be further evidence of the presence of a large number of undocumented workers in this population.

The senior data also provided a clearer look at the low consciousness of this group and the question of the role of what was referred to as the "infirmities of age" that limit action. What was found was further indication that physical limitations were not the whole story. Two findings point to political identity as having played a major role in the seniors' lower consciousness. First, seniors were more conservative and moderate and less liberal and progressive than any other age group;[5] and, second, their tenant consciousness was significantly related to seniors' political identity, even though their willingness to engage in action did not significantly vary across political identity. Further left seniors had higher consciousness because their greater support for rent control and constraints on landlordism were sufficient to outweigh the apparent general inability to engage in action.[6]

The Santa Monica seniors were one of the groups that showed signs of having been heavily affected by the political activity in that city. Evidence of this was accidentally obtained during the administration of the survey on which this work is based. In an attempt to find out about how important tenant issues were to the respondents, they were asked to name the three most important problems in their neighborhood. The results of this inquiry did not prove to be generally interesting. However, several Santa Monica seniors gave a rather remarkable answer. They responded that the number one problem in their neighborhood was "radical rent control organizers."

Changing Political Identity

The activists believed that engaging in collective resistance to landlord actions could radicalize tenants. This was the focus of much of the discussion in Chapter 6. To some activists, primarily those who were themselves economic or political radicals, the process of radicalization did not end with the formation of radicalized tenant consciousness but also led to radicalization of the tenants' overall political identities. They could not explain why some tenants went through this additional transformation and others did not, but they "knew" that a certain percentage of the time it did take place. It was this faith that kept them in the tenant movement. If they were right and this percentage became substantial with increased tenant-movement activity, the tenant movement could itself be a solution to the problem that political identity of tenants appears to pose.

The economic and political radicals saw the process of transformation as shifting the focus of the tenants' highly developed anger for landlords and landlordism to the entire system of private property in this country. This link between landlordism and the general institution of private property was seen as the key (Indritz 1971). In terms of this study, this is thought to entail moving tenants up the sophistication scale to increasingly more complex explanations of tenants' problems. In Gramsci's terminology this would mean escaping hegemony and adopting a counter-hegemonic position.

Unfortunately, in-depth histories of people who have gone through this transformation or time-series data, which might help explain such a transformation, are not available for those interviewed in this study. The best that can be done is to follow the logic dictated by the significant relationship between tenant consciousness and political identity and assume that, as the activists did, that as consciousness rises, shifts in political identity are likely to follow. The precursor to an identity shift should be higher consciousness. It is possible with the data available to see if the tenant consciousness of tenants within political identity categories was significantly affected by their experience as tenants.

To examine the possibilities of transformations in political identity taking place as a result of changes in tenant consciousness, two variables were selected to examine holding political identity constant. The first variable was the relationship of the tenants with their landlords. In the county sample, this variable had a particularly strong relationship to tenant consciousness.[7] The second variable was the short-term expectation of buying a home. This variable was particularly important in Santa Monica. The data set where the variable was strongest was used in the respective analysis.

When the effect of the relationship with the landlord on tenant consciousness within each political identity group was examined, it was discovered that only among moderates and liberals did the relationship to the landlord make a significant difference in the level of consciousness.[8] The identity of conservatives and progressives appeared to dominate consciousness to the extent that this aspect of the everyday experience became relatively unimportant in determining the level of consciousness.

Among the moderates and liberals the shifts in consciousness associated with varying relationships with landlords were quite dramatic, indicating the potential for a shift in identity. In both groups there was about a 20 percentage point difference in average overall consciousness between those who had very good relationships with their landlords and those who had fair to very poor relationships with their landlords. As seen in Figure 8.3, the resulting impact at the margins of consciousness, at antagonist and movement levels, was such as to make the percentage of moderates and liberals with very good relationships with their landlords in the antagonist category similar to that among the average conservative and the percentage of moderates and liberals with fair to very poor relationships with their landlords at the movement levels very similar to that of the average progressive.

When the impact of short-term expectations of homeownership were examined within each political identity category in Santa Monica, the results were even more dramatic. The impact was significant in

Figure 8.3. *Comparison of Tenant Consciousness: Conservatives to Moderates and Liberals with Very Good Relationships with their Landlords and Moderates and Liberals with Very Poor to Fair Relationships with their Landlords to Progressives (Los Angeles County Sample)*

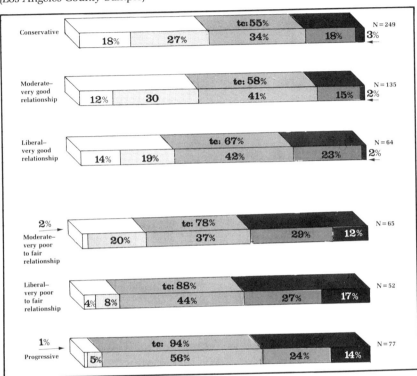

Note: *Please see Figure 4.1 for explanation of shaded bar codes. The classifications, in order, are: 1) Antagonist; 2) Individualist; 3) Defender; 4) Consumer; and 5) Radicalized.*

every category. The results also reinforced an observation made in the analysis of political identity and tenant consciousness: while certain people may be being radicalized, others may be being moved in a more conservative direction. Although the impact on consciousness was general, the most illustrative categories are the conservatives and progressives. Unfortunately, as seen in Figure 8.4, the number of respondents in these categories was low.

When the consciousness level of these groups was compared, exceptionally high consciousness among conservatives who did not expect to be able to buy in the next three years, and an exceptionally low consciousness among progressives who expect to be able to buy in this time period were identified. Among the conservatives who believed they

Figure 8.4. *Comparison of Tenant Consciousness: Conservatives and Progressive Respondents Who Wanted to Buy in the Next Three Years by Whether They Thought They Would Be Able to Buy (Santa Monica Sample)*

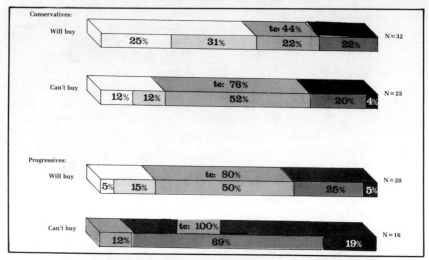

Note: *Please see Figure 4.1 for explanation of shaded bar codes. The classifications, in order, are: 1) Antagonist; 2) Individualist; 3) Defender; 4) Consumer; and 5) Radicalized.*

would not be able to buy, there was substantial decrease in the antagonists and individualists along with a substantial increase in the defender category. In addition there was the appearance of the only radicalized conservative tenant in the Santa Monica sample. Among the progressives who believe they would be able to buy, there was a substantial decrease in the movement levels of consciousness, a substantial increase to the defender category, and the appearance of the only individualist and antagonist tenants among the entire group of progressives in the Santa Monica sample.

While the data in both instances examined seemed to indicate tenant movement activity could lead to political identity changes, this conclusion should not be easily accepted. Political identity categories in the United States are thought to be very soft (Dolbeare and Edelman 1979, p. 153). Inconsistency in beliefs is thought to be the norm. And at least one tenant group that specifically set out to make this transformation happen, in this case to socialism beliefs, gave up, stating that organizing tenants only guaranteed that one would organize tenants and not make socialists (McAfee 1979). The question of whether such counter-hegemonic transformations are possible is one of the central issues in this study and will be examined in greater detail in the concluding chapter once the analysis of the remaining data is concluded.

Chapter 5 contained a brief discussion of the question of whether the consciousness measured in this study was a product of tenants' experiences or rather shaped those experiences. The conclusion of that discussion was consistent with Gramsci's point of view that the two are dialectically related. Experience and hegemony interact to form consciousness. The findings here could be interpreted as further evidence of the accuracy of this previously formulated conclusion.

The important role of consciousness, in the larger sense of political identity,[9] seemed to be indicated by the lack of significant impact on tenant consciousness of the quality of the relationship with the landlord among tenants with the strongest beliefs, the conservatives and the radicalized tenants. At the same time the significant impact on tenant consciousness of the quality of the relationship with the landlord among those with less extreme views, the moderates and the liberals, seemed to indicate a definite role for experience in the tenant consciousness formation process. This conclusion found additional support in the finding that in Santa Monica, whether or not the tenants thought they could buy a home in the next three years significantly affected the tenant consciousness of all the political identity groupings.

The tension between consciousness and experience indicated in the data also seems to express itself in the practice of the tenant movement. Consistent with the data, the tenant movement is always made up of tenants from the various political identity groups. This is possible because moderates with problems are just about as likely to be willing to participate in the movement as the average progressives. In fact sometimes a moderate in the movement with problems may have higher tenant consciousness than progressives in the movement without problems. This leads to the kind of divisions among the three types of radicalized tenants discussed in Chapter 3.

MOBILIZATION

A sense of competency, group identity and allegiance, and the will to act are generally seen as preconditions to the formation and mobilization of political consciousness. The absence of any of these elements is, conversely, seen as a major obstacle to the formation or mobilization of such consciousness. Authors such as Bertel Ollman (1972), writing about the factors that inhibit these processes, list the converse—alienation, isolation, and fear—as among the primary causal contributors to the failure of the predicted class consciousness and movement to manifest itself in capitalist society.

The focus here is on tenant consciousness, but it would also be expected that these elements would be factors in the formation or lack of

There is a movement in Santa Monica. It is unprecedented in the history of our city. It is quiet, strong and inevitable. The movement is your neighbors. The movement is you.

We now have a chance to control a major portion of our lives that has previously been beyond our control. We may have a word to say about what we pay to rent our home or apartment in Santa Monica.

Your wealthy opponents will try to frighten and befuddle you. They do not believe that Santa Monica should be a community based on care with restraint; profit with moderation; a community for the retired and employed; the young and the aged; the married and the single; the man or woman waiting for a home. They will tell you that you do not care for Santa Monica, your beach and the quality of your life.

A spirit is slowly, cautiously and conscientiously moving through Santa Monica. It is a belief in you and me and what we can do with our home and our lives.

COME WITH US AND VOTE YES.
YES ON PROPOSITION P.
The Fair Rents Initiative

Courtesy of Santa Monica Fair Housing Alliance. Reprinted by permission.

formation of tenant consciousness and the tenant movement.[10] Having the two data sets, the politicized tenant of Santa Monica and the relatively nonpoliticized tenants of the county,[11] provided a vehicle for observing the importance of these factors. However, causation cannot be fully established. While activism is thought to engender efficacy and allegiance, efficacy and allegiance are also thought to engender activism. Either may precede the other. Organizers in the county and Santa Monica had the broad reaction to Proposition 13 to build upon. In a successful organizing effort such as that in Santa Monica, efficacy, allegiance, and action appear to have fed upon each other. It will only be possible to measure the results of the process as of the date of this study.

Political Efficacy

Most studies of efficacy focus on individuals' sense of personal efficacy. For example, studies of efficacy that focus on political topics usually find that individuals with a personal sense of political efficacy are more likely to vote. This study, however, does not focus on individuals, but the potential of a movement. The question, thus, is not so much one involving individual sense of self-worth; rather, it is more one of "collective self-confidence," confidence in tenants as a group (Goodwyn 1978, p. XIX). To examine this collective sense of political efficacy, each respondent was asked how successful he or she thought tenants would be in gaining more rights if they were to become organized and active. The responses called for were a fixed set of four answers from very successful to not at all successful.

Consistent with the theory, the responses to the political efficacy question related significantly to tenant consciousness in both data sets. However, the relationship was, interestingly, more important in the county sample than in Santa Monica. The importance in the county was indicated by the responses to this question being entered second only to the allegiance variable (which we will discuss next) in the step-wise discriminant analysis in the county that included all significant variables reviewed in this book. The responses to this question were far down the list in Santa Monica. In Santa Monica the respondents' political identities were entered in the second position.

It seems of particular note that in the relatively nonpoliticized environment of the county, efficacy was a primary variable, while in the politicized environment of Santa Monica, political identity was a primary variable. As will be seen, efficacy of the type being measured was assumed in Santa Monica, while it was still an issue in the county where tenants have had more modest success. The dominance of political identity over other variables in Santa Monica seemed to suggest that once the question of efficacy was dispensed with, political identity asserted itself. Before that point was reached, the lines of political identity could and did remain blurred.

Indicative of the varying levels of success in Santa Monica and the county, the primary difference between the samples was in the percentage of tenants who believed organized and active tenants would be very successful or just somewhat successful. As seen in Table 8.4, 17 percent more of the tenants in Santa Monica answered "very successful" than gave this answer in the county. While more respondents gave the negative answers of "not very" or "not at all successful" in the county than in Santa Monica, in neither case was the percentage large.

Table 8.4. *Sense of Political Efficacy (Los Angeles County and Santa Monica Samples)*

Organized and Active
Tenants Will Be

	Los Angeles County		Santa Monica	
Very Successful	(424)	32.1%	(329)	48.9%
Somewhat Successful	(711)	53.8	(287)	42.6
Not Very Successful	(145)	11.0	(43)	6.4
Not At All Successful	(41)	3.1	(14)	2.1

In the county sample where the relationship between tenant consciousness and political efficacy was very significant, there was a substantial dropoff in political efficacy as tenant consciousness declined. Nearly one-half of radicalized tenants in the county sample believe organized and active tenants would be very successful, compared to only 14 percent of the antagonists. The relationship was not so dramatic in Santa Monica because even those who opposed the tenant movement had come to respect the movement's capacity for success. Just over half of the radicalized tenants in Santa Monica thought the movement will be very successful, a similar percentage as in the county, but the dropoff in the antitenant movement, antagonist category was only to 35 percent. Interestingly, it was not the radicalized tenants in Santa Monica that had the highest sense of efficacy. The consumers had the greatest sense of efficacy—60 percent answered very successful—perhaps indicating that radicalized tenants see limits that do not concern the more reformist consumers.

In Santa Monica the increased sense of political efficacy seemed to cut across all demographic lines. The result of the general high sense of efficacy was that none of the demographic characteristics under examination related significantly to political efficacy in Santa Monica. This was not true in the county. Of particular interest in the county was the relationship between political efficacy and the ethnicity/gender categories. Several important findings appeared in the analysis:

• The minority groups, including the low-consciousness Spanish speakers, had similar patterns (between 36 percent and 39 percent "very successful") of strong political efficacy.

• Whites, including both high-consciousness white women and low-consciousness white men, had substantially less of a sense of political efficacy. As with the minority groups, white men and white women had very similar patterns of responses (between 26 percent and 27 percent "very successful") to the efficacy question.

The finding that minorities had more of the type of political efficacy that was measured is consistent with the literature (Dolbeare and Edelman 1979, pp. 425–28). The general explanation for this finding is that such high scores result from the experience that minorities have had over the past decades with civil rights and other struggles. Whites, while they may be individually politically active, have not generally had experiences that include collective struggles. This alone, however, does not seem to explain all of our results. In particular it seems only a partial explanation of why the Spanish speakers and white women had levels of tenant consciousness inconsistent with their efficacy answers.

In the case of the Spanish speakers, the finding might be explained by the Spanish speakers' position in this society. It may be that they generally believe in the efficacy of collective action but do not see themselves as politically part of this society and, thus, are still not interested in joining in the political dimensions of U.S. tenants' struggle. The finding, with regards to white women, is consistent with the stereotype of women as feeling powerless in our society (McCourt 1977, p. 99). However, it may also be that women's close and intimate relationship with the low-consciousness white men additionally dampens their belief in what is possible. One can only hypothesize that the difficult economic situation women find themselves in leads them to high consciousness in spite of their relative pessimism.

The question of efficacy will again be a focus of the analysis when the role of activism is examined in a following section to determine the interrelationship between the two.

Allegiance

In order for there to be a sustained tenant movement, tenants must be

DEFEND RENT CONTROL

Don't take a chance!

The only candidates you can <u>trust</u> to protect rent control are those endorsed by Santa Monicans for Renters' Rights.

They are <u>honest</u> — and won't sell renters out to Big Real Estate.

FOR COUNCIL

Ken Edwards	3	⟶ ⊗
Dolores Press	4	⟶ ⊗
James Conn	7	⟶ ⊗
Dennis Zane	14	⟶ ⊗

RENT BOARD

Leslie Lambert	26	⟶ ⊗

Vote on Tuesday for the Renters' Rights Team

willing to follow the leadership of that movement (Ollman 1972, p. 8). This willingness to follow the leadership is called allegiance. To test for the level of allegiance, the respondents in both samples were asked how likely they would be to vote for a city council or board of supervisors' candidate recommended by their area's tenants' organization. The responses were a fixed set, including "very likely," "likely," and "not at all likely." In addition the answer that the respondent "would have to study the person running for office first" was recorded and coded as indicating a neutral response between "likely" and "not at all likely." The response to this question was, in effect, a measure of the amount of clout the tenant movement could muster in the political arena.

In both samples there was substantial allegiance, with over 60 percent of the respondents in both samples answering that they would likely or very likely follow the recommendation of their local tenant organization. As would be expected, the percentage of very likely responses was higher in Santa Monica. However, as seen in Table 8.5, the overall results were quite similar.

Table 8.5. *Allegiance (Los Angeles County and Santa Monica Samples)*

Likelihood of Following Tenant Organization Recommendation

	Los Angeles County		Santa Monica	
Very Likely	(389)	27.1%	(245)	34.5%
Likely	(492)	34.2	(200)	28.2
Have to Study Person	(408)	28.4	(194)	27.3
Not at all Likely	(149)	10.4	(171)	10.0

The similarity exists even though few of the respondents (7.1 percent) in the county sample were aware of the existence of a tenant organization in their area, while half of the Santa Monica respondents were aware of the organizations in their area. One would expect that this knowledge would have had more effect.[12] The county respondents showed an extraordinary allegiance by, in effect, granting a blank check to an unknown organization.

As shown in Figure 8.5, the tenants' responses on the allegiance question were very highly related to their tenant consciousness scores. The relationship was extraordinarily similar in both samples, with a high percentage of movement-level consciousness among the tenants who were very likely to follow the tenant organization's recommendation, and a substantial majority of those who were likely to follow the recommendation, at defender or higher level consciousness. An increase in the proportion of individualists was found among those who would have to study the candidate before making a decision, and a large proportion of those who would not follow the tenant organization's recommendation were at the antagonist level.

Figure 8.5. *Tenant Consciousness by Allegiance (Santa Monica Sample)*

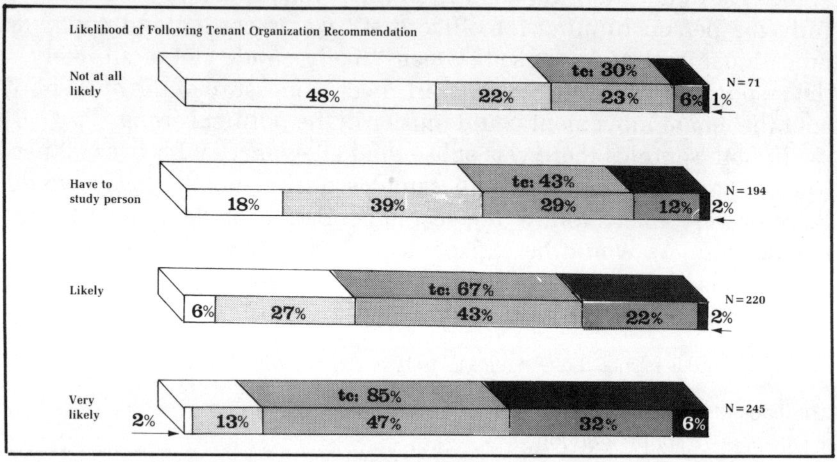

Note: *Please see Figure 4.1 for explanation of shaded bar codes. The classifications, in order, are: 1) antagonist; 2) Individualist; 3) Defender; 4) Consumer; and 5) Radicalized.*

The apparent similarity of the two samples on this point masked a very important difference between two that has contributed heavily to the continuing Santa Monica political successes. The allegiance of Santa Monica tenants has been captured in the electoral campaigns through voter registration drives and efforts to get out the vote. Two-thirds (471) of the Santa Monica tenants interviewed were registered to vote, compared to about one-half of the county tenant population. In addition the Santa Monica population that was registered turned out to vote. A nationwide study that examined voting patterns in the November, 1978, congressional election found that only 28 percent of tenants who were registered actually voted (U.S. Department of Commerce, Bureau of the Census, 1979). In Santa Monica in the election of April, 1981, 46 percent of the tenants registered voted.[13] In the national study they found tenants voted less than half as often as homeowners. Again, in Santa Monica, this was not true. In the 1981 election tenants voted in nearly (86 percent) the same percentages as homeowners.[14] If, as has been demonstrated in Santa Monica, tenants could be brought out to the polls across the country, the shape of politics in many jurisdictions would likely be altered.

The Tenant Vote:
How Groups Use Elections
to Win Political Power

From SHELTERFORCE, 1981 6(2): p. 1. Reprinted by permission.

The similarity of the primary results also fails to disclose that the underlying rationale for the allegiance in the two samples was quite different and may help explain the overall polarization that has been seen. The responses in Santa Monica appeared to be based on the success of the movement, while the responses in the county appeared to be based on frustration with the present situation. The quality of allegiance built on success may be much greater than that built on frustration.

To help understand the responses to the allegiance question, an additional question was asked about the respondents' beliefs about how elected officials were responding to tenants' problems. The effect of Santa Monica's successes was demonstrated by the finding that in the county, among those likely or very likely to follow a tenant organization's recommendation, a substantially higher proportion of respondents believed tenants' problems were not getting enough attention from elected officials than held that belief in Santa Monica (Very Likely: LA–70.2 percent; SM–50.6 percent and Likely: LA–57.3 percent; SM–39.0 percent). The impact of the successes also had its impact on those who did not support the tenant movement. Among respondents who would not follow a tenant organization's recommendations in Santa Monica, over half felt elected officials were paying enough attention (perhaps too much attention) to tenants' problems, compared to only 20 percent in the county.

The additional allegiance that existed in Santa Monica came from expected sources. Among tenants who were willing to follow the lead of the local tenant organization, there was an overrepresentation of liberals and progressives, younger, (below 60 years of age), lower-income (below $20,000 annual family income), college-educated whites (particularly men who were professional-managerial or petty bourgeois). In this group were tenants who had lived in the city less than five years, wanted to buy a home, but either believed they would never be able to or that they couldn't in the next three years, who had a history of multiple problems with landlords, and who had less than a very good relationship with their present landlords. This was consistent with the overall findings about tenant consciousness.

The sources of the increased allegiance in Santa Monica suggest that the amount of allegiance in the county might be expanded with organization and a worsening housing situation. At the same time, although Santa Monica results were positive, they also seemed to indicate that there may be a limit on how much allegiance the tenant movement can expect to gain, even with extraordinary organization. The large percentage of tenants in the Santa Monica population have made this level enough to be successful.

Activism

The question of tenant activism is of interest for two reasons. The first is to complete the analysis begun in Chapter 6. In that chapter the impact on consciousness of building-level activity was investigated and analyzed. The second is to understand the relationship between tenant activism and general political activism and social involvement. This will provide information on the extent to which tenant activism either builds off other types of activism or tends to generally activate tenants.

In Chapter 3 the extraordinary finding that over 40 percent of the respondents in each data set indicated that they had either previously participated in the tenant movement or were willing, if they could, to participate in the movement in the future was presented. Most of these respondents indicated they had or were willing to work in a rent control campaign, help organize tenant unions, or join an areawide tenant organization. A mobilization of 40 percent of a population would be quite phenomenal, and rather than viewing this as a likelihood, it should be viewed as the outside potential.

Anne Marie Staas Photos. Reprinted by permission.

In the county about 10 percent (66) of those who indicated interest in participation in the tenant movement actually had participated. This number was about 4.5 percent of the county sample. In Santa Monica the level of participation was substantially higher. A third of those who expressed interest, 13 percent (95) of the respondents, had actually participated. While these figures may be somewhat inflated by activists' willingness to participate in the study, they are still exceptional and indicate considerable political potential in the tenant movement. Because of the greater amount of participation in Santa Monica, the analysis will focus primarily on that data set.

Not surprisingly, the consciousness of those who had participated in the tenant movement was substantially higher than that of those who had not. This was true for all the elements of tenant consciousness as well. For example, in Santa Monica 75 percent of those who have worked in the tenant movement were very strong supporters of rent control, compared to 35 percent of the remainder of the respondents in that city. However, most surprisingly, only about a half of these activists have movement-level consciousness. Over 40 percent of the activists in both data sets were at the defender level, indicating that many of them may very well have been short-term or single-issue, rent-control activists. This seems confirmed by a substantial proportion of relatively low scores among this group (defender–activist) on the landlordism scale. Over 40 percent of the activists would not go beyond rent control and just cause to evict and support broad reform of the landlord-tenant relationship. Figure 8.6 illustrates these data.

Figure 8.6. *Activism by Tenant Consciousness (Santa Monica Sample)*

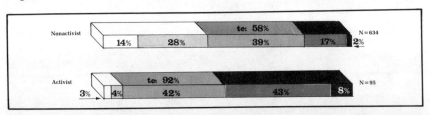

Note:*Please see Figure 4.1 for explanation of shaded bar codes. The classifications, in order, are: 1) Antagonist; 2) Individualist; 3) Defender; 4) Consumer; and 5) Radicalized.*

The connection between activism, efficacy, and allegiance was as expected. Nearly three-quarters of the activists in Santa Monica believed tenants would be very successful if they became organized and active, compared to under 50 percent of the remainder of respondents, and nearly 70 percent of the activists in Santa Monica would very likely vote as the tenant organization in that city recommends, compared to just under 30 percent of the remainder of the population.

Looking for groups that were overrepresented among the activists, it was found that tenants with the following characteristics were overrepresented in Santa Monica: under 40 years of age (77 percent), under $20,000 annual family income (80 percent), postgraduate educations (40 percent), lived in Santa Monica less than five years (91 percent), single, divorced, or separated (83 percent), professional-managerial or petty bourgeois (72 percent), and white (92 percent). In addition it was found that these tenant activists tended to be liberal or progressive in about equal proportions (60 percent in total), had multiple problems with landlords (48 percent), and believed either that they would never be able to buy a home or that their desires to buy a home in the next three years would be frustrated (50 percent). The comparable figures in the county were somewhat different, with an older, higher-income, and more racially mixed group of activists.[15]

The level of activity tenants engaged in in response to a problem at the building level discussed in Chapter 6 proved to be significant related to activist work in the tenant movement. As seen in Table 8.6, none of the tenants who moved and few of those who just talked to the landlord became active in the tenant movement. In both samples the level of

Table 8.6. *Proportion of Tenant Movement Activism by Response to Problem with Landlord at the Building Level (Los Angeles County and Santa Monica Samples)*

	Los Angeles County		Santa Monica	
Moved	(0)	0.0%	(0)	0.0%
Talked to Landlord	(4)	3.6	(5)	6.2
Took Individual Action	(19)	10.9	(27)	27.6
Joined with Other Tenants	(13)	14.8	(22)	34.9

participation in the broader movement increased significantly with those who took more aggressive action at the building level. In Santa Monica more than a third of those who organized in response to landlord actions at the building level were also active in the tenant movement.

The results of this analysis of the interconnection between building and movement activity would seem to indicate that the Santa Monica strategy of organizing at the building level to recruit tenants for the electoral campaigns was highly successful. While, as will be seen in the next section, these people may have been generally activated, it should again be noted that no permanent-membership tenant organization emerged from this process. Tenant groups in the county, without the immediate electoral battles present in Santa Monica, were seeking to build such membership organizations for the long-term struggle. This difficult task was taken on without the possibility of immediate reward that was present in Santa Monica.

The activists who were interviewed in this study stated that those who were already politically active were more likely to become active in the tenant movement and that conversely, that becoming active in the tenant movement tended to lead to broader political activity. Some of the activists also thought social involvement in the form of organizational membership would have the same interrelationship with tenant activism. Others did not. A few of the activists limited their prediction on social involvement to union membership. They felt union members would be more likely to see the wisdom of tenant activism, while members of other groups might or might not, depending on the political nature of the group.

As with tenant activism, the general level of political activism and social involvement in Santa monica was higher than in the county. The only exception to this rule was with union membership. A higher proportion of the county sample were union members, consistent with the earlier finding that a higher proportion of the county sample was working class. The data on this point is set out in Table 8.7.

Table 8.7. *Level of Political Activism and Social Involvement (Los Angeles County and Santa Monica Samples)*

	Los Angeles County		Santa Monica	
Political activism	(124)	8.5%	(106)	14.6%
Union membership	(292)	20.1	(112)	15.4
Organizational membership	(389)	26.8	(237)	32.6
No political or social activism	(790)	54.3	(352)	48.4

Table 8.8 shows that political activists were significantly more likely to have participated in the tenant movement than others. It also shows that political activism was also the best indicator of willingness to participate in the tenant movement, although in the county, union membership was a close second.

When the analysis was reversed to determine what other activities tenant activists were likely to engage in, it was found that tenant activists were generally otherwise involved. Only a quarter of the tenant activists had no history of either political activism or membership in a community organization or union. In Santa Monica they were approximately as likely to be a political activist (37 percent) or a member of a community organization (35 percent) and less likely to be a union member (23 percent). In the county they were most likely a member of a

Table 8.8. *Proportion of Political and Community Activists Who Engaged in Tenant Activism or Are Willing to Participate (Los Angeles County and Santa Monica Samples)*

	Los Angeles County		Santa Monica	
	Active	Willing	Active	Willing
Political activist	(23) 18.5%	(72) 58.1%	(35) 33.0%	(66) 62.3%
Union member	(23) 7.9	(159) 54.5	(22) 19.6	(56) 50.0
Community organization	(30) 7.7	(185) 47.6	(33) 13.9	(99) 41.8

community organization (46 percent) and less likely to be a political activist or union member (35 percent).

The findings here clearly establish a relationship between general activism and tenant activism. They do not, however, establish which comes first, general activism or tenant activism. For indications of the nature of the relationship between the two, it is necessary to look, in a more qualitative fashion, at Santa Monica's experience. Interviews with central figures in the Santa Monica movement suggested that participation in the movement was the catalyst that activated many tenants in the city. Many previously uninvolved people now hold office or serve on boards and commissions in the city (*LAT*, May 3, 1981, p. IX-1). In addition the Campaign for Economic Democracy, a member of the successful reform coalition, has been a direct beneficiary of the tenant movement in both gaining increased membership and an increased level of activity among its members. Also, in the city's Ocean Park neighborhood, a group named Ocean Park Community Organization has grown considerably with the tenant movement, and a community group named the Pico Neighborhood Association has been formed in the lower-income and minority neighborhoods along the Pico Corridor.

HEGEMONY

The findings of this study indicate considerable political potential in the tenant movement. In Santa Monica it has been demonstrated that it is possible, under certain conditions, to tap that potential. The trends in both rental and ownership housing seem to indicate that many of the conditions that led Santa Monica tenants to mobilize will become more common across the country. The finding that there is this potential in the tenant movement, however, does not tell us the substantive nature of what a powerful tenant movement is likely to achieve. Certainly, just cause to evict and rent control would accompany such a movement. In addition some broad increase in tenant power in relation to that for the landlord is predictable, including a tenant voice in whether a unit will be converted to a condominium. All of these reforms exist where tenants have successfully organized and become politically active. The question is, though, what more can we expect?

The predictions of how far the tenant movement could go range from revamping the national housing policy to an extreme of threatening the country's system of private property (Hartman 1975; Indritz 1971). In Chapter 1, we looked at the question of how far the tenant movement had tried to go in the past. In that chapter we found strong, historical, anti-landlord feelings and action for more aggressive housing policy, but little antiproperty sentiment. To the contrary, tenants have consistently been proproperty, complaining more that there has been a lack of access to ownership than complaining about the ownership of others.

In the urban setting the hegemonic dominance of the drive for accumulation through enterprise has rarely been questioned. Only speculation, monopoly, and vestiges of feudalism have been criticized. The socialization of property has not been the primary focus of tenant struggles. Rather, there have been repeated attempts at beating the laws of supply and demand in this century through stimulating housing production. Only in the Depression was there a serious loss of faith in the ability to win at this game, and even then there were few calls for socializing the existing privately owned housing stock. The programs put forward were rather liberal in nature, calling for government to provide that which the market could not. Today, we seem to be approaching another crisis and perhaps another period of loss of faith. There are early calls for beginning a process of socialization of the existing housing stock. Whether, in Gramsci's term, the movement is likely to become "counter-hegemonic" remains to be seen.

The data thus far have provided little evidence that the present crisis has moved this generation of tenants in a counter-hegemonic direction. In Chapter 7 an extraordinary drive for petty accumulation, that is, homeownership, was demonstrated by the tenants interviewed, including those at the movement levels. Another extraordinary finding reinforces the earlier finding regarding the drive for petty accumulation. Over 50 percent of the movement-level tenants in both samples expressed a desire to own rental property.

It would appear that the American dream may include more than just owning a home. It seems to also include the drive for at least modest accumulation of income-producing property. The data indicated, not only that this is part of the dream, but that the dream had become a reality at some point in their lives, for a substantial proportion of

present-day tenants. Among those tenants over 40 years of age, 17 percent in the county and 23 percent in Santa Monica had or at the time of
the study did own rental property.[16] The figures were substantially lower
among those under 40, with less than 10 percent in the present or past
ownership.

With this broad interest in ownership of rental property, together
with the amount of past and present ownership, it is not surprising that
the tenant movement, although potentially powerful, appears constrained. One has to assume, however, that the factors making it difficult
to attain homeownership will also restrict the possibilities of buying
rental property. Future generations of tenants may have the added frustration of being denied this additional avenue of accumulation, and the
tenant population, having less experience as landlords, may be more
easily radicalized.

To investigate further the degree of hegemonic domination of the
tenant movement, a scenario was formulated that assumed both broad-
scale increases in tenant consciousness and a shift left in the political
identity of the tenant population. To see the implications of this scenario, first the opinions of respondents about housing policy and landlordism were examined across the political identity categories. Then,
assuming a shift left in political identity and tenant consciousness had
taken place, these same opinions were examined for liberal respondents
with consumer consciousness and progressive respondents with radicalized consciousness. It was not until the opinions of this final group were
considered that hints of counter-hegemonic positions could be found.
The Santa Monica sample that represented a highly developed movement was used for this analysis.

To perform this analysis, the housing policy and landlordism questions discussed in Chapter 3 were employed. They were designed to test
tenants' positions on these subjects, as well as to test the implicit theories each position implies.

The common solution to the housing problem over the past few
decades has been to attempt to beat the laws of supply and demand
through stimulating construction through government subsidies to private developers. The first question asked was, therefore, about whether
the tenants supported such subsidies. For most of those who have assumed that this game could not be won, the alternate solution has been
government provision of housing for those the private sector could not
accommodate. The second question was, therefore about support for
public housing.

The next question asked attempted to measure whether there was
support for further government action in the direction of socialized
housing. Socialization of housing has come to mean either nationalizing

or cooperatizing the private rental housing stock. To test this tendency, the respondents were asked whether they supported the government's beginning either process of socialization. Hartman and Stone's (1980) scheme for beginning this process called for crediting tenants with an equity build-up in their apartment based on the rent they paid. To see if their approach could find a base of support, the respondents were next asked whether tenants who lived in a property five or more years should receive part of the proceeds if the building in which their apartments were located was sold.

An affirmative answer to the nationalize or cooperatize question need not have indicated a complete antilandlordism position. It could mean only that respondents were against big landlords while still maintaining the right of modest accumulation held so deeply in the consciousness of the U.S. population. To clearly identify those who were antilandlordism, those who supported socializing the housing stock were asked whether they would favor the elimination of all private ownership of rental housing. As was seen in Chapter 1, even holding this position is not a sure indicator of being deeply antiprivate property. To identify those against all private ownership of this form of property, those who favored the elimination of all private ownership or rental housing were asked whether they favored the elimination of the private ownership of all housing.

As shown in Table 8.9, the opinions on the housing policy and landlordism questions varied significantly with the respondents' political identities. As the suggested policy or reform becomes more radical,

Table 8.9. *Opinions About Housing Policy and Landlordism by Political Identity (Santa Monica Sample)*

	Conservatives	Moderates	Liberals	Progressives
Subsidized housing	(105) 70.0%	(134) 75.7%	(127) 84.7%	(48) 82.8%
Public housing	(80) 53.3	(100) 56.5	(105) 70.0	(41) 70.7
Nationalize or cooperatize	(10) 6.7	(18) 10.2	(20) 13.6	(21) 34.4
Tenant equity	(18) 12.4	(26) 14.8	(30) 20.5	(20) 34.5
No private rental housing	(0) —	(5) 2.8	(5) 3.3	(8) 13.1
No private ownership of housing	(0) —	(0) —	(0) —	1.7

the differences between the political identity groups increased. There was broad support for subsidized housing, but only liberals and progressives were strong supporters of public housing. When it came to either nationalizing or cooperatizing the private rental stock or providing for tenant equity build-up, only the progressives demonstrated substantial support. This support, however, was only a third of the population. Fewer still would go further.

When opinions of the liberal-consumers were examined, as shown in Table 8.10, a pattern very much like that of the liberals was seen, with the exception of less support for tenant equity.[17] A shift of consciousness

Table 8.10. *Opinions About Housing Policy and Landlordism of Liberal–Consumer and Progressive–Radicalized Tenants (Santa Monica Sample)*

	Liberal–Consumers		Progressive–Radicalized	
Subsidized housing	(35)	83.3%	(6)	60.0%
Public housing	(28)	66.7	(8)	80.0
Nationalized or coopertized	(6)	14.3	(10)	100.0
Tenant equity	(4)	9.5	(5)	55.6
No private rental housing	(1)	2.4	(7)	70.0
No private ownership of housing	(0)	—	(1)	12.0
	N = 42		N = 10	

and political identity to this point would apparently result in the return and reenergizing of the liberal housing policies of this century, but little more. At the extreme, with progressive-radicalized tenants, a different situation was seen.[18] The progressive-radicalized tenants were less supportive of subsidized housing than public housing. This group has apparently lost some of its faith in the private sector as did some housing reformers during the Depression and since. By definition this group supports nationalization or cooperatization of the private rental housing stock. However, while other groups appear to support the idea only to a point, progressive-radicalized tenants seem to predominantly mean their support as a step toward ending the institution of landlordism. Progressive-radicalized tenants also have given a majority vote for the tenant equity idea, although interestingly, the support is not overwhelming.[19] Few of these tenants, consistent with Hartman and Stone (1980), support the elimination of all private ownership of housing.[20]

The results of this analysis seem to confirm the finding of hegemonic domination of the tenant movement. It is clear that a radicalization and leftward political shift in the tenant population could contribute to a reversal in current trends away from direct government involvement in the construction and provision of housing. At the same time it is also clear that unless this transformation is extraordinary, landlordism, as an institution, is safe.

The premise employed here is that these findings resulted from the likely continuation of overwhelming support in this country for the right of individuals to accumulate property. Evidence supporting this premise was found not only in the nearly unanimous drive for homeownership and the majority desire for ownership of rental property, but in a further finding of the virtual absence of egalitarian feeling about the distribution of real property in the populations interviewed.

To test for the level of egalitarian feelings in the tenant population, the tenants in both samples were asked whether they would support a modern version of Skidmore's egalitarian, agrarian concept. The tenants were asked whether they believed that people should be able to buy as many homes as they wanted, and, if they stated they did not, whether homeownership should be limited to a single home until everyone has a home of their own. The questions were taken from a British study of attitudes of council housing (public housing) tenants in England (Moorhouse and Chamberlain 1974). The British study was conducted in the midst of a mass rent strike.

The sample interviewed in the British study was divided between those participating in the rent strike and those not participating in the rent strike. They found greater support for these measures of egalitarian feelings among strikers than among nonstrikers. However, even among nonstrikers, support was strong. Overall, over 50 percent of those interviewed supported the first proposition and just under 50 percent supported them both.

In the present study no such support for these egalitarian measures was found. As shown in Table 8.11, even among progressive tenants the support was only about half that found in the British study. Once again, the opinions of the liberal-consumers, as shown in Table 8.12, were not much different from the liberals as a group, and were far short of the British results.[21] As with the previous finding, it was only with the progressive-radicalized tenants that substantially different results were found.[22] Their support for the egalitarian measures exceeded that of the British council housing tenants.

The finding that the tenant population would have to move all the way to the progressive-radicalized position to support such egalitarian measures or the nationalization or cooperatization of the rental housing

Table 8.11. *Support for Limitation on the Number of Homes that an Individual Can Buy by Political Identity (Santa Monica Sample)*

	Conservatives	Moderates	Liberals	Progressives
Some limit	(9) 5.9%	(14) 7.8%	(20) 13.6%	(19) 31.3%
A one-home limit	(5) 3.3	(9) 5.0	(10) 6.8	(13) 21.3

Table 8.12. *Support for Limitation on the Number of Homes an Individual Can Buy of Liberal–Consumers and Progressive–Radicalized Tenants (Santa Monica Sample)*

	Liberal-Consumer	Progressive-Radical
Some limit	(5) 12.2%	(8) 80.0%
A one-home limit	(3) 7.3	(6) 60.0
	N = 41	N = 10

stock and tenant equity does not mean that such a shift of position will not occur. If either a depression or a return to stagflation follows the present period of economic stagnation, such a shift is conceivable. In either case the system would have great difficulty keeping its promises of upward mobility and homeownership to increasing numbers of people. What one author has referred to as the "tenantization" of the U.S. population would result (Stone 1978), and landlord-tenant conflicts would increase.

SUMMARY

This chapter explored the relationship between tenant consciousness and political identity, the potential for mobilization of tenants in the tenant movement, and the extent to which the Southern-California tenant movement had generated what appeared to be counter-hegemonic tendencies. Political identity was found to be significantly related to tenant consciousness. In Santa Monica this relationship was stronger than in the county. This was explained by the high level of politicalization in Santa Monica. Issues that were somewhat hypothetical in the county were very real in Santa Monica. The result was an apparent polarization in Santa Monica, particularly at the extremes of political identity, with the Santa Monica progressives having higher consciousness than those in the county and the Santa Monica conservatives having lower consciousness than those in the county.

Two conclusions of importance to the potential of the tenant movement were drawn from this evidence. The first was that the strong relationship between tenant consciousness and political identity, particularly with high levels of political activity, would seem to indicate that the tenant movement will be constrained unless there is a shift in the political identity of tenants. The second was that there was some evidence that the tenant movement itself might play a role in changing the political identity of tenants. With identity groups experience had a significant impact on consciousness. This finding also appeared to reaffirm the finding in Chapter 5 with regards to experience playing a role in the formation of consciousness. This second conclusion was tempered by the observation of political scientists that many people seem able to hold inconsistent beliefs and not go through substantial change in basic identity.

Three indicators of the potential for mobilizing tenants into the tenant movement were employed in this chapter. The first was the tenants' sense of efficacy, the second was their allegiance to the movement, and the third was their expressed willingness to work in the tenant movement. On all three measures Santa Monica tenants scored higher than county tenants, although, interestingly, the differences were more at the extreme than in the overall findings. For example, more Santa Monica tenants were ''very likely'' to vote as the tenant movement instructed, while more county tenants were just ''likely'' to vote as instructed. Taking the very likely and likely together, the percentages in the combined category were similar. This would seem to indicate substantial untapped potential for mobilization in the more general county population.

The question of efficacy, the belief that the tenant movement could improve the situation of tenants, appeared to be more important in the county where the issue of efficacy was unresolved. Efficacy was highly related to tenant consciousness in the county, but less so in Santa Monica. This seemed to result from the resolution of the question of efficacy in Santa Monica and the emergence of ''real'' politics.

Although the overall figures regarding allegiance, the extent to which voters would follow the lead of the tenant movement, were similar in the two samples, the findings were different in character. First, Santa Monica tenants voted in much higher percentages than is typical of tenants, and second, Santa Monica tenants had substantially more confidence in their elected officials than tenants in the county. The potential vote in the county appeared to be more a protest vote, while the potential vote in Santa Monica appeared to be more a support for the changes that had taken place.

The willingness to engage in tenant activism was significantly related to both efficacy and allegiance. It was also related to the building-level resistance to landlord actions discussed in Chapter 6. This was particularly important in Santa Monica where the organizers followed a policy of organizing tenants at the building level to recruit them into the various electoral campaigns that had taken place in that city. Tenant activism was also significantly related to general political and social activism. It appeared to politically activate tenants, giving more credence to the position that the tenant movement itself might be a catalyst to a shift in political identity.

In previous chapters, there has been little evidence of counter-hegemonic beliefs among the tenant population. Indeed, in Chapter 7, the evidence overwhelmingly indicated that tenants are still very interested in participating in the process of petty accumulation through purchasing a home. Additional evidence of the dominance of this element of the hegemony was identified in the finding that a majority of tenants with movement-level consciousness in both samples also expressed a desire to own rental property. It was only at the extreme that counter-hegemonic beliefs were common. Only the very small number of progressive-radicalized tenants seemed to hold counter-hegemonic beliefs. This was true for questions of housing policy, attitudes about landlordism, and for questions of egalitarianism in the distribution of property. The majority of potential tenant activists seemed to have attitudes well within the confines of the hegemony.

NOTES

1. The question inquiring about the political party affiliation was phrased: "Do you think of youself as a Republican, Democrat, or what?" In addition to recording party affiliation as reported above, the interviewers were instructed to record the response of "independent," if specifically stated. Respondents who stated they had no party affiliation or were not registered to vote were to be recorded as "unaffiliated."

2. Among conservatives and moderates with a party affiliation, party affiliation appeared to be much more important than political perspective. In addition conservatives and moderates within each party had similar levels of tenant consciousness, while there were significant differences between conservative and moderate respondents in various parties. The Democratic conservatives and moderates had higher consciousness than the Republican and the other party conservatives and moderates. Republican and other party conservatives and moderates were quite similar. In each group moderates actually had slightly lower consciousness than conservatives.

The finding that conservatives and moderates in each party had similar patterns of tenant consciousness was particularly important for Republicans because the overwhelming majority of Republicans in both samples were either conservative or moderate (about one-half of all Republicans in both samples were conservative). Among the Democrats, conservatives and moderates made up a majority in both samples, but the weight of the majority varied substantially between the two samples. In the county sample about two-thirds of the Democrats were conservative or moderate, while in Santa Monica, only just over a half fell in these categories (there were about twice as many Democratic moderates as conservatives in both samples).

Among liberals and progressive respondents, political perspective seemed to be more important than party affiliation, with progressives, as a group, having higher tenant consciousness than liberals. The only exceptions to this rule were the few respondents who identified themselves as progressive Republicans. They had tenant-consciousness levels more like the liberals.

The impact of political perspective on the independent and unaffiliated respondents' levels of tenant consciousness varied. Independents were the only group in which political perspective was the overall dominant factor. Conservative independents were like the conservative or moderate Republicans, moderate independents were like the Democratic conservative or moderate Republicans, while the liberals and progressives were similar to their respective political perspective categories. The opposite was true of the unaffiliated. Political perspective appeared to make no significant difference in the level of tenant consciousness, with the overall level of consciousness lying between that of the conservative and moderate Republicans and conservative and moderate Democrats.

3. Progressive–Consumer; Liberal–Defender; Moderate and Conservative–Movement levels and Antagonist.

4. We controlled for age, ethnicity, gender, class/gender, and income.

5. Data is set out in the following table:

Seniors	Los Angeles County		Santa Monica	
Conservative	(62)	27.9%	(49)	36.3%
Unaffiliated	(29)	13.1	(20)	14.6
Moderate	(105)	47.3	(46)	34.1
Liberal	(21)	9.5	(17)	12.6
Progressive	(5)	2.3	(3)	2.2

6. In the county, for example, 53 percent of the conservative seniors are strong or very strong supporters of rent control, compared to two-thirds of the liberals and 100 percent of the progressives. In Santa Monica the seniors vary significantly across political identity only in their support of rent control. Forty-three percent of the conservative seniors are strong or very strong supporters of rent control, compared to three-fourths of the liberals and 100 percent of the progressives.

7. In a stepwise discriminant analysis run on all the variables discussed in this study on the county data set, relationship to landlord was entered third only to the allegiance and efficacy variables discussed later in this chapter. When those variables were removed from the analysis, relationship to the landlord was entered first.

8. In the county there was a significant relationship between the relationship with the landlord and political identity. For example, 38 percent (92) of the conservatives had very good relationships with their landlords, compared to 19 percent (14) of the progressives. In contrast 28 percent (21) of the progressives had poor or fair relationships with their landlords, compared to 18 percent of the conservatives. Although the further left the tenant, the more likely he or she was to have a negative relationship, in Santa Monica the relationship between tenant consciousness and the relationship to the landlord was not significant. This seems another indication that the Santa Monica movement had transcended the expected base cause of tenant revolts.

9. Consciousness, as used here, means the product of previous interactions of experience and hegemony. It is assumed that political identity is generally representative of this former synthesis. As discussed earlier, the strong relationship between tenant conscious-

ness and political identity seemed to support this assumption.

10. We discussed the relationship between fear, the fear of eviction, and tenant consciousness in Chapter 6.

11. For a discussion of the politically alienating environment in Los Angeles, see Haas and Heskin (1981).

12. Actually, within each sample, knowledge of the existence of a tenant organization was significantly related to allegiance—in Los Angeles, 10.3 percent of those who answered very likely knew of a tenant organization; in Santa Monica, it was 59.4 percent. Respondents who answered that they would have to study the person were least aware of the existence of an organization (LA–4.9 percent; SM–3.0 percent).

13. This is based on an analysis of precincts that voted at least 60 percent for rent control in the successful 1979 election. In 1981, 12,662 of 27,323 registered voters in the 28 relevant precincts voted. In the lower-income, minority precincts analyzed the turnout was only about 40 percent, but this is still well above the national average.

14. This is based on an analysis of precincts that voted at least 60 percent against rent control in the successful 1979 election. In 1981, 3,872 of 7,188 (54 percent) registered voters in the seven relevant precincts voted.

15. The analysis also sought to determine who was most likely to be mobilized as opposed to simply expressing a willingness to become active. In both samples professional-managerial or petty-bourgeois tenants with college or postgraduate educations were most likely to have actually have been involved. In Santa Monica political identity was also significant, with 61 percent of the progressives, compared to 18 percent of the conservatives who expressed willingness, actually having participated.

16. The percentage of those who stated they presently owned rental property was a quarter of the respective totals in both samples.

17. Among progressive-consumers subsidized housing still is more favored (92 percent 23 to 80 percent 20). However, nationalization or cooperatization has a lot more support (44 percent 11), along with tenant equity (48 percent 12). Only 4 percent (1) supports eliminating private ownership of rental and other housing.

18. Radicalized tenants, as a group, have relatively left positions in Santa Monica: Subsidized Housing–78.3 percent (18); Public Housing–87.0 percent (20); Nationalized or Cooperatized–100 percent (23); Tenant Equity–50 percent (11); No Private Housing–52.2 percent (12); and No Private Ownership–13 percent (3).

19. In the county 63.6 percent (7) of progressive-radicalized tenants support tenant equity.

20. In the county 36.4 percent (4) of progressive-radicalized tenants support ending all private ownership of housing.

21. Only 16 percent (4) of progressive-consumers support a one-house limit.

22. Only 14 percent (1) of the liberal-radicalized tenants support a one-house limit.

CHAPTER

9

How Far Will the
Tenant Movement Go?

We began this study to determine the political potential of the tenant movement. Focusing on Santa Monica, we were able to examine the level of political consciousness generated in the process of, in Pickvance's terms, the transformation of a "social base" into a "social force" (1977). In Santa Monica tenants became, in this sense of the term, a "class-for-itself," overcoming both gender and social class divisions present in that city. An extraordinary mass of tenants were mobilized, and a sense of collectivity was generated. Tenants who were evicted in encounters with landlords, rather than shying away from future conflicts, became more aggressive; tenants permanently shut off from home ownership, rather than feeling personally defeated, became angered with economic forces contributing to their predicament; and tenants without landlord-tenant problems of their own, upon learning of the problems of others and sensing themselves to be part of a larger group, developed high tenant consciousness.

In the process of organizing tenants into a social force, questions regarding the efficacy of the tenant movement were dismissed, and the "real" politics of the community were exposed. In effect a single-issue movement was raised to the level of political struggle well beyond what is normally thought of when that term is used. People on the left were pushed further to the left and those on the right were pushed further to the right. People were forced to take their position and fight for it. Much of the city's population was activated, and a new government won the allegiance of a voting majority of its populace. As politicians say, "a mandate" for change was handed to a new force in the community. However, what this mandate consists of is not yet clear.

In part this lack of clarity exists because even with all the organizing

250

that has taken place in Santa Monica, little sign of a counter-hegemonic consciousness has emerged. The net result of the effort in Santa Monica has been only a distribution of tenant consciousness that approximated that present in the far less organized County of Los Angeles, taken as a whole. In particular the leveling effects of concentrated real estate speculation appeared to cause the consciousness of white male and petty-bourgeois tenants to raise to the level that other more structurally oppressed groups, more numerous in the county, occupied.

The Santa Monica population did show signs of greater sophistication in seeing speculators as the source of many of their problems, but it is difficult to know if this was more situational, resulting from the greater speculation in that city, or a sign of increased enlightenment. Certainly, the hegemonic domination of possessive individualism was not breached. If anything, it was that hegemonic domination, expressed in the frustration with not being able to buy a home, that strengthened the movement in Santa Monica.

For tenants in the tenant movement at the consumer level of consciousness whose goal it is to form a movement that will establish controls over the worse aspects of landlord and real estate industry behavior, this is quite enough. More successful organizing efforts such as those in Southern California, which appeared to be built on a coalition of tenants frustrated in their attempts at petty accumulation, tenants offended by the mistreatment they or their friends received from landlords, and tenants seeking legal protection from the rising cost of living because of their fixed incomes, may be possible. The hegemonic ideology can accommodate and even encourage such efforts. They do not interfere with the contradictions between the rights *of* property and right *to* property, while they give new vitality to the historically reified themes of antilandlordism, antispeculation, and democracy in this culture.

From the radicalized tenants' point of view, these findings leave much to be desired. A further transformation of tenant consciousness would have to take place before the movement they envision would have a change of becoming a reality. In Chapter 8 the evidence was that such further transformation would not come easily. The strong relationship between tenant consciousness and overall political identity indicated that political identity itself would have to be changed. This would seem to require a broader social movement than a tenant movement.

Within Gramsci's framework this would mean the formation of an "historic bloc" and counter-hegemonic consciousness (Adamson 1980, pp. 140–201). As in this study, Gramsci had a concept of levels of consciousness. What Pickvance called consciousness sufficient to form a class-for-itself, and we have called consumer consciousness, Gramsci called "economic-corporate" consciousness. At this level of consciousness, tenants, for example, would feel solidarity with each other in solving their economic problems, but this solidarity would not carry over to the formation of a larger counter-hegemonic coalition, what Gramsci called an historic bloc. For this more thoroughgoing movement to form, tenants, as well as other subgroups, would have to undergo a "catharsis" to a counter-hegemonic level of consciousness Gramsci called "ethico-political" consciousness. Gramsci is not explicit about how this catharsis takes place, much as the activists interviewed in this study were not specific about how tenants sometimes become radicalized. The catharsis is rather metaphorically described in terms of the emergence of the whole person and the end of alienation. What Gramsci does provide is a vehicle for the catharsis to take place. This vehicle is the "organic intellectual." The organic intellectuals lead[1] the population through a series of "negations" to lessen the bounds of the dominant ideology and then develop new ideas, which they "integrate" into the "very fabric" of the emerging movement's "culture, lifestyles, language and traditions." The intellectuals are organic in that they are from the class that is forming the new historic bloc.

The question of how the three types of radicalized tenants identified in this, acting as organic intellectuals, might try to induce such a catharsis remains. With the findings of this study in mind, the possible approaches the radicalized tenants might adopt will be examined. This investigation will conclude this study.

In Gramsci's terms, only the economic and political radicals would have to introduce truly "new" ideas. The tenantists and the extreme consumers would, rather, seek to renew and embellish the old tenant themes in this country's political history that we have examined. In the main they would replay the conflict between democracy and aristocracy of past years and try to move it beyond its previous political confines into the economic realm.

By definition the single-issue tenantists would not be interested in such a movement, but their antilandlordism themes might still make a contribution to a larger movement. Its strength helps explain why landlords are often singled out for economic regulation in periods of stress and suggests that tenants may, in fact, be a subgroup along with gender, race, and the like that should be considered in a larger coalition. Certainly in a period of increasing economic concentration and shadowy multinational enemies, landlords are a reachable target and a starting point for organization.

The extreme consumers' position is consistent with the formulation of a broader reform effort. Their analysis and ideas fit with the present drive for "economic democracy" and the efforts of the "new urban populists'' (Shearer 1982, p. 14). The movement in Santa Monica is seen as an example of building toward such a larger movement by some of its organizers, including, appropriately, the Campaign for Economic Democracy. The development of ''a concrete program of tenants' rights'' appears to be a clear extension of democracy from the political to the economic realm (Carnoy and Shearer 1980, p. 387).

What makes these concepts less than what Gramsci called for is that they are primarily antimonopoly rather than antiaccumulation. In this sense they are related to the Populist movement of the late nineteenth century and borrow many of their antimonopoly programs from that movement. There is, however, an important difference between the situation of the Populists and that of the economic democrats and ''new urban populists'' of today.

The Populists had their greatest successes with farmers, petty producers, who needed the process of production and distribution rationalized in order for their independent economic activity to remain viable. Their movement and the institutions they created were directed against the banks that threatened the stability of their lives with unreasonable credit terms, railroads that charged exorbitant rates, and grain elevator operators that usurped their profits to store their crops. The Populists were never as successful with the urban worker as they were with the farmer.

The agrarian Populists employed the clear image of the working farmer, the yeoman of the agrarian tradition, exploited by institutions away from the farm, in their organizing. The economic democrats and new urban populists replace this image with that of the ''community'' and organize against forces attacking that community, as they did in Santa Monica, for example, against outside speculators.[2] However, when it comes to social issues rather than communities, the distinctions become less coherent. In the tenant movement, for example, as noted in Chapter 3, they make the distinction between the small landlord and the big landlord. Consistent with this distinction, the Santa Monica rent control charter amendment contains an exclusion for small landlords, that is, the resident landlord who owns three or less units.

Where the line between small and big is drawn is not always so clear, particularly in the minds of the population. Historically, we have the example of Skidmore, who tried and failed to gain support for placing a limit on the amount of land that a family might own. At its base, the big-small distinction has as its premise egalitarianism. This sense of egalitarianism was not found in the tenant populations studied here. In a society in which petty accumulation is viewed as essential for security and often for success, it may be unreasonable to expect such egalitarianism.

The problem is compounded by the very base of such movements, in their support for the process of petty accumulation. They must seek to encourage this process while discouraging monopoly accumulation. To do this, programs of individual and collective forms of homeownership would be supported, along with antispeculation measures (Carnoy and Shearer 1980, p. 387). Whether this is politically possible remains to be seen. It is the problem that Henry George faced and was unable to politically resolve. Under pressure the successful petty accumulator often sides with the monopolist rather than with those who have not yet had their chance to begin the accumulation process. With such a turn of events, a "democratic" populist movement can turn "reactionary." The more radical proposal of Hartman and Stone is predicated on a collapse of the U.S. economy in another major depression. Their program goes beyond encouraging the transformation of current renters into petty accumulators, even in restricted, antispeculation forms. They contemplate converting all tenants and a sizable proportion of existing homeowners, when they face foreclosure, into a nonspeculation framework. The government would, in effect, guarantee tenants and homeowners security in return for giving up the right to use housing to accumulate.[3] Short of an economic collapse, it would be hard to imagine why existing or expectant homeowners would give up this "right."

The Stone and Hartman proposal would likely move us much closer to the European situation. In Europe working-class movements have produced social relations of consumption, what Castells calls "collective consumption," that are much closer to capitalist patterns of production (Castells 1977 p. 460). To the social and political radicals, a concomitant change in U.S. patterns of consumption could mean an unmasking of the class structure of this country and the merger of the tenant movement into a broader class-based movement.[4] The result could be a politics in United States much closer in form to that in England.

Even without the adoption of such a proposal, worsening economic conditions could result in a "tenantization" of an increasing portion of the U.S. population that could have the same tendencies (Stone 1980, p. 105). The nonclass-based, consumption-side movements of the recent past have been born largely in a period of economic expansion and, as in the case of Santa Monica, are responses to inflation rather than deflation. In a depression problems appear on both the production and consumption sides of people's lives, and movements become drives for both "homes and jobs." As a result, depression era movements, as seen in Chapter 1, tend not to be the consumption-side, isolated, single-issue movements, worrisome to some social and political radicals (Mingione 1977, pp. 104–5).

A truly counter-hegemonic, antiaccumulation model that would have a chance of gaining widespread popular support is hard to imagine in the context in which we now exist. As one author noted, in the present structural situation, people "may be 'forced' in a metaphorical, nondetermined sense to take advantage of the situation for the sake of their children if not themselves" and in the process, "become a part of the problem rather than part of the solution" (Duncan 1982, pp. 127–28). Only in a situation where nonaccumulators were in the overwhelming majority and faith in the possibilities of petty accumulation had been lost, could people be expected to turn away from petty accumulation and accept a counter-hegemonic collectivist's position.[6]

The problems facing the radicalized tenants, whatever their bent, lie ahead. At the present time the immediate problems of tenants once again threaten to grow worse. If the tenants in Los Angeles County are representative of tenants in other major cities in the United States, such worsening conditions should yield an increasingly powerful tenant movement. While Santa Monica's situation was in many ways unique and favorable for movement formation, the level of consciousness was no higher than that in the county. Movement formation appears to enhance the level of consciousness. Particularly, as an electoral force, the tenant movement appears a sleeping giant. The problems of organizing across race and ethnic lines, not faced in Santa Monica, will have to be overcome. This, however, does not appear to pose an impossible obstacle if the different structural situations faced by different racial and ethnic groups are addressed.[7]

The evidence of this study points strongly to the possibility of tenants becoming an "economic" class-for-itself. What remains to be understood is how such a class can go through that complex catharsis in the interaction of hegemony, everyday experience, collective action, negations, and counter-hegemony that Gramsci described. The activists could not shed light on how and why it sometimes happens. They did, however, state that it does happen. This leads us to continue to wonder whether this next episode of the tenant movement will be the one to escape the contradictions contained within the ideology of possessive individualism or once again replay the story from the past.

NOTES

1. Gramsci actually had a more dialectical notion than inferred by the word lead. In Gramsci's words "The popular element 'feels' but does not always know or understand; the intellectual element 'knows' but does not always undersand and, in particular, does not always feel" (Adamson 1980, p. 146).

2. For a discussion of this concept, see Lustig (1980) and the reply by Boyte (1980).

3. Programs like this presently have success with low-income renters, who, with government assistance, buy their apartments as limited equity co-ops. See, for example, discussion of Route Two in Hass and Heskin (1982).

4. Engels (1975, p. 48) did not include homeowners among the proletariat. They were not owners of capital unless they rented out property. It appeared that he saw them in an ambiguous category between the dominant class, consistent with the analysis in this study.

5. See the discussion of the English situation contrasted with that in the United States by John Agnew (1982).

6. Adamson (1980) notes that there is no guarantee that in such a situation the new hegemony will be socialist or democratic. It could also be fascist (p. 154).

7. A multiracial movement has been built in Baltimore (Leight et al. 1981).

Appendix—Methodology

One of the goals of this study was to classify the samples of tenants who were interviewed according to their level of tenant consciousness. This goal was met through methodological procedures that have not been described thus far in the text. In this appendix, after describing the overall methodological approach to classification of the random tenant populations, these procedures will be described.

STEPS IN THE METHOD OF CLASSIFICATION

The steps used in the classification process were:

1. Define the dimensions of tenant consciousness.
2. Determine the levels of tenant consciousness.
3. Create scales to test the level of consciousness of tenants on each of the dimensions.
4. Determine the pattern of scale positions at each level of consciousness.
5. Determine the proper weighting of the position on the four dimensions (a function).
6. Select a random sample of tenants.
7. Create a survey instrument with questions that will measure consciousness on all dimensions of tenant consciousness.
8. Create valid scales from the responses to the survey that match those used in the definition.
9. Classify the respondents according to their tenant consciousness.

Dimensions of Tenant Consciousness

As discussed in the Introduction, the work of John Leggett (1968) was particularly helpful in determining the dimensions of tenant consciousness. Leggett arrived at four dimensions through an analysis of Marxist literature. Initially, we took Leggett's four dimensions and modified them for tenant consciousness. An independent search of the consciousness literature confirmed Leggett's choices (see Chapter 3), and our analysis of tenant history suggested that the modifications of Leggett's dimensions were reasonable. The four dimensions were: "identification," "landlordism," "sophistication," and "action."

Levels of Tenant Consciousness

Our effort to identify levels of tenant consciousness again started with Leggett's work (1968, p. 41). Leggett formed five levels of working-class consciousness on his four dimensions. Using the Guttman Scale technique, he arranged the four dimensions in order of importance and used a single dichotomous test for each dimension. The levels on the scale were then determined mechanically by the number of tests the worker passed. If he passed none of the tests, he was at the bottom of the consciousness scale (Class Indifferent). If he passed all four he was at the top (Egalitarian Militant). The following table illustrates the dimensions. (Superscript 1 indicates class consciousness; superscript 2 indicates no class consciousness.)

Workers Typed According To Class Perspective	DIMENSIONS			
	Egalitarianism	Militancy	Skepticism	Class Verbalization
Militant Egalitarians	$+^1$	+	+	+
Militant Radicals	$-^2$	+	+	+
Skeptics	−	−	+	+
Class Verbalizers	−	−	−	+
Class Indifferents	−	−	−	−

While Leggett's scale was helpful in conceiving what the levels of tenant consciousness might be, his types were not themselves easily convertible to tenant consciousness categories. In part this appeared to be the case because Leggett's assumption that the four aspects could be measured with a single dichotomous test did not seem valid. None of the phenomena he sought to measure are dichotomous. For example people are not either skeptical or not skeptical; they are skeptical in degree. Each of the dimensions Leggett employed and we employed were scaleable variables rather than dichotomous. The categories, therefore, should be patterns of responses to scale tests rather than simply added responses to single questions.

While with what we knew about the tenant movement at this time we might have simply constructed levels of consciousness on our own, and created dichotomous tests and hypothesized what patterns of responses would fit each category, we decided to consult with tenant activists to obtain their opinion on constructing the tenant consciousness scale. As was explained in the Introduction, our levels of tenant consciousness had to relate to the tenant movement. Our concern was the potential for mobilizing the tenant population into the tenant movement. Activists were the ones who experienced tenants' political consciousness from this reference point and could, we thought, give us invaluable assistance in defining this form of consciousness.

The method of selection of the activists is set forth in Chapter 3. Each activist was interviewed according to a survey instrument composed of both structured and open-ended questions. We began part of the interview devoted to developing the levels of tenant consciousness by giving each activist a blank ladder which could have as many rungs (levels) as he or she wished. The activist was then asked to identify the level of consciousness at each rung by name. These names were then entered on the ladder. An open-ended description of each level of consciousness was then solicited. After all the open-ended descriptions were completed, the interviewer then returned to the ladder and asked for the position of each level identified on the four dimensions of tenant consciousness that had been previously created. Each interview was recorded and transcribed for analysis.

The transcripts were then read and coded (we will discuss the creation of the scales in following paragraphs). Starting with Leggett's five levels of consciousness and what we had learned about the tenant movement and political consciousness, we then examined the ladders the activists created, their open-ended descriptions, and coded information on the four dimensions of tenant consciousness to create the levels of consciousness employed in this study.

Employing scales rather than dichotomous tests resulted in our varying from what Leggett had provided. Leggett's top two types (militant egalitarians and militant radicals) considered all four dimensions of consciousness. These proved to be translatable to tenants active in the tenant movement who varied on their position on landlordism (radicalized and consumer.) After these two steps, however, Leggett no longer considered the action dimension. The activists made more variation in the action variable than working or not working in the tenant movement per se. The tenant movement involves confrontations between landlords and tenants at the building level and movement activity in a broader collective sense, such as working in rent control campaigns. The top two levels were those who would work in the movement. After this came the distinction about organizability at the building level. The next two levels then became those who were organizable at the building level (defender) and those who were not organizable (individualist). Again, because of this orientation toward the movement, the bottom level took on a more active characterization. Instead of being "nil" as Leggett had called it, the activists saw the bottom level composed of those antagonistic to the movement. At this bottom level, they made a distinction between consciousness, Landlord Lovers, and Unconscious, antagonism which did not prove measurable.

Tenant-Consciousness Scales

The construction of the four scales (one for each dimension) was done after reading the transcripts of the activists' interviews. The "ladder" approach not only provided a hierarchy of consciousness categories but also, in effect, provided scales for each of the dimensions. This information, along with what was learned from a review of the history and case study, was then incorporated into the scaling process. Standard five-point scales were used. There was considerable consistency among the activists on three of the four dimensions: identification, sophistication, and action. This made the construction of these scales quite straightforward. The activists were less consistent when it came to the landlordism scale, making the construction of this scale more difficult.

The fourth scale regarding landlordism was developed from a combination of "Likert"-like responses and specific examples of these "Likert"-like statements offered by the activists. The activists tended to respond in the following fashion to our questions regarding landlordism: "they totally support it", "they would support some self-interested restriction," "they are beginning to be suspicious and would support broad reform," "they are against it." For each of these "Likert"-like responses, the activist gave numerous examples. To make up the scale used in analyzing the results of the surveys of the tenants, the Guttman scaling technique was applied to various combinations of the examples given us by the activists. The result, as seen in Chapter 3, involved judgment of which of several possibilities would be most appropriate.

Coding the Activist Data

Thirty-two activists were interviewed. Twenty-eight of the activists created discernible tenant consciousness ladders and gave us codable responses on the positions of the levels on the four dimensions of tenant consciousness. Two tasks had to be performed before we could complete the definition part of the study. The levels created by the activists had to be translated into the levels of consciousness that were to be used in the study, and the responses about the position each level would take on the four dimensions had to be translated into scale points.

The 28 activists who completed the ladder exercise created ladders from 3 to 12 rungs. The mean number was four-and-a-half. Some of the activists created multiple types of tenants at a given level. In all, 107 codable types of tenants were created. Three members of the study team classified the 107 types into the six (later five) levels of consciousness and scored the responses. Because of the limited number of cases, disagreements among the coders were settled, when possible, by consultation, rather than by rejecting the disputed cases. Where this was not possible, the type was removed from the data set. Only four of the types created by the 28 activists could not be coded. However, the entire response set of a twenty-ninth activist who attempted the exercise was rejected because it could not be coded. This activist repeatedly changed his mind and reordered his types to the point that coherence was no longer possible. In sorting the levels created by the activists into the levels used in the study, the hierarchy of the activists was scrupulously observed, with the exception that some types created by the activists were collapsed onto the same level used in the study.

Weighting the Scale Points

The next problem we faced was how to replicate what we had learned from the activists in our responses from the randomly selected tenants. One possibility was that we simply add the points accumulated by the "archetype" tenant created by the activists at each level and divide by the number of cases at each level; then we could create even ranges around these averages in which we would place similar calculations made from the responses to the random surveys. We attempted this and attempted to reclassify the cases created by the activists into the ranges at each level. We found that the borders between levels were not coherent and that a substantial amount of misclassification resulted.

One of the problems in using simple mathematics was that it assumed that the points assigned on each scale were equivalent. We had no reason to believe this. To the contrary the impression we had from the literature and the activists was that the points on the scale were not always equivalent. Starting with this assumption, we sought a method of weighting the responses.

The method we decided on was discriminant analysis. As described in Chapter 3, discriminant analysis is a method for classifying cases according to predetermined patterns of multiple dimensions. This is what we had at this point, and we wanted to classify the tenants interviewed in the random sample to match the patterns provided by the activists. In order to use discriminant analysis, however, you must have more than quantifiably defined categories. You must also have the discriminant function from which the weights given the various points are derived and constants for each variable.

To obtain this function and constants, we performed a discriminant analysis (SPSS Package) on the data set created by the activists. (In naming the levels of consciousness and giving each level's responses on the four dimensions, the activists were, in effect, creating types of tenants. We treated the 107 types created as a data set for analysis.) The first function that resulted from this analysis explained a very high 93.5 percent of the variance in the activist data set. Two other supplemental functions were also derived to explain the rest of the variance. The function indicated that the activists had not given the dimensions of tenant consciousness equal weight. Landlordism was given the heaviest weight (.81), the next was action (.56), followed by identification (.28) and sophistication (.21).

We interpreted this function as giving more discriminating importance to the landlordism and action scales because most tenants support rent control and the activists' opinion that few tenants would be very sophisticated when it came to why rents increase. The variation is an interesting one. It could be interpreted as meaning that the activists gave more importance to theory over practice. Certainly at the top of the scale this was true. However, it also appeared to result from a belief that theory leads to action. As a tenant became more suspicious of landlordism, he or she would become more active.

We then used the function to classify the activists' data set. It is common to only use the first function when it explains such a high percentage of the variation. However, we decided to use all the functions (three—one less than the number of variables) that were derived. We did this because our task was to replicate the definition of consciousness we had developed from the activist interviews in the random data set as accurately as possible. When we used all the functions, then we were able to classify 92.5 percent of the activist cases correctly. Two functions yielded 88.79 percent accuracy and one function less.

Random Selection of Tenants

The method we used for selecting the tenants interviewed in this study was random digit dialing. In this method the prefixes for every phone in the area of study are entered into the computer, which then selected the next four digits according to a random number generator. All numbers generated are then called, through use of a screening instrument it is determined, in this case, whether a tenant household has been reached. If the number is a business or homeowning household, the interview is terminated. Four call backs were made before a number was abandoned.

If a tenant household was reached, then a Kish-type random selection table was used to select the person in the household to be interviewed. To use the selection table, the interviewer first lists the adult members of the household starting with the oldest male, lists all the rest of the males in order, and then lists the females according to age. The interviewer then asks to speak to the party randomly selected. If the person is not available, the interviewer makes an appointment to call back. Three call backs are attempted to complete this interview.

In all, 16,000 numbers were drawn in the county and 6,000 were drawn in Santa Monica. Of these numbers about 2,000 tenants were reached in the county and 1,000 in Santa Monica. Of those reached 79 percent (1,598) and 76 percent (758) completed the interviews. Twelve percent (246) and 14 percent (143) in Santa Monica refused to participate. About 1 percent in each sample terminated.

Consciousness Scales Used in Classifying Random Samples

See pp. 76–89 for a discussion of the scales in the classification of the random samples.

Classification of Random Samples

In order to classify a case, they had to have relatively complete sets of responses to scale questions. In all there were 31 questions that made up the scales. Depending on the skip pattern of an individual case, a respondent was asked 21 to 25 of these 31 questions. With this number of questions, it was more often the case than not that at least one response was missing in a case. The majority of the missing responses were to questions regarding why rents increase.

To deal with this problem, we devised a two-level test. The first level tested for the percentage of responses to scale questions and the second for the number of scale points left ambiguous by missing responses. The first-level test required that at least 80 percent of the scale questions appropriated to each case must have been answered. Applying this test, 27 cases (3.6 percent) from the Santa Monica sample and 135 cases (8.4 percent) from the county sample were removed from the study. Applying the second test, an additional 17 cases (1.1 percent) were removed from the county sample. No cases in Santa Monica failed this second test. In the case where a scale point was missing, the mean score was assigned.

Low-income, low-education, senior, Spanish-speaking, and Asian respondents were overrepresented in the cases removed from the study. They tended not to answer the more theoretical questions such as on the sophistication scale (60 percent of all "I don't knows" came on this scale). The higher-income, white, educated respondents were more likely not to answer the action questions.

With the exception of Individualists in the county sample, the classification of the respondents was within accepted levels of probability. Taking 75 percent probability as the test, the probability that the classifications were "correct" was as follows:

	Santa Monica	Los Angeles County
Radicalized	88.8%	95.6%
Consumer	78.1	74.8
Defender	85.2	88.8
Individualist	77.9	72.8
Antagonist	89.9	87.6

The slightly lower probability among county Individualists likely results from the difficulty in classifying Spanish-speakers, as discussed in Chapter 4.

Bibliography

PART I

Abrams, Charles. 1946. *The Future of Housing*. New York: Harper and Brothers.
———. 1950. "Rats Among the Palm Trees." *The Nation*. Feb. 25.
Adamson, Walter L. 1980. *Hegemony and Revolution*. Berkeley: University of California Press.
Agnew, John. 1982. "Home Ownership and Identity in Capitalist Societies." In *Housing and Identity—Cross-cultural Perspectives*. New York: Holmes and Meier.
Aronowitz, Stanley. 1973. *False Promises—The Shaping of American Working-Class Consciousness*. New York: McGraw-Hill.
Atlas, John, and Dreier, Peter. 1980. "The Housing Crisis and the Tenants' Revolt." *Social Policy*. January/February: 13–24.
Baar, Kenneth. 1977. "Rent Control in the 1970's: The Case of the New Jersey Tenants' Movement." *Hastings Law Journal* 28(3): 631–83.
Barton, Stephen. 1977. "The Urban Housing Problem; Marxist Theory and Community Organizing." *Review of Radical Political Economy* Winter: 16–30.
Beach, M. Y. 1845. *Wealth and Biography of the Wealthy Citizens of New York*.
Beard, C. 1913. *An Economic Interpretation of the Constitution of the United States*. New York: The Free Press.
Blau, J. L., ed. 1946. *American Philosophic Addresses, 1700–1900*. New York: Columbia University Press.
Blumberg, Richard E.; Robbins, Brian Quinn; and Baar, Kenneth K. 1974. "The Emergence of Second Generation Rent Controls." *Clearinghouse Review* August: 1974: 240–49.
Boggs, Carl. 1976. *Gramsci's Marxism*. London: Pluto Press.
Boyte, Harry C. 1980. *The Backyard Revolution: Understanding the New Citizen Movement*. Philadelphia: Temple University Press.
Braverman, Harry. 1974. *Labor and Monopoly Capital*. New York: Monthly Review Press.
Bridenbaugh, C. 1955. *Cities in Revolt*. New York: Knopf.
Burghardt, Nancy Romer. 1972. "More Than Just Rent Strikes:

Alternative Tactics." In *Tenants and the Urban Housing Crisis*, edited by S. Burghardt. Dexter, Michigan: The New Press.

Burghardt, Stephen, ed. 1972. *Tenants and the Urban Housing Crisis*. Dexter, Michigan: The New Press.

———. 1972. "Rent Strike or Tenant Union? The Building of a Permanent Organization." In *Tenants and the Urban Housing Crisis*, edited by S. Burghardt. Dexter, Michigan: The New Press.

Calverton, V. F. 1939. *The Awakening of America*. New York: The John Day Company.

Campbell, Angus; Gurvin, Gerald; and Miller, Warren. 1954. *The Voter Decides*. Evanston, Illinois: Harper and Row.

Campbell, Angus; Converse, Philip; Miller, Warren E.; and Stokes, Donald E. 1964. *The American Voter*. New York: John Wiley and Sons.

Carnoy, Martin, and Shearer, Derek. 1980. *Economic Democracy*. New York: M. E. Sharpe.

Carter, N. H., and Stone, W. L. 1821. *Reports of the Proceedings and Debates of the Convention of 1821*. Albany, New York: E. and E. Hosford.

Castells, Manuel. 1977. *The Urban Question*. Cambridge, Massachusetts: MIT Press.

Christman, H. 1978. *Tin Horns and Calico*. Cornwallville, New York: Hope Farm Press.

Clark, W. A. V., and Heskin, Allan David. 1982. "The Impact of Rent Control or Tenure Discounts and Residential Mobility." *The Journal of Land Economics* 58(1): 109–17.

Community Development Department, Housing Division. 1978. "Rental Policy Considerations." Los Angeles.

Community Ownership Organizing Project. 1976. *The Cities' Wealth*. Washington, D.C.: Institute for Policy Studies.

Cooper, J. Fenimore. 1846. *The Redskins*. New York: Burgess and Stringer.

Countryman, E. 1976. *Out of the Bounds of Law: Northern Land Rioters in the Eighteenth Century*. In *The American Revolution*, edited by A. F. Young, pp. 37–70. DeKalb: Northern Illinois University Press.

Deckard, Barbara Sinclair. 1979. *The Women's Movement*. New York: Harper and Row.

del Castillo, Richard Griswold. 1975. "A Preliminary Comparison of Chicano, Immigrant, and Native-Born Family Structures, 1850–1880." *Aztlan-International Journal of Chicano Studies Research* 6(1): 87–97.

de Mille, A. George. 1950. *Henry George*. Chapel Hill: University of North Carolina Press.

Dennison, G. M. 1976. *The Dorr War.* Lexington: University Press of Kentucky.

Dolbeare, Kenneth M., and Edelman, Murray J. 1979. *American Politics.* Third ed. Rev. Lexington, Massachusetts: D.C. Heath.

Downs, Anthony. 1978. "Public Policy and the Rising Cost of Housing." *Real Estate Review* 8(1).

Drellich, Edith Berger, and Emergy, Andree. 1939. *Rent Control in War and Peace.* New York: National Municipal League.

Duncan, Nancy. 1982. "Home Ownership and Social Theory." *Housing and Identity—Cross-cultural Perspectives.* New York: Holmes and Meir.

Ehrenreich, Barbara, and Ehrenreich, John. 1979. "The Professional-Managerial Class." In *Between Labor and Capital,* edited by P. Walker, pp. 5–49. Boston: South End Press.

Ehrenreich, B., and English, D. 1979. *For Her Own Good.* Garden City, New York: Anchor Press/Doubleday.

Ellis, D. M. 1946. *Landlords and Farmers in the Hudson-Mohawk Region 1790–1850.* Ithaca, New York: Cornell University Press.

Engels, Frederick. 1975. *The Housing Question.* Moscow: Progress Publishers.

Ermer, Virginia, and Strange, John H., eds. 1972. *Blacks and Bureaucracy.* New York: T. Y. Crowell.

Ernst, R. 1949. *Immigrant Life in New York City.* New York: King's Crown Press.

Fair Housing Project. 1979. *Discrimination Against Children in Rental Housing.* Santa Monica: Fair Housing for Children Coalition, Inc.

Femia, Joseph V. 1981. *Gramsci's Political Thought.* Oxford: Clarendon Press.

Foner, E. 1976a. "Tom Paine's Republic: Radical Ideology and Social Change." In *The American Revolution,* edited by A. F. Young. DeKalb: Northern Illinois University Press.

———. 1976b. *Tom Paine and Revolutionary America.* New York: Oxford University Press.

Foner, P. 1955. *History of the Labour Movement in the United States,* Vol. II. New York: International Publishers.

———. 1947. *History of the Labour Movement in the United States,* Vol. I. New York: International Publishers.

Ford, J. 1939. *Slums and Housing.* Cambridge, Massachusetts: Harvard University Press.

Fox, D. R. 1965. In *The Decline of Aristocracy in the Politics of New York, 1801–1840,* edited by R. V. Remini. New York: Harper and Row.

———. 1934. "New York Becomes a Democracy." *History of the State of New York,* Vol. 6. New York: Columbia University Press, pp. 3–34.

Friedman, L. M. 1968. *Governmental and Slum Housing*. Chicago: Rand McNally.

Frost, S. 1920. *Labor and Revolt*. New York: Dutton.

Garcia, John. 1976. "History of Chicanos in Chicago Heights." *Aztlan-International Journal of Chicano Studies Research* (7)2: 291–306.

Gates, P. W. 1973. *Landlords and Tenants on the Prairie Frontier*. Ithaca, New York: Cornell University Press.

George, H. 1955. *Progress and Poverty*. New York: Robert Schalkenbach Foundation.

Giddens, Anthony. 1973. *The Class Structure of the Advanced Societies*. New York: Harper and Row.

Glaab, C. N., and Brown, A. T. 1967. *A History of Urban America*. New York: Macmillan.

Goodwyn, Lawrence. 1978. *The Populist Movement*. Oxford: Oxford University Press.

Gorz, Andre, ed. 1976. *The Division of Labour: The Labour Process and Class Struggle in Modern Capitalism*. Hassocks, England: Harvester Press.

Gottlieb, Robert, and Wolt, Irene. 1977. *Thinking Big*. New York: G. P. Putnam's Sons.

Gramsci, Antonio. 1971. *Selections from the Prison Notebooks*. New York: International Publishers.

Grebler, Leo, and Mittelbach, Frank. 1979. *The Inflation of House Prices*. Lexington, Massachusetts: D.C. Heath.

Greenfield, R. J., and Lewis, J. F. 1980. "An Alternative to a Density Function Definition of Overcrowding." In *Housing Urban America*, 2nd ed., edited by J. Pynoos, R. Schafer, and C. Hartman. New York: Aldine.

Grier, William H., and Cobbs, Price M. 1968. *Black Rage*. New York: Basic Books.

Haas, Gilda, and Heskin Allan. 1981. "Community Struggles in Los Angeles." *International Journal of Urban and Regional Research* 5(4): 546–64.

Handel, Gerald, and Rainwater, Lee. 1964. "Persistence and Change in Working-Class Life Style." In *Blue Collar World*, edited by Arthur Shostar and William Gomberg. Englewood Cliffs, New Jersey: Prentice-Hall.

Handlin, O. 1979. *Boston's Immigrants*. Cambridge, Massachusetts: Harvard University Press.

Hartman, Chester. 1975. *Housing and Social Policy*. Englewood Cliffs, New Jersey: Prentice-Hall.

Hartman, Chester, and Stone, Michael. 1980. "A Socialist Housing Program for the United States." In *Urban and Regional Planning in* an *Age of Austerity,* edited by Pierre Clavel, John Forester, and William W. Goldsmith. New York: Pergamon Press.

Harvey, D. 1976. "Labour, Capital and Class Struggle Over the Built Environment in Advanced Capitalist Societies." *Politics and Society* 6(3): 265–95.

Hawke, D. 1966. *The Colonial Experience.* New York: Bobbs-Merrill.

Hawley, Peter K. 1978. *Housing in the Public Domain.* New York: The Metropolitan Housing Council.

Heskin, Allan David. 1978. "The Warranty of Habitability Debate: A California Case Study." *California Law Review* 66(1): 37–68.

Hofstader, R. 1973. *America at 1750, a Social Portrait.* New York: Vintage Books.

———. 1944. *Social Darwinism in American Thought.* Boston: Beacon Press.

Hofstadter, R., and Wallace, M. 1970. *American Violence.* New York: Knopf.

Homefront. 1977. *Housing Abandonment in New York City.* New York: Homefront.

Horowitz, Lucy, and Ferleger, Lou. 1980. *Statistics for Social Change.* Boston: South End Press.

Indritz, Tova. 1971. "Tenants Rights Movement." *New Mexico Law Review* 1, January.

Jennings, Thomas. 1972. "A Case Study of Tenant Union Legalism." In *Tenants and the Urban Housing Crisis,* edited by S. Burghardt. Dexter, Michigan: The New Press.

Joselit, Jenna Weissman. nd. "The New York City Rent Strikes of 1904 and 1907–08." Unpublished manuscript.

Keating, Dennis W. 1978. "Tenants Hound Landlords for Rebates." In *These Times,* September 6–12: 4.

Kim, Sung Kok. 1978. *Landlord and Tenant in Colonial New York.* Chapel Hill: University of North Carolina Press.

Kraus, M. 1971. "America and the Irish Revolutionary Movement in the Eighteenth Century." In *The Era of the American Revolution,* edited by R. B. Morris, pp. 332–48. Glouster, Massachusetts: Peter Smith.

Krohn, Roger G.; Fleming, Berkeley; and Manzer, Marilyn. 1977. *The Other Economy.* Toronto: Peter Martin Associates.

Lawson, Ronald, and Barton, Stephen E. 1980. "Sex Roles in Social Movements: A Case Study of the Tenant Movement in New York City." *Signs* 6(2): 231–47.

Legates, Richard, and Murphy, Karen. 1981. "Austerity, Shelter, and Social Conflict in the United States." *International Journal of Urban and Regional Research* 5(4): 255–75.

Leggett, John C. 1968. *Class, Race, and Labor.* New York: Oxford

University Press.

Leight, Claudia; Lieberman, Elliot; Kurtz, Jerry; and Pappas, Dean. 1980. "Rent Control Wins in Baltimore." In *Rent Control, A Source Book*, edited by John Gilderbloom, pp. 187–91. Santa Barbara, California: Foundation for National Progress, Housing Information Center.

Link, E. P. 1942. *Democratic-Republican Societies, 1790–1800*. New York: Columbia University Press.

Lipsky, Michael. 1970. *Protest in City Politics: Rent Strikes, Housing, and the Power of the Poor*. Chicago: Rand McNally.

Lockridge, K. 1971. "Land, Population, and the Evolution of New England Society, 1630–1790; and an Afterthought." In *Colonial America*, edited by S. Katz, pp. 466–91. Boston: Little, Brown and Company.Lockwood, Rodney. 1976. "What Has Happened to the New American Family's Ability to Buy New Homes?" *Urban Land* June: 3–6.

Loren, Charles. 1977. *Classes in the United States*. Davis, California: Cardinal Publishers.

Lowe, Cary. 1977. "California Housing Group Organizes." *Shelterforce* 2(4): l, 14.

Lubove, Roy. 1962. *The Progressives and the Slums; Tenement Housing Reform in New York City, 1890–1917*. Pittsburgh: University of Pittsburgh Press.

Lukacs, George. 1968. *History and Class Consciousness*. Cambridge, Massachusetts: MIT Press.

Lustig, Jeff. 1981. "Community and Social Class." *Democracy* 1(2): 96–111.

Mandelker, Daniel R., et al. 1981. *Housing and Community Development*. Indianapolis: Bobbs-Merrill, p. 210.

McAfee, K. 1979. "City Life: Lessons of the First Five Years." *Radical America* 13(1): 39–59.

McCarney, Joe. 1980. *The Real World of Ideology*. Atlantic Highlands, New Jersey: Humanities Press.

McCourt, Kathleen. 1977. *Working-Class Women and Grass Roots Politics*. Bloomington: Indiana University Press.

McDonnell, Timothy L. 1957. *The Wagner Housing Act*. Chicago: Loyola University Press.

Macfarlane, Alan. 1978. *The Origins of English Individualism*. New York: Cambridge University Press.

McGrady, Edward F. 1918. "What Labor Wants." In *Housing Problems in America*. New York: National Housing Association, pp. 297–302.

McGrane, R. G. 1924. *The Panic of 1837*. Chicago: University of Chicago Press.

McKenzie, Robert, and Silver, Allan. 1968. *Angels in Marble: Working*

Class-Conservatives in Urban England. London: Heinemann.

McLoughlin, W. P. 1892. "Evictions in New York's Tenement Houses." *The Arena* (December): 48–57.

MacPherson, C. B. 1962. *The Political Theory of Possessive Individualism.* Oxford: Oxford University Press.

Massey, Doreen, and Catalano, Alejandrina. 1978. *Capital and Land.* London: Edward Arnold.

Michelman, F. I. 1970. "The Advent of a Right to Housing: A Current Appraisal." *Harvard Civil Liberties-Civil Rights Law Review* 5(2): 207–26.

Miller, D. T. 1967. *Jacksonian Aristocracy, Class, and Democracy in New York, 1830–1860.* New York: Oxford University Press.

Mingione, Enzo. 1977. "Theoretical Elements for a Marxist Analysis of Urban Development." In *Captive Cities,* edited by M. Harloe, pp. 89–110. London: John Wiley and Sons.

Mohr, J. C. 1973. *The Radical Republicans and Reform in New York During Reconstruction.* Ithaca, New York: Cornell University Press.

Moorhouse, H. F., and Chamberlain, C. W. 1974. "Lower Class Attitudes to Property: Aspects of the Counter ideology." *Sociology* 8(3): 387–405.

Morais, H. M. 1971. "The Sons of Liberty in New York." In *The Era of the American Revolution,* edited by R. B. Morris, pp. 269–89. Glouster, Massachusetts: Peter Smith.

Morris, R. B. 1971. "Labor and Mercantilism in the Revolutionary Era." In *The Era of the American Revolution,* edited by R. B. Morris, pp. 76–139. Glouster, Massachusetts: Peter Smith.

Moskovitz, Myron, and Honigsberg, Peter. 1970. "Tenant Union— Landlord Relations Act." *Georgetown Law Journal* 58: 1103.

Myers, C. 1971. *The History of Tammany Hall.* New York: Dover Publications.

———. 1927. *History of the Great American Fortunes.* New York: Random House.

Nash, G. B. 1979. *The Urban Crucible.* Cambridge, Massachusetts: Harvard University Press.

Nie, Norman H., et al. 1975. *Statistical Package for the Social Sciences.* New York: McGraw-Hill.

Note. 1976. "The Great Green Hope: The Implied Warranty of Habitability in Practice." *Stanford Law Review* 28: 729.

O'Conner, H. 1941. *The Astors.* New York: Knopf.

Ollman, Bertell. 1972. "Toward Class Consciousness Next Time: Marx and the Working Class." *Politics and Society* Fall: 2–24.

Paine, T., ed. 1922. "Agrarian Justice." In *The Complete Political Works of Thomas Paine.* New York: Peter Eckler.

Penalosa, Fernando. 1971. *Class Consciousness and Social Mobility in a Mexican American Community.* San Francisco: R and E Research Associates.

Perin, C. 1977. *Everything in Its Place.* Princeton, New Jersey: Princeton University Press.

Peterson, M. D. 1970. *Thomas Jefferson and the New Nation.* New York: Oxford University Press.

———51 ed. 1975. *The Portable Thomas Jefferson.* New York: Penguin.

Pickvance, C. G: 1977. "From Social Base to Social Force: Some Analytical Issues in the Study of Urban Protest." In *Captive Cities,* edited by M. Harloe, pp. 175–89. London: John Wiley and Sons.

Piven, Frances Fox, and Cloward, Richard A. 1977. *Poor People's Movements.* New York: Pantheon Books.

Pole, J. R. 1978. *The Pursuit of Equality in American History.* Berkeley: University of California Press.

Poulantzas, Nicos. 1975. *Classes in Contemporary Capitalism.* London: Shield and Ward and NLB.

Rachlis, E., and Margusee, J. E. 1963. *The Landlords.* New York: Random House.

Rayback, J. G. 1959. *A History of American Labor.* New York: The Free Press.

Real Estate Research Council of Southern California. 1979. "Real Estate and Construction Report, First Quarter." Chapter VII, p. 287.

Reich, Wilhelm. 1972. *Sex-Pol.* New York: Vintage Books.

Reissman, Leonard. 1959. *Class in American Society.* Glencoe, Illinois: The Free Press.

Rex, John, and Moore, Robert. 1967. *Race, Community, and Conflict.* London: Oxford University Press.

Rodgers, D. T. 1978. *The Work Ethic in Industrial America, 1850–1920.* Chicago: University of Chicago Press.

Rose, J. G. 1973. *Landlord and Tenants.* New Brunswick, New Jersey: Transaction Books.

Rossiter, C. 1962. *Convervatism in America.* New York: Knopf.

Santa Monica City Council. 1978. Fair Housing Alliance Report, (July), Item 12B. City of Santa Monica, California.

Santa Monica Planning Department. 1978. "Everything You Always Wanted to Know About Santa Monica." Statistical Summary. City of Santa Monica, California.

Santa Monica Rental Housing Information and Mediation Service. 1979. "Report on Current Housing Problems." City of Santa Monica, California.

Schlesinger, A. M. 1929. *Political and Social History of the United States, 1829–1925.* New York: Macmillan.

Schnapper, M. B. 1975. *American Labor: A Pictorial Social History.* Washington, D.C.: Public Affairs Press.

Selltiz, Carrie; Wrightsman, Lawrence S.; and Cook, Stuart, W. 1976. *Research Methods in Social Relations,* 3rd ed. New York: Holt, Rinehart and Winston.

Shannon, F. A. 1966. "Not Even an Indirect Safety Valve Attracting Eastern Farmers." In *The Frontier Thesis,* edited by R. A. Billingston, pp. 41–50. New York: Robert E. Krieger.

Shearer, Derek. 1982. "How the Progressives Won in Santa ·Monica." *Social Policy* 12(13): 7–14.

Siegel, Mark. 1981. "Toward an Economic Democracy Housing Program." In *Rent Control: A Source Book,* edited by J. Gilderbloom, pp. 251–61. Santa Barbara, California: Foundation for National Progress, Housing Information Center.

Sinclair, Upton. 1933. *I, Governor of California and How I Ended Poverty; A True Story of the Future.* New York: Farrar and Rinehart.

Sisson, D. 1974. *The American Revolution of 1800.* New York: Knopf.

Skidmore, T. 1829. *The Rights of Man to Property!* New York: A. Ming Jr.

Soboul, A. 1965. *A Short History of the French Revolution, 1789-1799.* Berkeley: University of California Press.

Spiller, R. E. 1931. *Fenimore Cooper: Critic of His Times.* New York: Minton, Balch and Company.

Sternberg, Arnold. 1978. "Testimony, Assembly Committee on Housing and Community Development." In *Forum* 1(3): 10–12.

Sternlieb, George. 1972. "Death of The American Dream House." *Society* 9(14): 39–42.

Sternlieb, George, and Burchell, Robert W. 1980. "Multifamily Housing Demand: 1975–2000." In *America's Housing, Prospects and Problems,* edited by G. Sternlieb, et al., pp. 219–57. New Brunswick, New Jersey: Center for Urban Policy Research, Rutgers University.

Sternlieb, George, and Hughes, James. 1981. *The Future of Rental Housing.* New Brunswick, New Jersey: Center for Urban Policy Research, Rutgers University.

———. 1980. "The Uncertain Future of Rental Housing." In *America's Housing,* edited by G. Sternlieb and W. Hughes, pp. 257–67. New Brunswick, New Jersey: Center for Urban Policy Research, Rutgers University.

Stone, Michael. 1978. "Housing, Mortgage Lending, and the Contradictions of Capitalism." In *Marxism and the Metropolis,* edited by W. Tabb and L. Sawyers, pp. 179–209. New York: Oxford University Press.

———. 1980. "The Housing Problem in the United States: Origins and Prospects." *Socialist Review* 52: 65–119. Afterwords: 395.

Syzmanski, Al. 1979. "A Critique and Extension of the PMC." In *Between Labor and Capital*, edited by P. Walker, pp. 49–67. Boston: South End Press.

Thernstrom, Stephen. 1964. *Poverty and Progress*. Cambridge, Massachusetts: Harvard University Press.

Thompson, E. P. 1966. *The Making of the English Working Class*. New York: Vintage Books.

Touraine, Alain. 1971. *The Post-Industrial Society*. Translated by Leonard F. X. Mayhew. New York: Random House.

Tribe, Keith. 1978. *Land, Labor and Economic Discourse*. London: Routledge and Kegan Paul.

United States Department of Housing and Urban Development. 1980. "Measuring Restrictive Rental Practices Affecting Families with Children: A National Survey." Ann Arbor, Michigan: Survey Research Center, Institute for Social Research.

United States League of Savings Associations. 1980. *Homeownership: Coping with Inflation*. Chicago: U.S. League of Savings Associations.

United States Riot Commission. 1968. "Report of the National Advisory Commission on Civil Disorders." Official Records. Washington, D.C.: Government Printing Office.

Vaughan, Ted R. 1972. "Landlord-Tenant Relations in a Low Income Area." In *Tenants and the Urban Housing Crisis*, edited by S. Burghardt, pp. 77–89. Dexter, Michigan: The New Press.

Veiller, Lawrence. 1967. "Housing Evils and Their Significance." In *The Urban Community*, edited by R. Lubove, pp. 56–58. Englewood Cliffs, New Jersey: Prentice-Hall.

———. 1903. "Tenement House Reform in New York City, 1834–1900." In *The Tenement House Problem*, Vol. 1, edited by R. W. DeForest and L. Veiller, pp. 69–118.

Ware, N. J. 1964. *The Industrial Worker*. New York: Harper and Row.

———. 1935. *Labor in Modern Industrial Society*. Boston: D. C. Heath.

Warner, Sam Bass, Jr. 1972. *The Urban Wilderness*. New York: Harper and Row.

Warren, Frank A. 1974. *An Alternative Vision; The Socialist Party in the 1980s*. Bloomington: Indiana University Press.

Watts Labor Community Action Committee. nd. "Housing Needs and Demand in the Goodyear/Lindsay Village Green Project Area." Unpublished report.

Wekerle, Gerda R. 1980. "Women in the Urban Environment." *Signs* 5(3): 188–215.

Welter, R. 1975. *The Mind of America*. New York: Columbia University Press.

Williamson, A. 1973. *Thomas Paine*. London: George Allen and Unwin.

Williamson, C. 1960. *American Suffrage from Property to Democracy 1760–1860*. Princeton, New Jersey: Princeton University Press.

Willis, J. W. 1950. *A Short History of Rent Control Laws*. Ithaca, New York: Cornell University Press.

Wood, Edith Elmer. 1931. *Recent Trends in American Housing*. New York: Macmillan.

Woodyatt, Lyle John. 1968. "The Origins and Evolution of the New Deal Public Housing Program." Ph.D. dissertation, Washington University.

Wright, Erik Olin, and Perrone, Luca. 1977. "Marxist Class Categories and Income Inequality." *American Sociological Review* 42: 32–55.

Zahler, H. S. 1941. *Eastern Workingmen and National Land Policy, 1928–1862*. New York: Columbia University Press.

Zetnick, S. 1979/1980. "Melville's Bartleby, the Scrivener: A study in History, Ideology and Literature." *Marxist Perspectives* Winter 1979/80: 74–92.

Zusman, Marty E., and Olson, Arnold O. 1977. "Gathering Complete Response from Mexican-Americans by Personal Interview." *Journal of Social Issues* 33(4): 46–55.

PART II

Newspapers and Periodicals

Beverly Hills Post

Brentwood Hills Press

CED News (Campaign for Economic Democrats)

CES Newsletter (Coalition for Economic Survival)

Chain Letter (California Housing Action Information Network)

Daily News (formerly published as the *Valley News*)

Grassroots (Berkeley's Community Newspaper)

Housing Law Project Bulletin

Los Angeles Herald-Examiner

Los Angeles Sentinel

Los Angeles Times (abbreviated as *LAT*)

New York City Herald

New York Times

New York Tribune

Niles Weekly Register

Ocean Park Perspective

children as reason for, 255
class, 111
expectation to buy, 247, 251,
253–255
hegemony, xiii, 34–36, 214, 221,
239–41, 244, 254–255
land monopoly, 17–19, 23–26
ownership of rental property,
240–241, 244, 247
petty accumulation, xvi, xx, 10,
14–15, 23, 34–36, 40, 153–
154, 180, 215, 247, 250–251,
253–255
Poulantzas, Nicos, 110
Professional-managerial, 94, 113,
116–117
activism, 111, 113, 236–237
eviction fear of, 169, 171–172
expectation to buy, 100, 114–
115, 177, 186–188, 197–198,
200–201
expectation to buy of former
owners, 205
income, 198–199, 209
landlord-problems knowledge of
friends, 147
landlordism, 113
rent control, 113, 133
rent levels, 152
rental conditions, 131–132, 133–
134, 155
rents fairness of, 135
residential satisfaction, 133–134
Property Management Journal, 43

Rainwater, Lee, 111
Rayback, J. B., 5, 10, 15
Real Estate Research Council of
Southern California, 183
Reich, Wilhelm, xviii
Reissman, Leonard, 114
Rent control, 17–18, 29, 33, 36, 42,
61, 63–65, 69–73
activism, 42–43, 59–60, 85–86,
235
age, 96–97 (See Seniors)
allegiance, 249

class, 113, 133, 144–145
education, 100
ethnicity, 51–52, 75, 105–107,
133, 164–166
eviction, 168–170
gender, 99–100, 105, 122, 123
housing market, 35
income, 100, 122, 166
landlord-problems, 144–145
landlordism, 81
laws, 41, 45–47, 48, 50–53, 58,
164–166, 177
political identity, 216, 221
rental conditions, 131–133
seniors, 45, 150, 153–154, 221
sheltercost, 137
tenant movement, 49–51, 85,
240
Rental conditions, 126–128, 151–152
activism, 159–161, 163
age, 129 (See Seniors)
class, 131, 133–134
ethnicity, 128, 133
eviction, 168–169
landlord-problems, 159–161
landlord-relationships, 142
rent control, 133
rents fairness of, 126, 131–132,
154
seniors, 128
sheltercost, 137
Rents, xii, xxi, 3–4, 11–13, 15–28,
35–36
activism, 53, 71, 159–161, 163
class, 131–133, 135, 152
egalitarian concept, 244
ethnicity, 75, 107, 152
expectation to buy, 188, 191
fairness of, xxi, 4, 131–133, 135–
136, 142, 152–153, 154, 155,
194–195
gender, 98–100, 135, 152
housing market, 32–33, 40, 51,
53–54, 59, 63–65
increases, 43, 48–49, 70, 75, 99,
100, 107
land tax schemes, 5, 23–28

About the Author

Allan David Heskin is Associate Professor of Urban Planning at the University of California at Los Angeles. He teaches courses in housing in both the Planning and Law Schools, with an emphasis on the politics of housing.

Dr. Heskin was educated at the University of California, Berkeley, where he received a law degree in 1963, and at the University of Washington, where he received a Ph.D. in Urban Planning in 1975. He has been interested and involved in the tenant movement since the mid-60's, when he served as a Legal Services Attorney. Later he was attorney-in-charge of research and development in landlord-tenant law at the National Housing Law Project.

Dr. Heskin has published numerous articles on housing in planning, law, and economics journals, as well as having conducted a major study of rent control for the City of Los Angeles.